The Heresy of Self-Love

The
HERESY of
SELF-LOVE

A Study of Subversive Individualism

Paul Zweig

Princeton University Press
Princeton, New Jersey

Preface (1980)

During the dozen years since *The Heresy of Self-Love* was first published, cultural debate in America has teetered between extremes. In the late 1960s, an appetite for communal experiences of every sort gripped the country with millennial fervor. New ways of being together were offered as solutions to every kind of discontent, as if man could be made anew by some new configuration of sociability. There were communes to replace the harrowing strictures of personal intimacy; block associations and cooperative schools to dissolve the separateness of urban living, which had come to seem a special claustrophobia of our time. Political marches and meetings—rock concerts, too—became forms of exalting secular communion.

These were years when merely private experience tended to be thought of as an embarrassment, a form of personal failure keyed to judgmental words like "repression," and "alienation." At the same time, as if by paradox, a spirit of exuberant experiment with the limits of privacy became popular. "Liberation" through drugs, sex, and modes of dress; a growing fascination with experiential religion represented an attempt to transform the very nature of privacy. "Self," hypostasized into an oddly precise, delimited entity, entered the cultural vocabulary, either as a term of invective or as the watchword of a new form of freedom.

Yet again, it seemed, a legend of ancient Greece, one of the less dramatic of Ovid's little stories, had become an intimidating paradigm of the moral life: the story of Narcissus, who refused to love anyone but himself, and thereby loved himself to death.

While writing *The Heresy of Self-Love*, I had spent several years tracing the curiously persistent revivals of Narcissus in our cultural traditions. Over and over again, he became the figure of a powerful longing for inward autonomy, a sort of spiritual Robinson Crusoe, as in the fantastic poems of the Gnostic sects which competed with early Christianity; or else, a grim figure of warning: a starved lover staring into cold water; a woman gazing into a mirror, representing the Medieval sin of *luxuria*. In Milton's reworking of *Genesis*, Adam himself became a kind of Narcissus, doomed because he could not live without the "other self" God had made out of Adam's very flesh.

Narcissus was the failure of love, the fray in the social bond. He stood for a danger that has fascinated as well as repelled us for centuries: the danger that the individual will become so enamored of his mind and flesh, that society will go untended and God go unloved; or, perhaps more secretly, that each of us will go unloved. For Narcissus is never ourselves, he is always the other one who cannot see us.

The social effervescence of the 1960s quickly faded, and the vaunted revolution in personal style—what Charles Reich called "the greening of America"—never really took place. Yet those years have left behind the feeling of an unsolved problem, which has fed cultural debate in recent years. The galvanizing word of the debate is "narcissism," used to express a widespread nervousness that the social bond has somehow been drained of significance. The meaning of Yeats' famous lines: "Things fall apart, the center cannot hold," has been internalized and made nightmarish by a conviction that not only institutions and governments, but personality itself, is falling apart.

Magazines complain about the "new narcissism" and the "me generation." Psychiatrists remark a decline in once familiar personality problems, such as the neuroses, and an increase in a vaguer, less tractable condition characterized by feelings of inner emptiness and low key misery, a sort of lifelong psychic cold. This condition, they claim, results from an "inability to love," and is ultimately a form of loneliness which the psychoanalyst Heinz Kohut calls a "narcissistic personality disorder."

In the work of social critics like Richard Sennet (*The Fall of*

Public Man) and, in particular, Christopher Lasch (*The Culture of Narcissism*), "narcissism" has become the central concept in an attempt to define what they see as a broad collapse of cultural values and, maybe, of civilization itself. As a result of this widespread assault by journalists, social critics and psychiatrists, "narcissism" bids fair to replace "alienation" as the cant word of our decade, although, as with "alienation," no one seems quite sure he knows what the word means—supposing, as the psychoanalyst Leslie Farber wondered aloud to me recently, that it means anything at all. This doesn't prevent magazines from printing worried articles on the "new" social disease, and universities from setting up seminars on "narcissism" as they did only a few years ago on "alienation." Indeed, "narcissism" may simply be "alienation" rewarmed, i.e. the latest slogan for designating what theologians used to call original sin, meaning all the ways in which human beings dependably go wrong.

Here is Christopher Lasch's composite portrait of the contemporary narcissist: "facile at managing the impressions he gives to others, ravenous for admiration but contemptuous of those he manipulates into providing it; unappeasably hungry for emotional experiences with which to fill an inner void; terrified of aging and death." Lasch's description is drawn largely from the clinical literature developed by Kohut and Otto Kernberg. His contribution has been to take it from the clinic into the street, as the diagnosis, no longer of an individual "case," but of an entire society conceived of as a (possibly) terminal case. At times Lasch seems to be writing Dantean mythology rather than social criticism, as when he describes narcissistic America as "a lawless . . . society in which the normal conditions of everyday life come to resemble those formerly confined to the underworld."

Today's argument about "narcissism" amounts to a gloomy inversion of the exuberant hopes of the 1960s. In both cases, the merely private life is seen as a trap for man's nobler social energies. The sixties' hope to elude the trap has simply given way to a conviction that we are in it for good. We have also inherited from the sixties a curious historical amnesia, of which Lasch's work is an example. Although Lasch was trained as a political historian, his claim that contemporary society has been fatally weakened by the aggressive self-isolation of its members, gains its tone of apocalypse from an amazing failure of the historical imagination, a failure which may characterize our time more tellingly than "narcissism."

We seem to have forgotten that men have existed from age to age on the edge of social collapse and spiritual crisis. Candide didn't exactly live in happy times either, nor did the ancient Greeks, whose acrid wisdom Nietzsche quotes in *The Birth of Tragedy*: "Best is not to have been born at all; the next best is to die as quickly as possible." Civilized life has often been experienced as a borderline condition in the process of getting worse, and history is, ultimately, the story of bad times. The story, too, of an endless repertory of surprises: dead-ends which turn out to be new beginnings; disasters which fuel expansions of thought; desperate needs which create entirely unforeseeable fulfillments.

My subject in *The Heresy of Self-Love* is the West's millennia-long fascination with Narcissus: deploring his inhuman solitude, admiring him as a figure of fulfillment and transcendence. In the speculative fantasies of the Gnostics, in the programmatic self-indulgence of the Medieval Brethren of the Free Spirit, in the almost objectless love poems of Provence, in Adam Smith's theory of self-interest, in the radical social criticism of the nineteenth century, we find the same cult of self-love, along with the same foreboding that self-love will undermine the teetering fabric of sociability.

The recent invective against "narcissism" is finally an old story retold: not the final illness of "late capitalism," but an episode in the sinuous conflict between the individual and society which has been the signature of Western cultural history.

Part of the problem may lie in the very term "narcissism," with its psychiatric overtones. By absorbing history into case history, a precious dimension of cultural adventure is reduced to a "diagnosis." How impoverishing this is becomes clear if we try to imagine our chorus of psychiatric moralists parachuted, say, into the late eighteenth century. I wonder how they would diagnose the extravagant opening scene in Rousseau's *Confessions*, where Rousseau, his book in his hand, stands on the platform of the Last Judgment, inviting the human race to gather round and hear the story of his superbly "innocent" life? Could there be a more "narcissistic" inversion of the Biblical scenario of judgment?

Crossing the English Channel, one hears them inveighing gloomily against the gigantic, unhappy struggle with self which characterized seventeenth and eighteenth century England, among Protestants who were fanatically "narcissistic" in their devotion to the inner workings of their minds, and to the methodical increasing of their private wealth. Now, I am willing to believe that Puritan England was a very unhappy place, perhaps unhappier than our own. Yet the tensions of that grim, turbulent time gave rise to one of the wealthiest, most complex societies ever known. Narcissus, in Puritan England, was not the fifth horseman of the Apocalypse, but one of the tutelary gods of history, and he still is, I suspect, for all the moralizing of the social philosophers.

In this longer perspective, Narcissus is seen to be not so much the worm in the fruit of industrial society, as a perpetual devil's advocate to the longing for community, an arch-heretic whose refusal to fit represents that aspect of human personality which resists the social and has, presumably, always resisted it.

The Heresy of Self-Love is the story of these resistances, and of the ever-renewed attempt in the West to socialize them. It is a story of reversals, of heresies gravitating toward the heart of accepted values. Above all, it is the story of an irrepressible cultural dialectic: excoriating the sin of privacy, we have created a form of exhibitionism—what I call "public privacy"—which has fueled our most powerful cultural values.

New York   Paul Zweig
January 1980

Preface (1968)

Of all the tales which Ovid tells in *The Metamorphoses* that of Narcissus has been retold and reinterpreted more than any other. His mistaken love and his self-imposed death have never ceased to fascinate us, as if Narcissus were acting out a fate which we recognize all too well. Plotinus evoked him to dramatize the delusion of all worldly pleasures. For medieval iconography he represented the sin of self-indulgence and vanity; while in the traditions of courtly love Narcissus became a purified, more spiritual embodiment of "Daun Cupido." Self-love—that most undramatic of all emotions—has had an ever renewed currency in the cultural languages of Europe. Montaigne, Spinoza, and Rousseau gave it a philosophical prestige. The manuals of religious meditation diverted its emotional resources toward the goals of orthodox religion. The social philosophers of the eighteenth and nineteenth centuries set it up as a touchstone according to which they condemned the "alienations" imposed upon them by their society. The heresy of self-love has taken many forms. It has become a part of our cultural traditions, always condemned and yet central to our most familiar values.

In the pages which follow I have set out to explore these versions of Narcissus which have so powerfully shaped the attitudes of our culture. Only in the West, Burckhardt suggests, did the subversive genius of the individual become public and indispensable: a necessary troublemaker.

By describing a number of exemplary moments in our cultural history, I have attempted to dramatize and clarify this experience of self-cultivation and self-exaltation. My intention was not to make an exhaustive scholarly study of the subject. Instead, I set out to write a series of linked essays evoking the spirit of what I have called "subversive individualism," and the curious persistency with which it reappears throughout all European history. Much that might have been included in the book has been left out. Nothing is said of Renaissance philosophers like Giordano Bruno or Pico della Mirandola. Rabelais, Montaigne, and Pascal are referred to only in passing, as are Nietzsche and Dostoevski. These exclusions are to some extent arbitrary. But my choices, in the end, have revealed me perhaps as much as they have revealed my subject. By following my sympathies, I have perhaps given a certain unity to the arbitrary, which may be the best one can do with his ignorance.

I open my study with the Gnostics and end it with the nineteenth century. This too demands an explanation. Periclean Greece was obsessed by the mysteries of pride and self-love also. Yet I chose to begin my account with a number of obscure religious intellectuals vaguely organized into sects and crushed by the worldly weight of the Church during the first centuries after Christ. Their "alienation" from worldly experience, their antisocial doctrines, their extreme spiritual self-reliance mark a break with the Hellenistic past and, as Hans Jonas has suggested, prefigure the mood of modern existentialism. They embodied a conflict which has never ceased to harass the culture of the West, often driving it to its greatest achievements, yet perhaps also forcing it to pay a price in anxiety and spiritual restlessness which makes it so different from the great civilizations of the East.

PAUL ZWEIG

New York
September 1968

Contents

Part One

1 THE GNOSTIC MIRROR

History, it is said, is like the river in which we can never bathe twice. The waters change, the events replace one another. In naming it, already we are mistaken, for we are naming yesterday's river. Yet the changes of history often assume patterns which seem familiar, as if the repertory of human forms were limited. The historian then discovers similarities from one age to another, only partly concealed beneath the surface of the events themselves. Such a resemblance has often been felt between the modern period and the late Roman Empire. During the centuries after Augustus, a curious double language became current among the citizens of Rome. The *res publica* continued to command a range of ceremonies and allegiances whose performance was scrupulously observed; but increasingly the citizens acted out his "duty" in a spirit of passiveness and perfunctory obedience.

Rome, with its military conception of government, demanded no more than this language of conformity. And this, as Burckhardt has pointed out, allowed a zone of private values to appear, entirely divorced from the *res publica*. Here a second language came to be spoken, a language parallel to the public one and unperturbed by it. It was, on the whole, a religious language, charged with emotion, one whose intimate concerns were not only anti-authoritarian but, ultimately, antisocial. The spiritual allegiance which their emperor no longer demanded of them the Romans gave to Oriental deities whose cults became universal. As the Roman's public language became one of empty obedience, his private language expressed need for emotional communion. As publicly he was victimized by the law, and by sweeping economic forces, privately he searched for some form of personal salvation. It is notorious that official culture deteriorated under the Empire, but this private, religious culture continued to flourish, until forced by its very triumph to betray its origin and become public, in officialized Christianity. This double language of orthodoxy and subversion, which so well characterizes our own society, was unprecedented before the years of the late Empire. For the first time, a citizen could organize his sensibility around a system of antisocial, and even antiworldly, values.

It is not surprising, therefore, that our modern distrust of "society," and our own "romantic" traditions of revolt against conformity, should lead us to find a congenial spirit in the society of the corrupt Empire. In the second and third centuries, as in the nineteenth century, a new kind of "individualism" came to be valued, all of whose energy was devoted to subverting the powers of worldly authority, in the name of some entirely private range of emotions.

The Pax Romana had made the Empire into what Gibbon described as a vast prison, with no escape for those who resisted its authority. It was a prison as vast as the world; and this is recognized in the religious terminology of the Neoplatonists, the Christians, and especially the Gnostics, for whom "this world" was literally a prison, enclosing each citizen in his own isolated predicament. But if the world was a prison, then the only appeal could be "out of this world," away from its authority and toward some new authority whose main evidence lay not in laws, no matter how brilliantly codified, but in a certain quality of experience. Such was the atmosphere in which Christianity first gained its strength, rejecting the legalistic aspect of Judaism, along with the authority of the Empire, while it appealed, in the writings of St. Paul, to spiritual conviction as individual as that of "grace."

Yet from the very first the Christians moderated this Pauline "individualism," limiting its mystical bias with a shrewd sense of organization and earthly responsibility. Already during the first and second centuries the new Church showed signs of an absolutist tendency. In each city of the Empire, the Christians assembled under the authority of a bishop, whose word was spiritual law. Their religion made them citizens in the City of God, but it also made them members of a strict, increasingly organized community. The Christians owed their success as much to this organizational shrewdness as to the richness of their doctrine.

But the double allegiance which characterized the spirit of the Empire soon became a problem for the Church as well. By the fourth century, the success of Christianity was so widespread that Constantine could appeal to its organizational genius in order to consolidate his own power. As the Church allowed itself to become a political instrument, identified now with the maintenance of law and order, it had to confront its own radical message in the doctrines of various heretical movements, and even more spectacularly in the spiritual anarchism of Egypt, where the desert saints had begun to perform their feats of extreme asceticism, often in defiance of the Church itself. Of the sects and heresies which competed with Christianity during the first centuries, the most dangerous, if we are to judge from the polemics of the early fathers, were the numerous, highly individualized sects which we characterize commonly as "Gnostic."* They were dangerous because their ethical and

---

* This term is used to designate a highly fragmented religious movement of late antiquity with which the early Church came in contact. Gnosticism seems to have flourished most vigorously during the second century, though the first Gnostics may well have been contemporaries of Christ or St. Paul; the Manicheans of the fourth and fifth centuries are also thought of as belonging to the Gnostic movement. The mystical preoccupations of the Gnostic sects formed a kind of bridge between pagan and Christian spirituality. Gnostic influence was felt throughout large portions of the late Roman Empire: from Rome to Egypt, Syria, and

soteriological concerns were so close to those of Christianity; but especially also because they embodied the uncompromising individualism which the Christians themselves had been led to modify, in the interests of Church discipline. R. M. Grant has indeed wondered whether certain early Gnostic sects, like that of Simon Magus for example, were not simply radical Paulinians, and therefore all the more troubling for the Church.

The Gnostics—like the Christians and the Neoplatonists—described life on earth, and the earth itself, as a tragic corruption of the Spirit. Mankind, indeed the entire cosmos, lived under the stigma of original sin. The spiritual duty of each individual became to undo this sin in himself by undoing all his ties with worldly experience. The Gnostic sects, despite vast differences among them, were uncompromising on this point. Unlike the Christians, who believed that even the fallen earth had been divinely created, the Gnostics condemned the world entirely. God was absent from it, they felt; its laws and conditions were entirely perverse. Even the stars were signs of worldly oppression, and therefore hateful. The only trace of the hidden God that men could discover lay buried in their souls, "sleeping" or "drunk" with earthly poison. By awakening this "spark," the Gnostic escaped from his earthly prison.

The Gnostic imagination is powerfully subversive. Nothing in the world claimed their allegiance if not that concealed fragment of their being which they were taught to cultivate. This extreme "individualism" is reflected in the chaotic organization of the sects, but also in the freedom with which Gnostic doctrines were continually changing in the hands of imaginative individuals with a gift for poetry or speculation. The sects attacked by Hippolytus,* in the *Philosophumena*, belong

---

Greece. The development of Christian doctrine was, to a large extent, a reaction against the competing doctrines of the Gnostics.

* An important theologian and martyr (165–235), who lived in Rome during the bulk of his ecclesiastical career. The *Philosophumena* is his

to a single milieu, that of third-century Rome. But the innumerable variations among them, the shifts in doctrine from sect to sect, show the small value these Gnostics placed on orthodoxy, and the great individual freedom their vision necessarily allowed.

The Gnostic treatment of Biblical and Greek themes shows how conscious they were of the subversive energy released by their theology. They reversed traditional values, turning the Old Testament God into an inferior Demiurge (Marcion); the serpent into a "pneumatic" agent whose role was to induce men to eat of the Tree of Knowledge (the Ophites). Cain, the rebel and wanderer, became a hero (the Cainites); while Prometheus was invested with the glory of having transgressed Zeus's law, in favor of mankind. Long before they were rediscovered by nineteenth-century romanticism, Satan and Prometheus were admired and praised by the Gnostics.

At the center of Gnostic speculation is bewilderment at the overwhelming presence of evil in the world, and a need to account for this evil while preserving the absolute goodness of God. Their most extravagant fantasies are meant to answer this need for "understanding" which is expressed in the famous Valentinian* formula: "What liberates is knowledge of who we were, what we became; where we were, whereinto we have been thrown; whereto we speed, wherefrom we are redeemed; what birth is, and what rebirth. . . ." To the Christian emphasis on love and faith the Gnostics add a desire for knowledge, though by this they mean not only rational but also mystical knowledge;

---

most important work. In it he seeks to show that the various Christian heresies are traceable to false pagan philosophies.

* Valentinus founded the most profound and influential Gnostic school of the second century. He was born in the Nile delta, and received a Greek education in the schools of Alexandria, where he became a religious teacher and a Christian. According to Tertullian, Valentinus was at first a member of the orthodox Christian community in Rome where he was highly regarded "because he was brilliant and most eloquent." Little is known of the rest of his life. After he broke with the local Church, he is thought to have returned to Egypt where he was probably accepted as a loyal member of the Egyptian Church.

the speculative gnosis imparted by their treatises is meant only as preparation for that moment of illumination when the "sleeping" spark in the soul will be reawakened.

Their speculative gift led many Gnostic sects to elaborate long, sometimes impressive, metaphysical poems in order to answer the questions asked in the Valentinian formula. The most extravagant fantasies were proposed to explain God's original act of creation, the fall from Light into Darkness, man's painful fate as an "alien" in the world of matter, and the "way" he must follow back into the world of Light. When the inspiration of such great second-century Gnostics as Basilides, Valentinus, and Marcion deteriorated in the hands of later followers, the cosmological fantasies tended to become excessive, filled with repetition and mediocre allegory. Texts like the *Books of Pistis-Sophia* or the *Book of Jêou* are characterized by this speculative extravagance which has led all but the most recent religious historians to accept more or less at face value the accusations made by Irenaeus, Tertullian,* Hippolytus and other Church Fathers, who brushed aside the whole mood of Gnosticism as a kind of religious madness.

Yet the Gnostic poems, at their best, reveal a moral awareness far more sensitive than any to be found in second- or third-century Christian writings. Valentinus, from what little we know of him, was surely one of the great religious minds of his century. The subversive energy of the Gnostics gave shape and insight to their fantasy, leading them often to discover themes of religious psychology that are of the greatest interest

---

* Tertullian is one of the greatest early Christian writers (b. 155). He was a stern polemicist and is credited with having formulated a central paradox of Christian faith: "I believe because it is absurd." Born of pagan parents in Carthage, he was converted to Christianity relatively late in life, before gradually drifting into violent disagreement with the Church. Irenaeus (130–200) was presumably born in Asia Minor. His life was largely devoted to formulating and defining the Christian canon of Biblical texts, setting firm limits to orthodox doctrine, in opposition to the syncretic tendency of the Gnostics.

to us, for these themes will be rediscovered by a whole tradition of subversive individualism in the West.

Although the first Hermetic book,* entitled *Poimandres*, belongs to a Pagan strain of Gnosticism, it elaborates material common to the entire mood of Gnostic speculation, including typical references to the Old Testament story of Genesis. It is particularly interesting because the author is concerned, at crucial moments, with providing a motive for the cosmic events he describes. In doing so, he treats openly themes which remain implicit or are merely alluded to in other Gnostic writings. The treatise takes the form of a vision that has possessed the author in a moment of meditation, "his mind mightily lifted up . . . his bodily senses curbed." In this state of heightened awareness, he "sees" an answer to those questions of whence, why, and wherefore which obsessed the Gnostic mind:

> Suddenly everything was opened before me in a flash, and I beheld a boundless view, everything became Light, serene and joyful. And I became enamored with the sight. And after a while there was a Darkness borne downward . . . appalling and hateful, tortuously coiled, resembling a serpent. Then I saw this Darkness change into some humid nature, indescribably agitated and giving off smoke as from a fire and uttering a kind of sound unspeakable, mournful.

---

* The body of the theological writings known as the Corpus Hermeticum probably dates from the first three centuries A.D. They were popularly attributed, as their name indicates, to the god Hermes Trismegistos, as he was called in Greek, or Thoth, as he was called in Egyptian. The Hermetic Corpus as a whole is not particularly Gnostic, though it contains elements related to Gnosticism, as in the *Poimandres*. The books of the Corpus are marked by a turgid mystical piety. On the whole it seems unlikely that there was any well defined Hermetic community or "Church." The Hermetics were more concerned with magic, alchemy, and occult medicine, and it is this connection which accounts for the frequent references to Hermes Trismegistos in Medieval and Renaissance literature.

The boundless Light preceding all creation allows "after a while" a contrary force of Darkness to arise within it. This, in turn, becomes the "humid nature," or alternatively the "Boulé" or Will of God: a female principle, cut off from the Light which gave birth to it. From here on, the treatise describes the various confrontations and complicities that arise between the Light and its own emanation, the Darkness, leading to the formation of the Cosmos, the imprisonment of humanity within the Cosmos, and finally the ascent of man back into the Light. To this extent, the *Poimandres* is typical of most Gnostic writings.

After its creation, the feminine "humid nature" "receives" into it the *Logos,* or Word of God—the sexual connotations here are obvious—which then contributes to fashioning order out of chaos. It rises above the water and earth and becomes the highest portion of the Cosmos, the element of air and fire, akin to the Demiurge who then completes the work of ordering the Darkness into a world.

It is at this point that the tragedy of man's fall begins. God, once the Cosmos has been created, allows the energy of His divine Love to operate once again. Now that the spheres have been set whirling "with thundrous speed," a new desire moves inside the Light:

> Now the Nous, Father of all, being Life and Light, brought forth Man like to Himself, of whom he became enamored as his own child, for he was very beautiful, since he bore the Father's image; for indeed even God became enamored of His own form, and He delivered over to him all His works.

The Primal Man described in this passage will, through his own fall, give birth to fallen humanity, playing the same role for the Hermetics as does Adam in the Genesis story, which is probably alluded to here. The figure of Primal Man has its equivalent in other Gnostic texts, but the *Poimandres* treats him differently, for it makes his creation appear gratuitous. Elsewhere

Man, Adam, Primal Man, Anthropos play a definite role in the creation of the cosmos; they complete some part of the work which here is entirely attributed to the Logos and the Demiurge. Apparently for this Hermetic author, God created Primal Man simply for the delight He then felt in loving His own image. Echoes of this theme can be found elsewhere among the Gnostics, especially among the Valentinians, who avoid, as the *Poimandres* also does, the extremes of Persian dualism. In the *Philosophumena,* Hippolytus reports the speculations of a third-century Valentianian sect. God, they said, is love. But love cannot exist without an object; therefore it is in God's nature to create something separate from Himself, so that He may exist fully by loving it. What He creates, however, must be worthy of His love; He therefore allows to emanate from Himself the "Pleroma," a presence which is and yet is not Him. By creating the Pleroma, and subsequently the entire cosmos, God remains both the object and subject of His own love. This theme of divine self-multiplication also appears among the Simonians, for whom "there is one power, divided into upper and lower, begetting itself, increasing itself, seeking itself, finding itself, being its own mother, its own father . . . its own daughter, its own son . . ."

At some point, God is moved to an act of pure self-delight; and this, in turn, gives rise to a series of cosmic intrigues which transform the original creation, luring it down to its final degraded kingdom: mankind and his earth. For man's tragedy, in the Hermetic account, has only just begun. The "humid nature," fashioned into a cosmos, with ascending spheres and hierarchies, is ruled over at God's behest by the Demiurge. Meanwhile, beyond the outer limit of the cosmos, Primal Man lives on, a pure duplicate of the Light, until, weary of his idleness, he asks God for the power to rule and create in his own right. God grants the request; He associates Primal Man with the hierarchies of the Demiurge, until one day, out of restlessness, pride, or curiosity, Man violates the limit of his power:

He [Primal Man] who had full power over the world of things mortal and over the irrational animals bent down through the Harmony and having broken through the vault showed to lower Nature the beautiful form of God. When she beheld him who had in himself inexhaustible beauty and all the forces of the Governors combined with the form of God, she smiled in love; for she had seen the reflection of this most beautiful form of Man in the water and its shadow upon the earth. He too, seeing his likeness present in her, reflected in the water, loved it and desired to dwell in it. At once with the wish, it became reality, and he came to inhabit the form devoid of reason. And Nature, having received into herself the beloved, embraced him wholly, and they mingled: for they were inflamed with love.

Primal Man has broken through the ordered circuit of the spheres; like Narcissus, he has fallen in love with his image reflected in the water, and this inordinate love makes him a captive of the dark world he was meant to rule over. Once again the downward progress of God's creation turns upon an act of self-delight: Narcissus loves his image; watery Nature, spying this emanation of God's splendor, becomes infatuated with it. Her chaotic waters draw down the straying self-lover, until they have imprisoned his beauty in "the form devoid of reason." Because of Primal Man's uncontrollable love, death and suffering are introduced into the world. A portion of the Light world— i.e., God's image—has been forceably mingled with the Darkness, where it will be imprisoned until some future time. Meanwhile, these "sparks" of light, fragments of the Primal Man, wander in exile through the world, "asleep" in the "souls" of mankind.

Thus man's fate of exile in the world originates with this wrong imitation of God's self-delight. Just as the cosmos itself is a deformed image of the archetypal Light world, so the fall of Primal Man is a replica of God's original self-mirroring through which Primal Man himself was created. But while

God's self-love was creative and pure, Man, through his "error," "has become a slave . . . though he was androgynous, having issued from the androgynous Father . . . he is conquered by love . . ."

These two acts of self-love lie at the heart of the Hermetic vision, in the *Poimandres*. They help us to understand certain obscurities in the text, such as the seemingly redundant role of Primal Man. As we now see it, Man's presence contains the key to the poem, for he embodies the original self-delight which first impelled God to create. The Darkness was "borne downward" through the Light because of this impulse to love Himself which is part of God's nature. There remains, however, another question to which the text yields no immediate answer. Why must the androgynous purity of God's self-delight be reversed by Man's self-delusion, which, instead of Joy, brought guilt and pain into the world? The Gnostics' mythical turn of mind led them to project their speculative insights onto heroic figures, who then reveal themselves to us by acting out their part in the tale. Their metaphysical poems are allegories of religious psychology. In this case, the *Poimandres* projects onto its allegorical heroes an insight into the nature of pride: that its self-delighting purity implies as well a painful loneliness. This mythical division into purity and guilt dramatizes the hidden complexity of self-love. It is the technique of storytellers, who make the opposite sides of a dilemma come alive in the characters of the hero and the villain. Hero and villain belong to one another, and therefore must choose a common ground on which to meet. Yet one acts out his fate and is wrong; the other, for deeds not unlike those of his enemy, is glorified. In the same way, the *Poimandres* dramatizes the two inextricable passions of self-love. God's act is all Light; it is generous, self-contained, and free. Man's act is all Darkness; it is rooted in arrogance, delusion, and loneliness. When Man and Nature embrace each other, they abandon themselves to a false love; for Man has seen only his image, while Nature has seen only a reflection of God's beauty. Their sexual union is based on blindness to each other, and humanity is born out of their deluded egotism.

Variations of this theme are found often in Gnostic writings. The potency of the mirror and its image, recognized in magico-religious practices throughout the world, was of great service to the Gnostic poets as a narrative device for conveying the transmission of being from one level of creation to another. With the Gnostics, however, it is a story of degradation, a fall from the creator into His image; as in this Mandaean poem:

> Abathur [one of the Uthras, plotting the creation of a world] goes into that world [of darkness] . . . He sees his face in the black water, and his likeness and son is formed unto him out of the black water.

In a text closer to the atmosphere of Christian Gnosticism—the recently published *Hypostasis of the Archons*—the figure is employed in a way not unlike that used in the *Poimandres,* as an instrument of self-delusion by which the Higher is lured down into the Lower:

> The Incorruptibility looked down upon the regions of the water. Its image revealed itself in the water and the powers of darkness fell in love with it. The archons took counsel and said, "Come, let us make a man from dust . . ." they formed [this man] after their own body and after the image of God which had revealed itself in the water . . . "We will equal the image in our formation, so that it [the image] shall see this likeness of itself, [be attracted to it] and we may trap it in our formation.

Self-reflection, the fashioning of an alter-ego, plays an important part in the Gnostic myths of creation. In each case, self-love is portrayed as a gateway to man's fall. But the *Poimandres,* the *Hypostasis of the Archons,* and indeed all the major Gnostic works, are concerned with the fall only as a necessary prelude to their doctrine of man's redemption. They are, in the main, treatises of salvation. Their speculative poetry is no idle fantasy; it is an initiation into the gnosis which will enable straying souls to discover the true "way." They go on, therefore, to describe how that spark of divinity in man, through which he may climb back into the lost Heaven of Light, is also impelled by the energy of self-love. Because God loves Himself, He will overcome the barriers of material corruption, in order to draw back into His original Light the fragments of His image in men. This is the second half of the Gnostic story: the painful climb of the soul back to God.

According to the Gnostics, therefore, man's fate is circular. But the mounting of the arc is not simply a reversed image of its descent. Between the two movements, a change has occurred. The story of man's fall is exactly that of the world's creation: God, the Demiurge, and Primal Man engage in a series of cosmic events through which God's image is lured down to imprisonment in the world. Only at the nadir of the fall is the human race born out of the strayed pieces of the Light. From now on, each exiled individual carries a fragment of God within him, at the "apex" of his soul. It is by looking inward, by awakening this divine spark, that one can eventually free it from its earthly prison, allowing it—and oneself—to rise up through the material spheres to Heaven. If the fall of man takes on the aspect of myth and allegory, his ascent back to God becomes an affair of individual psychology. Each of us carries God back to Himself, when we accept the revelation of inward knowledge—gnosis—and free ourselves from bondage to the laws of the world. This is the meaning of the advice attributed by the *Philosophumena,* to a certain Monoimus:

> Do not look for God and the creation and other like things, look for Him by starting in *yourself* and learn who it is *in you,* that possesses all things without question, and says, "*My* God, *my* spirit, *my* thought, *my* soul, *my* body." Learn where sorrow, joy, love, and hate come from; why we come without wishing

it, and love without wanting to. If you look for these things correctly, you will find it in *yourself*.

By sinking passionately into oneself, the individual restores the spark of God—his own true self—to its divine origin.

The Gnostic thus finds himself engaged personally in the adventure of the universe. He struggles up out of the world's impurity by turning inward and fanning the divine spark in the soul. In so doing, he neutralizes the self-infatuation of Primal Man and soothes that other, better love of the Light for its luminous self. His arm in this struggle of Light against Darkness is still another nuance of self-delight: the mystical inward turning counseled by Monoimus.

If there are any doubts about the meaning of this psychological-mystical ascension, they will be resolved, I think, by one of the loveliest Gnostic texts, *The Hymn of the Pearl,* located in the apocryphal *Acts of the Apostle Thomas.* The hymn tells the story of a boy, raised in "the kingdom of (his) father's house," who is sent one day by his family on a journey to the East, in search of a certain pearl. Once arrived in the Eastern land, he loses his way and forgets his original mission. This is a symbolic narrative of the soul's descent into bondage and its "sleep" in the world of Darkness. But one day the lost boy receives a message from above, which awakens him from his forgetfulness. He remembers now who he is, and where he comes from—those very things which Valentinus' formula counsels the Gnostic to seek for in himself. In this state of awakened knowledge he seizes the pearl and starts his upward journey. As he approaches the confines of his true home, the poem continues:

> I went forth . . . My robe of glory which I had put off and my mantle which went over it, my parents . . . sent to meet me by their treasurers who were entrusted therewith. Its splendor I had forgotten, having left it as a child in my father's house. As I now beheld the robe, it seemed to me suddenly to become a mirror-image of myself: myself entire I saw in it, and it entire

I saw in myself, that we were two in separateness and yet again one in the sameness of our forms.

The boy of the hymn represents the archetypal savior, the messenger from above, the alien wandering in the desert of the world who is common to most of the Gnostic poems. But the gentle humanity of the text adds another dimension to its meaning. The archetype melts into the human, the cosmological actor becomes also the humble Gnostic awakening to knowledge of his divine origin. The boy who has put off his soiled earthly garment—his body—in exchange for his "robe of glory" is the "awakened" individual who has discovered, at the heart of knowledge, the object he has been seeking: the "mirror-image" of his true self. In the Gnostic imagination, the seeker is identical with what he seeks. Looking for God, he is looking for himself; while God, who draws man up out of bondage, seeks nothing less than His own image.

What the Gnostics give us, finally, is a universe of passional laws, where half-mythical, half-abstract figures project their desires into space and bring about, almost as a by-product, the material Darkness of creation. But when we inspect these passions and their aborted results, we find that we are dealing at every level with interlocking circles of Narcissi, each desiring only himself—God, Primal Man, earthly humanity: three great actors on the stage of the world, each seeking blindly, or lucidly, for his own image. Of the three, the part of earthly humanity is the most difficult, because in it good and evil are equally present. To the extent that man shares the fault—the illusory self-delight —of his ancestor, he is confined to his prison and must suffer death. To the extent that he can accept the divine self-seeking of the Light, he is freed and puts on the "robe of glory": the "mirror-image" which he had forgotten in his father's house.

According to this view, good and evil are not two opposing forces ranged against each other in the battle for man's soul. Instead they are like strange twins, so much alike that one can easily be mistaken for the other. Indeed, to love one means to have dangerous intimacy with the other. In striving to rise up and "become" God, nothing is more perilously easy than to curve away from the goal of divinity and to assume the hubris of the Demiurge, that minor God of matter who thought he was godlike, when he was only devilish.

This brings us to one of the strangest figures in the pantheon of Gnostic heroes: that saint of holy self-indulgence, Simon Magus.* Although cast by the Church Fathers in the role of arch-heretic, Simon Magus so transforms the Biblical message as to place himself all but outside the atmosphere of Christian thought. The Simonians, whose doctrines were recorded during the second and third centuries, place at the center of their vision the usual Gnostic poem of the creation: emanations of Light and Darkness descend, embodied in ranks of allegorical figures, until their final degradation, when one of the heavenly entities, the Sophia, or Thought of God, is detained by the powers of Darkness and made prisoner on earth. The duty of the Simonians was to enter the cosmic struggle, by aiding the Sophia to undo her earthly bonds and return to God. They could do this by accepting the revelation of the sect, thereby furthering the Sophia on her journey and accompanying her ascent. Simon acknowledged Jesus as a precursor, a first "messenger" sent to awaken the sleeping spark in men. But the striking originality of Simon's religion lay in the personal role he himself played. For if Jesus was a precursor, he Simon was the actual messenger and member of God, whose duty was to lead the fallen Sophia

---

* Presumed to have lived in the first century A.D. According to Acts 8:5–24, he was a magician who had great influence in Samaria. He was converted and baptized by Philip the evangelist but later offered money to several of the apostles in order to obtain from them the power to impart the Spirit (cf: the word "simony"). He is said to have repented, though Irenaeus, Hippolytus, and others later accuse him of being the first Gnostic. There is some doubt, however, on the part of scholars, as to whether the Simon mentioned in Acts and the Simon accused by Irenaeus are indeed the same person.

through the world and finally out of it. Here lay Simon's greatest genius, if it can be called that. He brought with him on his missionary wanderings a certain Helen whom he claimed to have discovered in a brothel in Tyre; this woman, he preached, was the last and lowest incarnation of the Sophia; she had been redeemed by him, Simon the messiah, and so would all be redeemed who acknowledged them both. Simon went on to draw a conclusion from his antiworldly doctrine which is not typical of most Gnostic religions, though it reappears regularly enough not only during the first centuries but far on into modern times. Because the world is a prison, its conditions and laws are unjust. But one who has been illuminated has found in himself the spark of a higher dispensation; he is in a state of "grace" and can no longer be held accountable in ordinary terms of justice. It is in this sense that Simon can be called a radical Paulinian, for, like other, later heretics, he draws strictly antinomian conclusions from Paul's doctrine of grace. In the words of Irenaeus' accusation: "Those who place their hope in himself and his Helena need no longer heed them and might freely do as they like. For by his grace were men saved, and not by righteous deeds." This state of grace seems largely to have been translated in terms of sexual liberation, which makes the Simonians the originators of that libertine gnosis which reappears in later centuries with the Messalines, the Heretics of the Free Spirit, and the whole antinomian strain of modern culture.

Simon's immense "pride" never ceased to fascinate Christianity for he embodies one of the permanent temptations of the Christian mind: the irrepressible desire to wield for oneself those powers of divinity that are revealed to a man who has opened the right doors in his spirit. Simon exemplifies a "confusion" inherent in the Gnostic—and later on, though to a lesser extent, in the Christian—experience. Love of God and self-deification are so closely related that the Gnostics, like the Christian mystics later, often use the language of one to express the other. The interlocking self-loves of the universe blur into a single passionate involvement with self. What emerges, finally, is one who loves God and who, because of this, is God. Here too the seeker has become identical with what he seeks; and Simon is perfectly within the logic of his vision when he declares that he is none other than the divinity Himself.

Although the Gnostic cosmology erects a staunch barrier between the Creator and His fallen creatures, with eons and imprisoning spheres between, it allows a paradoxical intimacy between the illuminated individual and his God. For the spark in the soul which marks each of us as an alien in this world is not merely a reflected light, or a mirror, or a divine signal, as it was most often for Christian theologians; it was thought to be a fragment of God Himself. By awakening it, one in fact became God. Most Gnostic sects allowed for a simple hierarchy among their initiates, the highest rank being that of Perfecti: those whose spiritual gift was so apparent that they were considered to be already "perfect," more God than man. This trait also characterized the neognostical Cathars a thousand years later; though the "confusion" it implies between God and man gave rise, among the Cathars, to the strictest asceticism.

Simon Magus dramatizes still another paradox of the Gnostic imagination which was inherited, in one form or another, by the traditions of Christian heresy. The condemnation of bodily existence becomes, with the Gnostic, a masterful defense of interior freedom. The profane world is described as an aborted unreality; yet each individual harbors within him a pure road starting in his soul—in his imagination—and ending in God. By giving free rein to his religious fantasy, the Gnostic poet created a world with his words. His imagination itself became godly as he promulgated Light and Darkness, Pleroma, Demiurge, and Cosmic tragedies. This poetic self-transformation takes on another more radical form with Simon, who turns not only his words but his gestures and his very being into a god.

This "excess" of spiritual pride crops up in the Christian world with fascinating regularity during the next nineteen hundred years. For example, the resemblance, between the Simonians and those later, eschatological sects of Eudes de l'Étoile and of Tanchelm in the twelfth century is striking. We are told that Simon was known in Latin surroundings by the name of Faustus, the favored one. And it has been argued that the European legend of Faust descends ultimately from this "arch-heretic" of the first centuries. Faust's lust for power represents one of the constant passions of the European psyche: the longing for a final, all-powerful solitude to which the world itself must submit. Faust, like Simon the Gnostic, wanted to become the god of a universe which mirrored his most hidden potentialities.

2 THE MYSTIC SELF

The *Chandogya Upanishad* tells how Virochana and Indra came one day to Prajapati in order to question him about the true nature of the Brahma. Prajapati welcomed his divine disciples; but instead of answering their demand, he gave them a set of false instructions. He told them to put on their finest robes and then to look at themselves in a mirror: the image they saw there, he said, would represent the highest Brahma. Satisfied with their new knowledge, the two gods left Prajapati, though later Indra returned, unable to believe that nothing higher could be found than the pleasures of earthly self-delight.

The success of Prajapati's ruse depends on a distinction which not even the gods, it appears, could always make. The truth of mystical union, we learn, is revealed only to one who has undone his ties with the world of experience, having gathered to a single point the scattered parcels of his selfhood. This is a theme of mystical theology common to East and West alike. In the words of an Arab mystic, "To mount to God is to enter into oneself. For he who inwardly entereth and intimately penetrateth into himself, gets above and beyond himself and truly mounts up to God." Yet as the mystic gathers himself into that circle of "inwardness" which he calls the "apex" or "spark" of his soul, he encounters an obstacle, the last and subtlest of all: the strands of his passion become confused, he cannot be sure to choose rightly between the "true self" at the apex of his soul and the "false self" of earthly experience.

The Hindu parable is meant as a warning to those who have undertaken the mystical journey into themselves; for when they arrive at this difficult fork in the "way," they must learn to con-

tinue inward to the spark beyond their selfhood, and not downward into the self-deluding pleasures of the ego. Between the
true "way" and the false, the resemblance is bewildering to any
but the wisest disciple.

The Gnostics also knew this strange difficulty of "knowledge,"
projecting their insight onto the figures of the good and bad
Narcissus, God and man, who work out the psychology of their
self-delight in a fresco of cosmological events. And indeed the
mystical traditions of the West, from Plotinus onward, have at
their disposal an image which they will use again and again to
express the dilemma of the spiritual journey. In a text which had
a forming influence on much of Christian mysticism, Plotinus
describes the distracting "beauty" that can lead men astray:

> Let him who can arise withdraw into himself, forgo all that is
> known by the eyes. . . . For if one pursue what is like a beau-
> tiful shape moving over water—is there not a myth about such
> a dupe, how he sank into the depths of the current and was
> swept away to nothingness? Well, so too one that is caught by
> material beauty and will not cut himself free will be precipi-
> tated . . . down into the dark depths . . . where . . . he will
> traffic only with shadows, there as he did here.

The worldly soul is compared to Narcissus, whose life and love
is wasted in the pursuit of shadows. For all earthly experience is
bathed in the false glitter of the senses; our changing passions
dissolve at the touch like an image on water, clouding the
true permanence of the self, of which Buddhist scripture writes,
"Have Self as a lamp, Self as a refuge, and no other refuge."
Also "Through Self one should urge on the self, one should
restrain the self by Self—for Self is the lord of the self."

The mystic "way" contains at the outset this subtle danger
which will haunt the ethics of Christianity, shaping its doctrines,
feeding from within its ever-renewed insistence on orthodoxy
and spiritual obedience.

In the Ninth Book of his *Confessions,* Augustine echoes
Plotinus, as he describes the experience revealed to him in the
garden:

> The good which I now sought was not outside myself. I did
> not look for it in things which are seen with the eyes of the
> flesh by the light of the sun. For those who try to find joy in
> things outside themselves easily vanish away into emptiness.
> They waste themselves on the temporal pleasures of the visible
> world. Their minds are starved and they nibble at empty
> shadows.

The resemblance between the two texts is not surprising, for
we know that Augustine practiced the *Enneads* diligently, and
was in fact largely responsible for bringing the speculative
genius of the Neoplatonists into accord with the more properly
religious vision of Christianity. Yet something has become
blurred in the passage from Plotinus to Augustine. The image
of Narcissus has disappeared, and with it the troubling awareness that Self and self are brothers to the unpracticed eye. The
worldly passions of the ego speak a language strangely similar
to that of this high Ego, concealed by the changing surfaces
of sense and illusion.

Plotinus, like Prajapati in the Hindu parable, and like the
Hermetic poet of the *Poimandres,* understood this deceptive
danger of the "way," and the need to preserve, within the re-
nunciatory discipline of the senses, the goal of a purer, more
permanent Self. With Augustine, however, all this has become
less clear; perhaps because the task he set himself was more
difficult. Augustine, with his Christian sensibility, is less interested in the frescoes of cosmology and speculative metaphysics
than in the elusive psychology of revelation. He needed to "reduce" the mythical insight of the Gnostic, and the vast speculative vision of Neoplatonism, to the experience of the Christian
mind, with its spiritual energies and worldly obstacles. For this

reason, undoubtedly, he has remained the most "modern" of his contemporaries.

But in the transposition, the psychology of Narcissus has gone underground. Augustine seems not to have trusted that fine difference between Self and self which Prajapati tricked his divine disciples into understanding. In his treatise *De Musica,* Augustine analyzes the psychology of transgression. Things of the body, he writes, are dangerous because they "strongly fix in the memory what they bring from the slippery senses." Later, these traces of past experience—Augustine calls them "phantasms"—float dangerously in the mind; they have become images of potential delight, drawing the consciousness of the individual away from the naked otherness of God, into this circle of self-delighting fantasies. A man sins, according to Augustine, because he has lived too often and too intensely among the images of his mind. All such indulgence of the self is dangerous, for it leads one never closer, always further from God. To preserve himself from sin, the Christian must terrorize his inward life; he must flagellate his spiritual energies and extinguish the "pride" of the self.

We must not forget, however, that Augustine wrote in an atmosphere of polemics and religious contention. His goal was to defend the Church, and the "dangers" he warned against were palpable in the rival doctrines of pagan and heretic alike. Elsewhere in the *Confessions,* we read:

> There are many abroad who talk of their own fantasies and lead men's minds astray . . . These people want to be light, not in the Lord but in themselves, because they think that the nature of the soul is the same as God. In this way their darkness becomes denser still, because in their abominable arrogance they have separated themselves from you.

Augustine speaks here to defend Christian orthodoxy against the anarchic vision of the Gnostics and Manichaeans, both of whom accorded a powerful freedom to those idiosyncrasies of the individual spirit which the Church so mistrusted. By castigating the "pride" of self, and emphasizing the terrible abyss which separates God from man, Augustine strengthens a traditional bulwark of the Church that will continue to serve throughout its history, setting definite limits to the spiritual autonomy of the individual. The Christian lesson of humility will have as its counterpart, from the very first, an exhortation to obey the doctrines and dogma of the Church. The mystical purgation of the self is reshaped by official Christianity into a moral homily; the first article of Christian virtue becomes abdication of the individual will which humbles itself before the authority of God's representative on earth. The flight from self to Self, which is at the heart of Gnostic speculation, has become a flight from self to the infallible authority of the Church. It is no wonder, then, that the greatest of the Church Fathers should have allowed certain distinctions to become blurred. In doing so, he sets the tone of Christian morality, and defends the authoritarian order of the Church which was to become so overpowering during the Middle Ages.

This vision of humility conceals within it, however, a power of imagination that will never cease to strain at the limits of Christian dogma. The themes of Gnostic speculation, in particular, will continue to erupt, inherited or reinvented in the heat of mystical adventure by many illustrious, if marginal, Christians.

Like the Gnostics before them, the Christian mystics and theologians used the dialogue between the image and its object to characterize the mysterious transfer of divinity from God to His creation: the divine gift which alienates nothing from the giver, for what He has given He still retains.

As early as St. Paul, we read, "We all with unveiled face reflecting as in a mirror the glory of the Lord, are transformed into the same image from glory to glory." In later centuries, the sense of the spiritual journey is revealed in this description of man as a mirror for the divine light. Scotus Erigena calls man's soul "the purest mirror in the world," while Bonaventure's *Itinerarium Mentis in Deum* is described as an upward journey of the soul, which learns first to discover God "mirrored in the external world"; but then we move beyond this, to encounter, there "in the sanctuary of our souls . . . God reflected in His image." At this inmost point of the spiritual journey, the Christian rejoices to "behold the reflection of God as in the light of some candelabrum."

Although Christian philosophers have rarely been interested in cosmology, when the Cambridge Platonist, John Smith, turns to speculations it is in terms that are now familiar to us. The entire creation, according to Smith, can be thought of as a mirror; for "God made the universe and all the creatures contained therein as so many glasses wherein he might reflect His own glory. He hath copied forth Himself in the creation." The examples could be multiplied, from sources as mild as Smith, the Anglican Brahmin, to the heretical German cobbler, Jacob Böhme,* who wrote in his *Six Theosophic Points:*

> Seeing then the first will is an ungroundedness, to be regarded as an eternal nothing, we recognize it to be like a mirror wherein one sees his own image . . . Thus we recognize the eternal Unground out of Nature to be like a mirror . . . The eternal Unground eternally takes rise in itself, enters into itself, grasps itself in itself, and makes the center in itself . . .

Böhme, in his eccentric language, goes on to elaborate this image of God's self-creation with all the freedom of a Gnostic poet. The intertwining energies of Will, Fire, and Erotic Passion

---

* Böhme was an idiosyncratic German theologian and mystic (1575–1624) who lived an obscure life as a shoemaker. He wrote numerous books and tracts wherein he sought to reconcile the speculative thought of his century with a more traditional mysticism. His writings, couched in strange visionary language, had a great influence on the Romantics, as well as on later philosophers such as Schelling, Hegel, and Nietzsche.

which animate his vision articulate the original act of self-delight by which God gave Himself to man and to the world.

But Böhme did not stop here. Like the Gnostics, he sought to embrace in a single sweep the violence of the Cosmic struggle and the spiritual psychology of man. Between one and the other he found occult resemblances which he was careful to point out. In doing so, he warned against a temptation which lay beneath the surface of Christian morality, ready to draw even the most devout believer into its "error." The vast mirror of the Unground, Böhme wrote, is closer to man than he may realize; for the "fire" that surges within him, disturbing his serenity, propelling him toward the most unreasonable ambitions, has its source in a similar mirror: the "fiery mirror" of his pride. Pride causes man, in love with his own "great glory and beauty," to reach out after the properties of the unsurpassable "center." In Böhme's language, this meant that man, because of his pride, has sought to equal God: he has forged, within his own imperfect experience, a mirror in which he means to take pleasures like those taken by God in the great mirror of the universe. Such is the meaning of this lovely passage from Böhme's early work, *Aurora*, in which he warns man against the bewildering mirror he carries in his soul:

> Now being that he was so beauteously and gloriously Imagined or formed as a King in Nature, his beauteous form and feature tickled him, and so he thought with himself, *I am now God. . .* I will prepare and erect for myself a new kingdom; for the whole Circumference, Extent, or Region is mine, *I am God alone,* and none else. . . And in his pride he struck and smote himself with darkness and blindness, and made himself a *Devil. . .* He wrestled with the Salliter of God in the flash of fire and anxiety.

The danger for man, according to Böhme, lies in his very nobility. Because he has been endowed with a shadow of spiritual greatness and is capable, therefore, of great things, he may climb to that dangerous height from which his all-too-human frailty will betray him into pride. His fall is a dark measure of the height to which he had risen. We find echoed here, in Christian language, the tragedy of human greatness that so tormented the Greeks, finding its most powerful expression in the anguished choruses of the *Agamemnon*. Although the language of Christian piety since Augustine had concealed those uneasy brothers—the light and dark Narcissi of the *Poimandres,* or the self and Self of Buddhist scripture— beneath the surface of the language they continued nonetheless to shape our response to the dilemma of personality and spiritual ambition.

The mirror as it was used by Saint Paul, Scotus Erigena, Saint Bonaventure, and others, describes the danger, but also the ecstatic challenge concealed in the Christian vision, despite its authoritarian bias. In every case, the miracle of God's intimacy with man—the miracle of His immanence—is described as an act of self-delight. The image of the mirror enabled theologians to solve a paradox which troubled their understanding of God and His creation. How could God be present in the world of matter, even if it was only at the apex of man's soul? How could He be mingled with imperfection, though remaining flawless? How, above all, could He love what was less perfect than Himself, giving and yet somehow retaining what He gave? The image of the mirror, and the corresponding vision of God's generosity as an act of self-delight, allowed these questions to be answered. God came down into the world as into a mirror. He came down in order to possess an image of His own divinity. And He will allow man to be "saved," in order to save that fragment of His image captured in the human soul. Man is at best an invisible partner in this exchange between God and Himself.

This feeling of man's nothingness in the face of the Divinity, what Rudolph Otto has called the overpowering sense of his "creatureliness," is undoubtedly an element in all religious experience. The Christian must acknowledge his infinite dependence in the face of God's self-delight. He is exhorted to efface the movements of his will, in order to reflect more perfectly the image of his Master. For the only virtue the good Christian must traditionally seek is to become less and less himself, so that God, through this act of personal self-effacement, may delight more purely in His own reflected image. It is this complicity in God's pleasure which lies behind passages like this one, by that somber moralist, Thomas a Kempis: "The highest and most profitable learning is this: that a man have a truthful knowledge and a full despairing of himself." Or this one, by the German mystic Meister Eckhart: "It is always you yourself that hinders yourself. . . . Therefore begin first with yourself and forsake yourself. Truly you will then flee first from yourself, whatever else you may flee."

Because God seeks Himself, man must flee himself. Such is the moral dilemma of Christianity. Yet, as Prajapati sought to teach his disciples, the mirror can "betray" those who cultivate it. This is what Böhme clearly saw when he warned man against the mirror in his soul which was also his greatest glory. When man looked inward, past the deforming veils of his ego, he might discover in the soul's mirror another image: not God's but his own. Indeed, in the pure heat of the mystical experience, the distinction between the two, so important to Christian morality, becomes secondary. Instead there is a powerful sense of God's nearness to the soul, a glory at the "presence" which has drawn one so completely into its Light that such distinctions need no longer be made. The distance between God and self has become so diminished that the very words, in mystical language, are interchangeable. At the end of the *Poimandres*, we see the purified souls "rise up toward the Father, and give themselves up to the Powers, and having become Powers themselves, enter the godhead. This is the good end of those who have

attained gnosis: to become God." Such is also the language of
the great German mystics Eckhart, Suso, Tauler, Ruysbroeck,
and others who will repeat, with Eckhart's *Sermon on the Just
Man,* that "if a man is in justice, he is in God and he is God."
Pursuing the logic of their experience, the mystics restore to
Christianity the suppressed Self inside the ego whose virtue is
to be both human and more-than-human, both man and God.

The very warmth of the Christian vision, the growing experience of personality that begins to animate its doctrine—following the example of Augustine himself—charges this moral
dilemma with all the bewildering attraction of a loving, highly
personalized God. When Dante, in the *Paradiso* (Canto xxxiii),
renews the traditional image of the mirror, his language radiates
a mood of sensuous delight that was unknown to the Gnostics:

> Eternal light, that in Thyself alone
> Dwelling, alone dost know Thyself, and smile
> On Thy self-love, so knowing and so known!
>
> The sphering thus begot, perceptible
> In Thee like mirrored light, now to my view—
> When I had looked on it a little while—
>
> Seemed in itself, and in its own self-hue,
> Limned with our image.

This self-loving, self-delighting God is not only a term in the
speculative logic of theologians. He is sensuous and attractive;
He draws the imagination to Him, and troubles the all-too-
human emotions of the believer. The explosiveness, the tension
of Christian morality can be traced, surely, to this image of a
God who exalts those very qualities of emotion which are forbidden to man. The ever-repeated injunctions against pride,
the authoritarian rigor of the Church, the terrible lesson of
humility repeated century after century, point to a living

presence always ready to surge into the light and claim its own:
the repressed, tantalizing Self which Christianity has alter-
nately fed and starved with an ever-renewed energy of contradiction. Given this confusion in the Christian experience of
grace, one can hardly blame the Italian mystic Angela of Foligno
for the cruel story she tells of her progress toward God:

> In that time and by God's will, there died my mother, who was
> a great hindrance to me in following the way of God; my hus-
> band died likewise; and in a short time there died all my chil-
> dren. And because I had begun to follow the aforesaid way, and
> prayed God to rid me of them, I had great consolation of their
> deaths, although I also felt some grief; wherefore, because God
> had shown me this grace, I imagined that my heart was in the
> heart of God and His Will and His Heart in my heart.

Angela is a ruthless penitent. Because "God had shown her
this grace," she will allow no earthly attachment to stand between her self and that high ground in the soul toward which
she travels. She had "great consolation," and also "some grief;"
yet it is clear that the consolation far outweighed the grief.
Surely there is something inhuman in Angela's passion for
grace. The death-wish become reality which she evokes with
such serenity of conscience recalls the extreme individualism of
certain heretics, of whom we will speak in their turn. Indeed,
to be fair, Angela's zeal has often been blamed by "wiser"
doctors of the Church. Yet the way she has taken is the high
road to Heaven, the goal she sets is the noblest that Christianity
can offer. And the infantile selfishness of her experience is as
deeply embedded in the spiritual vision of Christianity as is its
exhortation to humility.

Of all the great mystics, Eckhart* is perhaps closest to under-

---

* Meister Eckhart: probably the greatest German speculative mystic,
born at Hochheim, near Gotha (1260?–1328?). His voluminous writings
helped to form the tradition of medieval German prose. He taught and
preached actively in Strasbourg and later in Cologne, where he became
the most popular preacher in Germany, though his mystical doctrines

standing not only the danger of this egotistical backsliding, but
how closely it is bound to the nature of the mystical experience
itself. Like all mystics, Eckhart knew that the only way to meet
with God was to dissolve the boundaries of the self. The mystic
was precisely a man who had learned to reach beyond the
frailty of his ego. Yet, in a famous parable of the mystic way,
Eckhart begins, "A nobleman went out into a far country to
obtain for himself a kingdom, and returned." As Böhme was
later to point out, the man who sets out on the journey must
already be noble; for he who abandons the self must already be
self-possessed; in giving up his selfhood, he must have something to lose. But then, when at last he does rise beyond the
ego, it is to obtain an even greater wealth: the title to a kingdom.
The seeds of his humility are endowed with a powerful grace.
Eckhart quotes St. Matthew, who says, "He who forsakes
anything for My sake shall receive a hundredfold as much
again." The mystic abandons the self, because he knows he will
receive it back a hundredfold. His humility is an adventure, and
a harsh constraint, but it is also a delight; the "nobleman," after
his long journey, returns loaded with "riches."

Eckhart, it is true, argues that the noblest Union, at the far
end of the journey, can never again be contained in the com-
pressed circle of the self. But such stability, he adds, will be
possible only "in eternity." We, who are still anchored in the
flesh, are condemned to backslide from the joy and terror of
Illumination, into the old self. Yet what a strangely exalted ego
Eckhart proposes to us! After having journeyed to the end of
the way, Eckhart writes:

> I can do all things by my will. I can bear all the hardships of
> all men, and feed all the poor and do the work of all men, or
> whatever else you can imagine. If you do not lack the will, but
> only the power, you have really done it in the sight of God . . .

were at times suspect to the Church and accused of heretical tendencies.
Eckhart was the shaping influence on fourteenth-century German mysticism.

> If I wanted to have as much will as all the world has . . . then
> I have it, for what I want I have.

Simon's vision was not bolder than this. Eckhart unleashes the
power of his imagination. He expresses the thirst for solitary
greatness that will be echoed in Goethe's *Faust,* in Hegel's image
of the history-devouring sage, in Hölderlin's *Empedokles,* in
Lautréamont's *Maldoror,* in Nietzsche's character of Zarathustra.

When, centuries later, the German mystic Angelus Silesius
attempted to capture in verse the loving exaltation he felt during
such moments of grace, he wrote:

> I am rich as God. Dear friend, believe me:
> No particle of dust that is not His and mine.
> I know God cannot live a moment without me:
> If I should come to nothing, God shall cease to be.

The "way up" leads past this country of the emotions, where
the strands of self and Self are woven into a single fabric. The
final glory of the way, all seem to agree, lies beyond such pleasure-
ful exaltation, in a *coincidentum oppositorium* of plenitude and
emptiness, Light and Darkness, Height and Depth. Yet something in the Western sensibility is irrevocably pleased by the
transvalued selfhood which it encounters on the way. The yogi,
in his mystical wisdom, was familiar with this dilemma. As he
mastered, step by step, the complexities of his body, he was said
to reach a degree of discipline so extreme that he acquired unequaled magic powers. Nothing on earth could resist his will.
At this stage, the yogi was said to have ended his climb from the
world of change into the world of eternity. He had risen above
imperfect experience by mastering it entirely. But the yogi
understood at this point the futility of such magical powers. The
same movement of wisdom which had led him so far, now led
him still further. He renounced the magic and the will, moving
beyond them into the pure impersonality of Union. But we in the

West have been fascinated by the magic, we have been fascinated by the rich possibilities of character and individuality. The delight of God's mirror has tempted us to apply it to the dilemma of our earthly frailty and to the "unreasonable" humanity of our ambitions.

3 THE HERESY OF THE FREE SPIRIT

The Wheel of Fortune is a favorite image in medieval iconography. It is an emblem of earthly insecurity, and it corresponds to a permanent anxiety in the medieval mind: a fear of unforeseeable change, of the disasters, famines, and wars which cast a shadow of apprehension over the medieval world. The Wheel of Fortune was a reminder that the greatest success, poised at the summit of the ascending arc, would be shattered tomorrow as the wheel spun full circle. Thus the legend inscribed on one anonymous image of fortune: "I have no kingdom; I will reign, I reign, I have reigned." Success was already an omen of disaster; a good year, by the logic of inconstancy, was the harbinger of a bad one. Huizinga, in his history of the declining Middle Ages, speaks of "wars and brigandage, scarcity, misery and pestilence."

This mood of insecurity, symbolized by the Wheel of Fortune, lies behind the medieval dream of a divinely inspired social order. It explains the eagerness with which the Pseudo-Dionysian vision of spheres, hierarchies, and angels was adopted in the thirteenth century. "This world," condemned to perpetual change, was the realm of unreality. Misfortune and change were the work of the devil. Anything, therefore, which violated the harmony, any initiative contrary to the spoken Authorities of order, was sinful. The whole notion of sin became highly "legalistic": a question of broken rules, while "virtue," divorced from any practical experience of "grace," became an act of conformity, a "spontaneous" agreement with the framework of the official reality.

The cult of Authority, during the Middle Ages, is undoubtedly rooted in this feeling of worldly insecurity. Obedience to the traditional models absolved men from responsibility for their own fates. It is a reaction described by Mircea Eliade in *The Myth of the Eternal Return:* the heroic model stands at the entrance to culture, an "archetype" whose authority comes from an absolute fullness of being. In "primitive" cultures, all life is regulated on the model of this mythical hero; the society is ruled by repetition. By repeating the original gestures of the hero, man neutralized time and leapt outside of change; he returned to the harmony of the "former times," by abdicating everything that was "merely" personal. During the Middle Ages, Boethius, Augustine, the Bible, and later Aristotle, became heroic Authorities: bulwarks against new thought and against the harsh insecurity that men continued to feel.

This meant, in effect, a culture based on suppressed individuality. The Church, whose obsession with orthodoxy became exacerbated at this time, gained a repressive energy unequaled before. Its antiworldly morality taught that the body was a prison, the passions a highroad to hell. Without strict obedience to Church ritual and dogma, the spirit was doomed to follow the way of its flesh into perdition. It was a simple morality, fitted to the tendency of the medieval mind to see violent contrasts in the world: Light and Darkness, Summer and Winter, Heaven and Hell, Good and Evil, Matter and Spirit. The ground was well prepared for the dualist heresies of the thirteenth century, for there was an implicit Manichaeism in the way people grasped their experience of the world.

The thirteenth century was a time of awakening energies. The repressive medieval vision, rooted in the cult of authority, gathered momentum now, at first condemning even the new Aristotelian spirit. It was this "police force" mentality, as Burckhardt put it, that would eventually animate the Inquisition and witch hunts of later centuries. But this strengthening of authority drew its new harshness from a more general awakening that stirred all of European culture and led, in particular, to a revival of heretical movements unprecedented since the days of the early Church.

For centuries, it would seem, the peoples of Europe had ceased to respond to their own experience. Instead they had been content to transcribe the wisdom surviving from a time when everything human and divine had been decided once and for all. In those former days—the half-mythical memories of Rome—the world had been younger and therefore richer in signs for man.

By the twelfth and thirteenth centuries, however, the rootless society of the early Middle Ages had acquired a measure of stability; the feudal order had gathered riches and momentum; the Authorities of the religious and secular branches had ramified with renewed vigor. First, pioneers like Abelard, and then the Schools themselves, fortified by a new familiarity with the Aristotelian corpus, began to extend the scholastic method, to interrogate, and to follow their personal dialectics to conclusions that were often of doubtful orthodoxy. A whole tradition of vernacular literature, owing little or nothing to classical models, began to gain an audience, outside of the increasingly specialized circles of Latin culture.

The resurgence of heresy belongs to this atmosphere of renewed energies. These defections from the orthodox vision of the Schoolmen challenged the discrepancy between the dream and the reality; between the Pseudo-Dionysian hierarchies and the repressive world they were meant to justify. In this unstable atmosphere of resistances, defections, and mystical enthusiasm, the undermining spirit of the individual—that creature suspect above all to the medieval mind—began to exercise itself and transmit its new experience to the modern world.

Little evidence remains of the heresies which spread through Europe for more than two centuries. The Church was a thoroughgoing persecutor, manipulating its secular arms with skill and consummate brutality. It dismantled the heretical sects, brought them to trial, refuted their arguments in due scholastic style, and then left behind pyres of their burned books, and more pyres for the unrepentant heretics themselves, who often leapt joyfully into the flames, like the martyrs of the early Church itself.

What we know of the heresies comes, most often, from copious papers of accusation compiled by the Inquisitors, whose method of question, argument, and refutation led them to give more or less honest accounts of the doctrines they accused. This is supplemented by occasional surviving documents, which more often than not verify the accuracy of the Church records.

Of all the Neognostic heresies which agitated Europe during these centuries, surely the most curious is that sect of wandering spiritual anarchists, the Heretics or Brethren of the Free Spirit. In their lives as well as in their doctrine the Brethren expressed a spirit of subversive egotism which has rarely been surpassed; its effect was to undermine completely the medieval vision of a divinely inspired universal order. Not until the far more literary visionaries of the nineteenth century—Emerson, Stirner, Nietzsche, et al.—had begun to write, have such antisocial doctrines been expressed and widely adhered to.

The Brethren of the Free Spirit offered their initiates nothing less than a prospect of self-deification, accompanied by an extreme spiritual libertinism, which, for centuries, scandalized more timid believers. From the ninety-seven counts of accusation against the Brethren made by Albertus Magnus* during the

---

* Albertus Magnus was also known as Albert of Cologne (1206?–1280). He was one of the widest-read and most learned men of his time. As a member of the Dominican order, he publicly defended the Dominicans against their many detractors. He engaged in extensive preaching toward the end of his life, mostly in and around Bavaria. It was in his Inquisi-

late thirteenth century—one of the first traces we have of the heresy—to the outraged texts of Richard Baxter, the English puritan, who accused them of every "abominable filthiness of life," the Brethren of the Free Spirit willfully shocked the religious and moral sensibilities of their contemporaries.

The movement itself is difficult to trace and has, on the whole, been neglected by historians. During the repeated waves of repression that harassed the heretics during the fourteenth century, they disguised themselves so well that it became hard to distinguish them from many other groups practicing voluntary poverty. The Church was puzzled by the spread of the movement but also by its elusiveness. Papal delegates were often warned against bringing innocent victims to the stake in their zeal to stamp out the offenders. Unlike the Cathars in Southern France,* who founded a secular power and provoked a political response from the Church, the Brethren of the Free Spirit were able to disappear in the confusion of minor orders that prevailed during the thirteenth and fourteenth centuries. They preserved their antinomian doctrine by infiltrating groups of wandering beggars known as Beghards and Beguines, who traveled throughout medieval Germany crying *Brot durch Gott* ("Bread for the love of God").

---

torial capacity as a Dominican that he confronted the Heretics of the Free Spirit.

* The Cathars were a heretical Christian sect that flourished in many parts of western Europe during the twelfth and thirteenth centuries. Their stronghold was southern France where, for one hundred years, they managed to supplant the orthodox Church almost entirely. The Cathars inherited the radical dualism of the early Gnostics, probably through a chain of obscure historical influences—neognostical sects are known to have survived for one thousand years in parts of eastern Europe. The Church of the Cathars declined in the thirteenth century, after Simon de Monfort led a crusade against them (the Albigensian Crusade), burning and destroying all of their strongholds in southern France. The Dominicans were first formed by the Catholic Church in order to combat the influence of the Cathars, using methods of Inquisition conceived for that purpose. The Dominicans also imitated the piety and poverty for which the Cathars were known.

Their elusiveness, however, was not only a response to the persecuting monolith of the Church. The very nature of their doctrine led the heretics to live outside of society, for that doctrine embodied, essentially, a flight from social order and responsibility. The Brother of the Free Spirit was taught to assume, in and through his own exalted sensuality, a lasting communion with the highest of all Authorities: God Himself.

Their doctrine of an emotionally charged divine knowledge belongs to the same current of Neoplatonic thought which, from Scotus Erigena on, had inspired more orthodox mystics such as Eckhart, Ruysbroeck, and Suso. But the antiworldly bias of the heretics led them to blur the distinctions between God and man, as the early Gnostics had also done; they preached instead a more radical form of illumination in which the divine source and its earthly receptacle became one. The heretic underwent a permanent transfiguration of his very flesh, such as no mystic, in the usual sense, had ever aspired to.

Illumination is usually described as overpowering but brief. For a moment, the self is dissolved into the sea of its God. Later the mystic recalls this flash of erotic harmony, as it continues to shed its Light over his stay in the body. In the Christian as in the Buddhist traditions, the mystic reconciles his intense solitude with a life of good works, within the framework of the Church and of the existing society. Like St. Theresa and St. Francis, he founds monasteries; like Eckhart, he preaches. He may bring new insights and fresh attitudes to his work; he may give free reign to a spirit of criticism and innovation; but he makes terms with the world and in particular with his Church, however imperfect they may be.

The heretic of the Free Spirit accepted no compromise with the world. When, after long discipline and fasting, he had achieved unity with God, he believed his illumination was anchored permanently in the flesh, elevating his entire life onto a plane of mystical transparency. The experience of mystical knowledge was entirely renewed for the Brethren of the Free

Spirit. Instead of succumbing to the weight of his "creatureliness"—a sense of the infinite nothingness of self—the heretic never ceased to exalt his transfigured individuality. With God's help, the self was transformed into a durable focus of the divine light which then could be, as Christ had been, a kind of God on earth.

In the *Liber Manualis* Albertus Magnus accuses the heretics of rejecting "Christ's divinity, the authority of Scripture and Church, the value of the sacraments," because they claimed to have become more divine than Christ Himself. According to their doctrine, Albertus continues, "Man must abstain from exterior things, and follow only the signs of the spirit within." By peeling away the constraint of earthly law and necessity, the soul "can become God; the soul is eternal and can, through self-exaltation, become the principle of universal life." They believed, therefore, that "it was enough to act like Christ in order to equal Him, and to outdo in saintliness all those revered by the Church."

One result of this strange doctrine was a theory of mystical libertinism, in which self-indulgence and erotic freedom become signs of godliness. According to the indictment of Albertus Magnus, the heretic claims that "we become God in all the powers of our being, down to the last elements of our body; we must give to the body everything it violently desires." It becomes an act of cosmic piety to satisfy one's needs, a mystical joy to obey the wildest caprice of the emotions. Like the Gnostics before them, the heretics invoked St. Paul's doctrine of grace: "To the pure all is pure." But they interpreted it in keeping with their system of mystical license. Adultery, blasphemy, lying, and even murder were no longer considered to be sins. On the contrary, if they were done freely, in a state of illumination, they were so many signs that God was acting inside the ego.

During the fourteenth century, after cruel repression had forced the movement underground, a certain Johann of Brunn recanted after having lived for twenty-eight years among the heretical Beghards in Cologne. He entered the Dominican order, where he was asked, as penitence, to write a complete confession of his errors. Johann had been living with his wife in the town of Brunn, when he felt called to lead "the perfect life." He took the advice of a friend and went to live in Cologne with a community of Beghards who were widely known for their piety and observance of the Christian life. Before he was accepted in the group, however, he had to sell all his belongings and take a vow of voluntary poverty. He was then given a ragged tunic and told to beg his livelihood in the streets of Cologne, crying the watchword of the heretical Beghards, *Brot durch Gott*. The discipline at first was hard. He was taught to stifle every movement of the will; to spend his days in continual prayer and meditation; to engage only in acts which were distasteful to him. But when he finally crossed the threshold of initiation, all constraint was lifted. "The free man had the right to give in to all his desires, to satisfy all his caprices: his own nature blossomed in all the works of nature. God was in him totally and corporally; all his movements were divine."

Once this inner freedom was achieved, Johann continues, all humanity was thought of as a servile mass to be manipulated at will. The Brethren could steal from the weak and crippled, or "kill whoever bothered them." They lied to priests, gaining thereby a great reputation for piety. The hospices of these mendicant brothers were used for secret orgiastic ceremonies, in which God was said to descend into the very heat of the erotic excitement.

The antiworldly vision of the heretics differed from that of other medieval dualists in another important detail. Though the material world was considered to be evil, the Brethren of the Free Spirit felt that they were endowed with a mission of rehabilitation. Since their own wills were godly, they could lead worldly things back toward the light, by desiring them and using them. By indulging their desires, they not only demonstrated the presence of God in their ego, they also did a work of redemption, spreading God into the world which He had abandoned.

Johann's confession resembles the outcries that were raised in England three centuries later against the doctrines of the Ranters, who were probably the last resurgence of the medieval heresy. The Episcopalian, Edward Hyde, makes his Ranter opponent claim "that they are very God, infinite and Almighty as the very God is . . . That the acts of adultery, drunkenness, swearing, and the like open wickedness, are in their own nature as holy and righteous as the duties of prayer and giving of thanks . . . That all the women of the world are but one woman's husband in unity; so that one man may be with all the women in the world for they are her husband in unity . . ." Other texts by and against the Ranters give a picture of the movement consistent with Hyde's accusations. Surprisingly enough, the Ranters were often linked with another, more respectable group, the Quakers. The two sects seem to have been rivals for the same clientele; indeed, the Quakers have been credited with outbidding the libertarians and drawing off many of their adepts. The "inner light" of the Quakers, their experience of violent possession, is not unlike the gnosis of the Free Spirit; though the Quakers, of course, rejected any hint of the antinomian conclusions drawn by the heretics.

We come now to the final audacity of the heretical vision. The Brethren of the Free Spirit did not hesitate to pursue the logic of their gnosis to its furthest extreme. Once the self had become a permanent vessel for the divine energy, it was only a step to believing that the energy originated there where it seemed to appear. Once more the self was transfigured. It had been a lens through which God expressed His light, or a receptacle harboring the divinity on earth; now it became the very light itself, the original source of all godliness. To the more exalted heretics, God Himself was an appendage to the divine will of the ego: "When God created all things, I created all things with

Him . . . I am more than God." The mystic Ruysbroeck puts the following words into the mouth of his heretical opponent:

> When I dwelt in my original being and in my eternal essence, there was no God for me. What I was I wished to be, and what I wished to be I was. It is by my own free will that I have emerged and become what I am . . . God can know, wish, do nothing without me. With God I have created myself and I have created all things, and it is my hand that supports heaven and earth and all creatures . . . Without me nothing exists.

There is undoubtedly a kind of madness in the libertarian attitudes of the Brethren. Modern psychology has given clinical names to such "delusions of grandeur" which seem to cross the line into psychosis and give rise to entirely unsocial modes of behavior. We remember that Schreber, in Freud's case history, believed that his body had become the focus of divine rays; and the crank libertarian mystic Jean Antoine Boullan, whose cult swept through eastern Europe during the nineteenth century, was found to be "a typical paranoiac, obsessed by delusions of grandeur and persecution." The extreme unsocial behavior of the Brethren draws on energies that are normally repressed by civilized morality. It expresses a refusal of society which we associate with extreme neurosis or psychosis. Yet to call the permanent illumination of the Brethren madness is to blur several important distinctions. For one thing, the heretics organized their lives according to doctrines which were taught, either orally or by means of special documents, from generation to generation. They "learned" their mad response to the world, and shared it with other Brethren toward whom their behavior remained perfectly "normal." The utter solitude and the ego disintegration which characterize psychotics were in no way part of their experience. The English psychoanalyst, R. D. Laing, points out that a number of extreme schizoid personalities preserve their "contact" with reality by adhering to some sect, or esoteric group, whose bizarre doctrines they appropriate for themselves. By "sharing" their system of experience they remain whole, and live their lives this side of complete isolation. Strindberg is a literary example of one who was able to make such a choice: during his entire life his strange delusions and obsessive psychological insecurity brought him close to the limits of sanity, until he found a "system" of metaphysical doctrines in the work of Swedenborg (and later the Cabalists) which allowed him to organize his madness by expressing and communicating it. Similarly, the Brethren of the Free Spirit, living in a world whose obsession with insecurity we have already described, fortified themselves by their doctrine of mystical exaltation.

A more important distinction, however, has to do with the attitude of medieval society toward the heretics. The failure of historians to trace definite limits to their influence is instructive here, for it emphasizes not only the elusiveness of the movement but the widespread attraction it exercised over large numbers of people. The heresy is hard to pin down because it expressed an omnipresent mood, apt to crystallize almost anywhere.

Trithemius, abbot of Sponheim, still found traces of the Brethren in Germany toward the end of the fifteenth century, a hundred years after the fanatical policing of Charles IV had sent hundreds of heretics to the stake. Trithemius was convinced that the founder and first adept of the heresy was a certain Tanchelm, a wild "messiah" who appeared near Antwerp during the twelfth century at the head of a ragged horde and claimed to be a reincarnation of Christ. The relation between Tanchelm and the sect of the Almoricians, who were brought to justice in Paris some sixty or seventy years later, remains a mystery. Yet the doctrines of the Almoricians leave no doubt as to their heretical allegiance. Again no link has been detected between the Parisian sect and the dominant form of the movement in Germany during the next two centuries. Nor can any be found between the German movement and the Ranters, in seventeenth-century England.

Apparently something in this strangely subversive doctrine was so attractive to medieval society that the heresy was able to flourish throughout a large portion of Europe, despite the greatest of difficulties.

If the Brethren of the Free Spirit were mad, the madness was closely linked to the nature of medieval society and religion, for it awakened a new and vigorous response in those who needed to resist the oppressive authority of the feudal order. Here is where the distinction between "mental illness" and the self-exalted mood of the heretics becomes interesting.

Distinctions of this kind have been made before. The connection between neurosis and history was brilliantly analyzed by the psychoanalyst Erik Erikson in *Young Man Luther;* while, as long as a century ago, the French historian Jules Michelet described the psychic and social energies released by those medieval madwomen, *les sorcières*. But it is modern anthropology that has done most to broaden our understanding of the dialogue between madness and society. Claude Lévi-Strauss points out that the shaman, who is a source of sacred power in certain societies, must by all Western standards be described at best as an unstable character and at worst as a psychotic delusive. Yet such a description, though true enough, entirely misses the point, he says. The shaman's folly is alive with meaning for his fellow tribesmen; it is a powerful madness, feeding its energy into precise rituals and thereby helping to preserve the spiritual health of the community. The shaman, because he is "mad," cannot live in normal society; but his madness traces a limit within which others can lead their lives, assured of that mysterious energy which the shaman has guaranteed them.

Between the shaman and the Brother of the Free Spirit there is this common genius: each enabled society to recognize a meaning in his madness; to discover its meaning and madness in his own. The idea of the exemplary neurosis—or psychosis—

has been largely discussed in recent years. Luther's neurotic crises, and the language he found to resolve them, stirred a similar impulse in the men of his time. His religious genius enabled him to broaden the terms of his anxiety, making his problem theirs, and his solution theirs as well. The same can be said for the Heretics of the Free Spirit. Their doctrine of permanent illumination expressed a need that was everywhere on the point of being recognized; a need that had been held in suspension in the work of men like Scotus Erigena and Amaury de Bène, awaiting a voice that could dramatize it for the popular imagination. With Tanchelm, and so many anonymous heretics, that voice was found.

We find that we have qualified our initial verdict of psychosis and accepted a more puzzled sense of the relationship between certain kinds of behavior and the society in which they appear. It is useful to make such distinctions now, for the charge of insanity has often been brought against the men who will be considered in these pages. The "madness" of Whitman, Rousseau, Nietzsche, Kierkegaard, Baudelaire, even Pascal, has caused a great deal of ink to flow. And the diagnoses which have been made are probably correct, as far as they go. The problem is that they do not go far enough.

The conversation of psychotics is, according to popular opinion, meaningless. This has not always been the case. The shaman's madness was charged with meaning for his people. During the Middle Ages, the Inquisitors did not mistake the importance of the antinomian heretics. The heretical doctrine was considered aberrant and excessive, but its meaning was not underestimated; it had to be stamped out but also refuted. Important theologians like Albert the Great countered the heretics' arguments point by point. Even the great Duns Scotus was tempted to enter the lists against them, not to accuse them of incoherence but of grave error.

It is possible, in fact, to make a different "diagnosis" of the

Free Spirit, one having nothing to do with mental illness. The heresy can also be understood as an extreme resistance to every principle of order in medieval society. Against the mediation of the Church and the scholastic obsession with dogma, the Brethren offered an emotionally charged communion with God and the Gnostic experience of divine knowledge. Against a secular community in which every soul was completely identified with its place and social function, the Brethren offered the subversion of all social functions without exception. Against a Cosmos of interlocking hierarchies, rising in orderly fashion toward God, the Brethren offered a world of chaos in which the only traces of Light and order were found in their own wills and passions. Against the vision of man as the smallest unit—the microcosm—in a vast macrocosm which was the source of his humanity, the Brethren offered a self-generated, self-exalted individual who was the source of all Light in a darkened world.

Between the Pseudo-Dionysian dream and the quicksand on which, for centuries, daily experience had been raised and demolished, there had opened a gap wide enough for desperation to enter, provoking new thoughts in the minds of those who had begun to doubt. A popular belief, in the thirteenth and fourteenth centuries, held that no soul had entered Paradise since the splitting of the Churches. It is from this mood of desperation, in a world abandoned by grace, that the antiworldly, antiauthoritarian dualism of the heresies drew its strength. In the light of medieval experience, it could be argued that the heretics were far closer to the reality than were the Schoolmen with all their pomp and magnificence.

4 THE MOOD OF MEDITATION

In Georges de La Tour's painting "La Madeleine au Miroir" (seventeenth century), we see Mary Magdalene looking to one side, quietly attentive. The only light in the painting comes from a candle, glowing behind the death's head which the Magdalene fingers absent-mindedly. At first her eyes seem to be gazing beyond the painting itself, as if no earthly object could explain the emotion in them. To the left a mirror hangs from the wall, and this, we soon discover, is what Magdalene has been looking at. We can only guess at what she sees in the mirror. But we, outside the painting, see the reflected image of a skull, lit by a point of candlelight: death repeated in its image, enforced and clarified by its doubleness. De La Tour's painting conveys the intense calm of meditation; the vision of eyes directed inward, beneath the illusory veils of the body. Yet, despite the morbid quality of the scene, Magdalene has lost none of her sensuality. The dress she wears hangs loosely over her breasts; her face is mobile and emotional. This image of the sensual woman gazing into her mirror—for centuries the conventional figure of idleness, luxury, or self-indulgence—has been transformed by De La Tour into that of a saint whose mirror reflects back to her the transcendence and the harsh solitude of death.

"La Madeleine au Miroir" expresses a new feeling in Catholic spirituality: a need to enter into the hard mysteries of religion, not despite the senses, but through their very power and fascination. We do not see Magdalene purging the "phantasms" of her inner life with guilt and self-mortification. She knows that the impulses which first led her into sin contain a principle of transcendence; their very strength reveals to her a path inward to the "apex" of the soul.

The religious and cultural upheavals of the sixteenth century had brought about a far more subtle awareness of the intricacies of the self. The Catholic Church, in particular, saw quickly how important it would be to cultivate this newly valued "individualism." It set about readjusting its spiritual goals in order to make them more attractive to the new sensibility. To meet the need, a great emphasis came to be given, throughout Europe, to the practices of meditation. Manuals of Meditation recommending entire programs of spiritual discipline were popularized; the programs included exercises in concentration, models to be followed, subjects fit for different occasions and personalities. The manuals of Loyola, Luis de Granada, François de Sales, to mention the most popular, were translated into all the European languages, transforming the spiritual habits of the entire continent.

Theologians had always made a distinction between the intellectual practice of "meditation" and the higher state of mystical "contemplation." Meditation, properly speaking, was thought to prepare the spirit, by initiating it into divine matters "in which our mynd, not as a flie, by a simple musing, nor yet as a locust, to eate and be filled, but as a sacred Bee flies amongst the flowers of holy mysteries, to extract from them the honie of Divine Love" (François de Sales). To meditate meant to consider the various articles of faith, to explore their ramifications in religion and thought, and finally to grasp them, not only with the intellect, but with all the awakened strength of the emotions. During the sixteenth century, however, this "lower" activity of the spirit was enriched by the practice of the manuals, which served to strengthen the emotional resonance of meditation and make it more attractive to large numbers of people. François de Sales' definition, quoted above, has a decidedly mystical tone, as if the "understanding" he refers to carried with it already a grain of the ultimate sweetness. This new attitude, popularized by the manuals, blurred the line between meditation and contemplation, as the former drew the latter down and absorbed it. This helps to explain the great popularity and the ease of sixteenth-century mysticism. It accounts also for the warning thundered by St. John of the Cross, during the next century, against the illusory pleasures of meditation: those sudden flashes of light which even the beginner could experience, though his imperfect self was still too weak to resist the temptation of "spiritual pride and gluttony."

From the height of his medieval grimness, John of the Cross understood the "danger" of these newfangled disciplines which taught the initiate to prey on his own feelings, cultivating the "phantasms" of his inner life almost to the point of hallucination. "These persons," he writes, "in communicating, strive with every nerve to obtain some kind of sensible sweetness and pleasure, instead of humbly doing reverence and giving praise within themselves to God. [They tend to act as if] their own satisfaction and pleasure were the satisfaction and pleasure of God." But already John of the Cross was an isolated figure. For another spirit had begun to stir at the heart of Christian devotion. Those very "phantasms" which the medieval ascetic had struggled to purge from his imagination because they smacked of temptation and the devil had, by the sixteenth century, become a bulwark of the religious experience. A brief account of the practice of meditation will make this even clearer.

According to most manuals, the work of meditation itself is preceded by a short preparatory exercise known as the "composition of place." In order to mobilize his faculties, the initiate is taught to evoke all the visual details related to the subject of his meditation. He sees "the places where the things [he] meditated on were wrought by imagining [himself] to be really present at these places." The meditation will grow out of this imaginary landscape whose purpose is to disorient the senses by loosening their contact with profane reality while it creates

another, more spiritual world, impressed upon the mind of the
initiate with all the driving force of a hallucination.

But the composition of place does more than disorient the
senses and stimulate the emotions. It is highly articulated, complex, convincing. If the subject of the meditation is Heaven, for
example, one should evoke:

> the spatious pleasantnes of that celestiall Countrie, the glorious
> companie of Angels and Saintes. Yf on God's judgment which
> must passe upon us, our Savior sitting on his Judgment Seate,
> and we before Him expecting the finall sentance: if on death,
> ourselves laied on our bed, forsaken of the Physitians, com-
> passed about with our weeping friends, and expecting our last
> agony.

This amounts to a visionary poetry located only in the mind; a
garland of highly sensuous images, woven about a fixed center:
the exalted selfhood of the initiate. For the "hero" in each of
these scenes is the meditator himself. When God appears on the
Judgment Seat, His business will be only with this strangely
exalted ego who has dared to evoke Him in the space of his
mind. Again the creative imagination is turned loose, in the
service of religion, as it once had been for the Gnostics, transforming the self into an impassioned actor, a protagonist in the
great drama of salvation.

This is made even more apparent in a passage from the Latin
exercises of the English Catholic, Robert Southwell. Southwell
suggests that the reader begin his meditation by considering how
he himself had been enslaved by the devil, until one day the
"King" heard of his plight, laid aside his royal robes, and came
down dressed as a beggar, to save the doomed sinner. "For
thirty years he sought thee . . . etc." The exercise goes on to
describe how each fatal step of the Savior was a personal gesture made toward the reader himself and culminating in this
moment of awful intensity when "at length He found thee
among the wolves. He freed thee, but the wolves have attacked

Him and He has been slain." In Southwell's exercise, God moves like a vast influence about the willful center of the ego. All the will and emotion of the initiate, we are told, must be directed toward this one goal: to re-create the drama of salvation in the single space of the mind; to withdraw all emotion and concern from the profane world, replacing them with a circle of sacred "phantasms" whose very intensity will raise the self to its highest possibility: its own, and the world's, salvation.

These techniques of meditation compose a private rhetoric, a controlled colloquy of self with self, which is no longer condemned but has instead been made into a rich mode of religious experience. As we read the description of another meditative practice, known as "application of the senses," we seem to be reading, point by point, a reversal of Augustine's inquiry into the psychology of the sinful mind. Ignatius Loyola explains, in the following passage, how to obtain the greatest effect when meditating on the life of Christ:

> The first point is to see the persons with the eyes of the imagination . . . The second is to hear what they are saying, or might say; and by reflecting on oneself, to take some fruit from this. The third is to smell and taste the infinite sweetness and delight of the Divinity . . . reflecting on oneself, and deriving some fruit from this. The fourth is to feel with the touch; as, for example, to kiss and embrace the spots where such persons tread and sit, always endeavoring to draw fruit therefrom.

There is a strong egotism in this vision which turns the holy events of Christianity into a grove for the hungry self, who is taught to stroll along the paths of his imagination, gathering their best fruits.

Despite St. John's warning in *The Dark Night of the Soul*, the strength of Christianity from the sixteenth century on has been centered in this "middle range" of the spirit, where the desires, images, and passions of the individual become protagonists on the stage of religion. Eckhart, in the fourteenth century,

knew that man was condemned to slide back into the limits of
the self, even after he attained the mystical heights. That, for
Eckhart, was the price of man's all-too-human frailties. But the
language of self-delight, which Eckhart knew so well how to use,
suggests a secret preference for these middle ranges of an experience which has partially "decayed" into selfhood. By the
sixteenth century, however, this evidence of man's weaker nature
has been openly revalued and the pleasures of self-concern re-
instated—as if centuries of praising God's self-delight had provoked a secret desire in men to do as much for themselves.

A shift in the emotional resources of religion can be seen
in the following poem by Robert Southwell:

> O Lord, my sinnes doe over-charge thy breast,
>   The poyse therof doth force thy knees to bow;
> Yea flat thou fallest with my faults opprest,
>   And bloodie sweat runs trickling from thy brow:
> But had they not to earth thus pressed thee,
>   Much more would they in hell have pestred mee.
>
> This Globe of earth doth thy one finger prop,
>   The world thou doo'st within thy hand embrace;
> Yet all this waight of sweat drew not a drop,
>   Ne made thee bow, much lesse fall on thy face:
> But now thou hast a loade so heavie found,
>   That makes thee bow, yea fall flat to the ground.
> . . . .
> O Prostrate Christ, erect my crooked minde,
>   Lord let thy fall my flight from earth obtaine;
> Or if I needes must still in earth be shrin'd,
>   Then Lord on earth come fall yet once againe:
> And either yeeld in earth with me to lie,
>   Or else with thee to take me to the skie.

The theme and imagery of the poem are entirely conventional:
the poet accuses himself, mortifying his sinful nature at the

thought of God's overpowering sacrifice and suffering. He evokes remorse at the hugeness of man's fault, joy at the thought of His mercy, elaborating those thoughts in a series of highly charged emotional images. But there is another energy which runs in the poem, an energy half-concealed by its rhetoric, as if the poet, caught up in the experience of his meditation, had released it unawares and then allowed it to carry his poem in a direction for which he was not entirely prepared. God is described, in the second stanza, in all His power, as He holds the world in His hand and props it with a single finger. Yet, though "all this waight of sweat drew not a drop," one creature in the world has discovered that God Himself can be made to bend without fail; that the Divine Will can become subject to the faulty human will. The paradoxical lever by which the creature gains this power is none other than his own all-too-human sinfulness. For God falls flat, "with [man's] faults opprest" and "sweat runs trickling from [His] brow." The poet's suffering has brought God to His knees; his own small tragedy has caused a change and a trouble in the divine order.

Southwell's stanzas reveal a taste for paradox and verbal surprise which is intended, surely, to dramatize the purely orthodox emotion of gratitude for God's sacrifice. But his language has carried him further than he seems to realize. For the pain he describes—his own human suffering—has acquired the strength of an incantation to which even God must yield. According to the religious economy of the Hindu Vedas, the man who performed the required sacrifices gained a precise measure of power over the gods, who could not refuse his prayer. The feeling we get from Southwell is not unlike this. By behaving in a certain way, he tells us—by sinning and duly suffering for his sin—the poet becomes a cosmic actor; he requires that God deal with him on the highest level. Despite the self-mortification and the humility, which the poem never ceases to express, the poet's rhetoric has carried him beyond supplication. In the final stanza he appears to be giving orders, demanding that God "yield in earth

with me to lie, / Or else with thee to take me to the skie," as if
his very sinfulness had given him some infallible right to God's
consideration. Christian humility has been undermined here by
a subtle pride which is based, paradoxically, on the poet's capacity for sin and suffering.

This unexpected reversal of roles is implied by the whole
practice of meditation, which exalts the resources of personality.
Southwell's poem only brings to the surface an attitude which
lies concealed in the meditative mind. To adore God in this
way means, in fact, to elevate the self until it is God who has
become the mirror and the poet who is secretly glorified.

Another poem in which this paradoxical energy can be detected is George Herbert's "The Crosse." Again the reversed
values of selfhood hover at the threshold of the poet's language,
organizing the poem almost despite his intention:

> What is this strange and uncouth thing?
> To make me sigh, and seek, and faint, and die,
> Untill I had some place, where I might sing,
>   And serve thee; and not onely I,
> But all my wealth and familie might combine
> To set thy honour up, as our designe.
>
>   And then when after much delay,
> Much wrastling, many a combate, this deare end,
>   So much desir'd is gi'n, to take away
>   My power to serve thee; to unbend
> All my abilities, my designes confound,
> And lay my threatenings bleeding on the ground.
>
>   One ague dwelleth in my bones,
> Another in my soul (the memorie
> What I would do for thee, if once my grones
>   Could be allow'd for harmonie):
> I am in all a weak disabled thing,
> Save in the sight thereof, where strength doth sting.

The poet explains how the sight of God has troubled him, how his faith has weakened and his will fallen short of its goal: again the conventional language of Christian humility. But the real source of his suffering enters the poem without ever quite being stated. It is betrayed rather by a curious mood, and by the repetition of certain words. We discover a surprising insistence, for example, on the "I," the "my," and the "me," conveying a strong sense of personal willfulness. The poet has been wrestled to the ground, wounded by his own sinful energies, and by his awe at the sight of God's perfection. Yet nowhere does he loosen his hold on the rhetoric of personality: his elaborate suffering seems to strengthen him, and give him a more acute sense of "what (he) would do for [God], if once [his] grones / Could be allow'd for harmonie." Yet the work of the poem, like the analogous work of meditation, is precisely to evoke the "grones" with an art which makes them over into "harmonie." This "weak disabled thing" is indeed overwhelmingly present, overwhelmingly insisted upon; as if the very intensity of its suffering drew it further into a true relationship with God, enabling it to "do" for Him what He could not do for Himself.

The last two lines in stanza one contain an ambiguity which can only strengthen our sense that a contradiction lies hidden within the poem: "But all my wealth and familie might combine / To set thy honour up, as our designe." Ostensibly the poet means to explain how much he and his are devoted to the praise of God's "honour." But since the word "designe" can also mean plan or blueprint, he may be saying that God's honor is his, the poet's own, blueprint: the sinner is the source of God's power; surely an unexpected reading, if we remember Herbert's mild Anglican orthodoxy. But Herbert was immersed in the mood of meditation, and this brings him closer, at times, than he may have thought to the hyperbolic language of Eckhart and the fourteenth-century mystics.

The disciplines of meditation served to strengthen one of the deepest inclinations of the Christian mind: the secret fascination with self which had always lain just under the surface of the religion, only partly concealed by its rhetoric of humility. After the sixteenth century, Narcissus openly fascinated the cultural imagination of Europe. He has enchanted psychologists, philosophers, poets, and sociologists until the intricate powers of the self have been granted an importance equaled only in the cosmic vision of the Gnostics or in the wildest medieval heresies.

It is fitting to close this chapter on the psychology of meditation with a text taken from Gerard Manley Hopkins' commentary on Loyola's *Spiritual Exercises.* Immersed in a Jesuit tradition which had long acknowledged the spiritual resources of personality, Hopkins saw into the heart of Christian meditation:

> I find myself both as man and as myself something most determined and distinctive, at pitch, more distinctive and higher pitched than anything else I see; I find myself with my pleasures and pains, my powers and experiences, etc. . . . more important to myself than anything I see . . . And this is much more true when we consider the mind; when I consider my self-being, my consciousness and feeling of myself, that taste of myself, of *I* and *me* above and in all things . . . Nothing else in nature comes near this unspeakable stress of pitch, distinctiveness and selving, this self-being of my own.

If Ovid's Narcissus had been a philosopher, a Christian, and a Jesuit, he might have expressed himself in just these words.

Part Two

5 LA FOLIE TRISTAN

The wandering monks and beggars of medieval Europe form a curious parallel to another group of wanderers whose prestige, though more "literary," has also been more enduring. The knights of courtly fantasy stray from kingdom to kingdom, through the expanses of the medieval forest—a realm of hostility and shadow, abandoned to the devil; they retire to solitary places and do penance; they lead admirable lives of discipline, abstinence, and loyalty; and they may, like Chrétien's Perceval, even be chaste, though their chastity often has about it the ambiguity of Provençal love. Above all, their devotion has only one goal: to seek adventure—as the anchorites sought bizarre varieties of asceticism—in order to uphold virtue and protect men from those demonic creatures, inspired by the "Enemy," who assail them.

Lancelot, Perceval, Gawain combine the ferocity of their pagan ancestors with a wholly Christian concern for good works, to form a new kind of hero, surpassed perhaps only by Homer's epic warriors. Their nobility is all the more imposing because it is self-conferred. A high lineage is important, not for its birthright, but for a greater aptness to valor which it may pass on to the aspiring knight. No one is born into King Arthur's court. Only the highest ambition, and the greatest worth in chivalry, prepare a knight for the honors of the Round Table.

Yet something in the chivalric ideal remains troubling; for the knight errant succumbs to a curious blindness. When Perceval rides off to be knighted, his mother, in most versions of the story, falls senseless with grief on the doorstep behind him. The aspiring knight, one supposes, might have returned to comfort his mother. Yet Perceval sins by omission, for never once does he turn his head; his mind is too inflamed with chivalric fantasy. Only years later does Perceval learn how his mother had been a first victim to his all-consuming thirst for glory.

After a life of questing, both spiritual and worldly, Perceval transcends the blindness of earthly chivalry; he overcomes his pride and becomes a Christian hero, a knight of the Grail. But Lancelot and Gawain remain faithful to their pride. Their lives are devoted to the good works of chivalry, like pagan sun gods—from whom Gawain is thought to be descended—they radiate their strength over the weak and the oppressed; yet their real concern is less with the good works than with a need to be well thought of for their deeds and, above all, well spoken of. The knight's "renown" precedes him over the earth, as if his fame were somehow the source, and not the result, of his heroic abilities. For the Arthurian knight is nourished on applause. He will risk everything, life included, to defend his rightful "name," but little to defend anything else. A famous example is Lancelot's shame at the prospect of riding in a peasant cart, though the success of his "adventure" depended on it. The adventure was honorable—the rescue of Guinevere, Arthur's wife and Lancelot's liege lady—but there are gestures so contrary to the decorum of knightly behavior that Lancelot was overcome at the thought of injuring his "reputation": yet he would have fought armies of cavaliers single-handed and undertaken the most arduous pilgrimage at the drop of a handkerchief, for that is what "names" are made of.

When, in the hands of Robert de Boron, the Arthurian cycle was transformed into an allegory of Christian revelation, replacing the earthly with a celestial chivalry, the scale of virtues was reversed. Lancelot, the greatest knight to have been seated at the earthly table, is denied entrance to the heavenly table of the Grail. The anonymous author of *La Queste du Saint Graal* describes the faltering Lancelot, "hard as stone, bitter as old wine, barren as a fig tree." Lancelot fails above all because of his pride: "In place of humility, you welcomed pride, valuing no one if not yourself."

"Other sins find their vent in the accomplishment of evil deeds, but pride lies in wait for the good deeds to destroy them." Augustine learned this during his own long struggle with pride; and though he tells us that he conquered his fault, we are not always convinced the victory was final. Much later he was to describe the Christian paradox that "God humbled Himself in order to be exalted." This strange reversal is at the heart of Christian revelation. But in the ambiguous hands of men whose devotion was of a more earthly quality, it opened the door to all the excesses of spiritual pride. For Augustine knew well that humility itself could become an "exploit," as the "athletes" of the Egyptian desert demonstrated. Among the knights of medieval fantasy, only Perceval wrestled with the "fault" of pride and won. For the other, more pagan heroes, there was no fault. Nemesis did not walk behind them to deflect their virtues. They were splendid and valorous, humbling themselves at the feet of their ladies, in order to be more completely exalted. Their lives resemble a trick done with mirrors, reflecting and transforming their deeds in the glass of reputation.

We recognize in these medieval knights a resemblance to Burckhardt's portrait of the Renaissance hero: the powerfully self-cultivated individual, ready to challenge heaven with his many perfections. The ritual boasting of the knight recalls, even more closely, that modern "child of nature," the American backwoodsman: a rootless, lonely man, enveloped in the language of his self-esteem. We cannot help paraphrasing Gregory the Great's portrait of the proud man: When he thinks he surpasses others in all things, he walks with himself along the broad spaces of his thought, loudly uttering his own praises.

The imagination of the later Middle Ages manifested a divided allegiance to these "individuals" in literature whose lives were solitary, austere, unfitted for the "ideal" order of feudalism. By the thirteenth century the rights of community had come to be inviolable; they formed part of an organic unity linking the lowest to the highest by gentle gradations of rank and precedence. From this point of view, the "individual" was by nature a suspicious character—the nuance persists in some uses of the French word *individu*. He was banished into exile, which was then thought to be a kind of spiritual death, for life without a prepared function was an absurdity. Madmen, lepers, thieves were made to wander from town to town; or, as on the *nefs des fous,* were floated aimlessly down rivers, belonging to no place or people.

Yet these banished "individuals" continued to exercise a strange fascination. Like *les sorcières,* they were thought to converse with the suppressed pagan gods, who had a great though underground influence on the people, as Michelet has pointed out. Their exile forced them into intimacy with the enormous forests making them natural allies of the supernatural. But more than that, the solitaries and the "fools," because of their very indigence, recalled the prestigious image of Christ, the great exile. The community that banished them felt an uneasy need to conciliate their influence. Fools and lepers were maintained somewhere in sight, near the city walls, and it was a blessed act to give them alms. The famous *nefs des fous* is a more spectacular image of this need to keep the exiled "individual" near the edge of society, in troubled view of all.

It is around this time that the desert saints, St. Anthony, St. Gerolomo, St. Simeon Stylites, and others, became major Christian figures. Their extreme asceticism, their rejection of all social bonds, made them heroes of the people, often against the very Church which was identified with oppression and class privilege. The forests and mountains of the thirteenth century harbored numerous anchorites, who were loved by the peasantry. In the more Christianized tales of chivalry, these *prud'hommes* are figures of sanctity; they guide the cavaliers, interpret their dreams, and warn them repeatedly against their inveterate pride and sensuality.

Some of this fascination with solitude and rootlessness undoubtedly contributed to the knightly ideal, explaining, in part, the success of chivalric literature in the courts of Europe. The wandering exile carried with him a prestige which already hinted at the supernatural. It was thus an easy task for Robert de Boron to transform the knightly quest into an allegory of Revelation in which the knights, above all Galahad, became analogues of Christ.

There is at least one other source for the prestige of the chivalric ideal. By the thirteenth and fourteenth centuries, medieval society had settled onto the soil. The feudal nobility had become fixed and prosperous, identifying the prestige of their names with the very land they occupied. The wandering knights of the epics belong to an earlier history; they idealize the more frankly heroic centuries of the Dark Ages when landed immobility was the exception and homelessness common to the noble as well as to the villein. As feudal society became more complex and more finely organized, it gave a new consistency to this past. During the eleventh century the older ranks of the nobility had found a way to enforce their military strength by conferring knighthood, along with fiefs, on many of their retainers. In return the ennobled vassals owed a military service to their benefactors. The practice became so current that these petty nobles soon outnumbered by far their liege lords, introducing new aspirations and a new sensibility into the world of the feudal gentry. According to the entrenched social order, the recently ennobled vassals were confined to a second degree of nobility; they were permanently dependent on the superior "names," and the half-mythical ancestry of their lords. But the knights themselves developed a different view of the matter, which went far toward transforming their very notion of nobility. According to Maurice Valency they tended to put a greater accent on "prowess . . . loyalty, (and) honor, upon the high standard of the class, and the personal worth of the individual." A distinction came to be made "between the nobility of birth and the nobility of personal merit, and it was normal for those who had not the former to insist on the unique importance of the latter."

If the poetry of knighthood can be said to express—and idealize—real aspirations in the medieval world, they are undoubtedly those of this small, dependent nobility. This is all the more probable since the poets themselves usually belonged to this class and were in a position to feel their dependency even more acutely than most. As poets, their prestige at court was clearly secondary. Like Chrétien de Troyes, they were themselves often noble; yet their skill put them in a situation more like that of the wandering *jongleurs,* whose affair was to distract the prince when his leisure weighed too heavily. The poets of chivalry were sure to respond sensitively to such a situation of dependence, using their imaginative power to enhance the code of personal nobility to which their social status would, in any case, have inclined them.

In their tales the heroic knight is always a vassal, seated at the table of his liege lord. The true mark of his blood, however, lies not in his rank but in his personal qualities, above all his courtesy and military prowess. Although he remains faithful in all things to his lord, he is, in a deeper sense, his own lord; he chooses his adventures, relies on his own wisdom, and is usually at the center of whatever dilemma, moral or military, he is called on to solve. The conflict of authority implied by such a situation is rarely dealt with openly by the tales, but it is present. The cavalier swears fealty to his lord; he describes in strong language his humility and readiness to serve. Even Tristan, the renegade, tries to preserve the honor of his uncle, King Mark. Surely it is not the nephew's fault if Mark is a weak, sensual, old man, who can never make up his mind. The same stuffiness and hesitation characterize Arthur, and even old Charlemagne. In the world of chivalry, the noble selves are always ready to serve, but somehow the fathers are not equal to their sons. Therefore Roland dies in ambush, and Tristan cuckolds Mark. They are almost forced into assuming their heroism, though when they do there is little that can stop them.

Tristan stands apart from these heroic silhouettes as a peculiarly modern figure. Something in his fate touches us more closely than the bizarre adventures of Gawain or Lancelot: there is more emotion and less heroic violence in the legend that is ascribed to him. Thomas places Tristan a generation later than King Arthur's court, and Gottfried* follows his example, thereby marking even more clearly the change he has conceived in the character of his hero. For Tristan's truest adventures are invisible; they are fought within, between conflicting passions. This shift from the ideal of manly knighthood to the hidden adventure of the passions is crucial. In Gottfried's *Tristan,* the exotic threads of Celtic legend mingle with more recent ideals— those of the Provençal court—to produce a new kind of emotional experience.

But are we right in insisting only on what is new in the vision? The Tristan legend is interesting because it reveals so clearly the transitions that have been made. Unlike the sudden

---

* Thomas wrote his version of the Tristan story between 1160 and 1170, probably while he was attached to the Angevin courts in France. Although he wrote in the literary style of the French courts, Thomas is thought to have been Anglo-Norman. Only the last sixth of his poem remains. Its greatest importance lies in the fact that Gottfried chose it as the narrative model for his own, far more elaborate poem.

Gottfried von Strassburg is one of the greatest of all medieval German poets. He wrote and flourished in Strasbourg around 1210, when his *Tristan* is thought to have been composed. Although Gottfried's poem is unfinished, it is considered one of the finest versions of the Tristan legend, and one of the most perfect embodiments of the medieval courtly spirit. Almost all we know of Gottfried must be inferred from the style, elevation, and wide learning displayed in his poem.

flowering of the Provençal lyric, *Tristan* allows us to follow a singleness of theme, apparent in the early material as well as in the later.

King Arthur's knights fought for the sake of glory. The ladies in distress, the ghosts and devils, the mystic fountains became mirrors in which the knight discovered a heightened image of himself. And yet it was a worldly glory that he sought, for the knight required an audience; without applause his heroism became meaningless. Indeed, the adventure cannot be said to have taken place until the knight was able to tell it, or have it told. Don Quixote, in his forlorn way, knew this and made no bones about it. After his encounter with a lion who refused to do battle but instead yawned and turned his lazy backside, the knight calls to the lion's keeper:

> Come then, shut the cage door, my honest friend, and give me a certificate under thy hand, in the amplest form thou canst devise, of what thou hast seen me perform; how thou didst open the cage for the lion; how I expected his coming, and he did not come; how, upon his not coming, I staid his own time, and instead of meeting me, he turned tail and lay down. I am obliged to do no more. So, enchantments avaunt! and heaven prosper truth, justice and knight-errantry. Shut the door as I bid thee.

In the eyes of the court, the certificate of applause imported more than the deed itself.

Tristan violates this decorum of knightly behavior. His taste for manly acts of heroism remains strong until the end; but the meaning of his legend, for Thomas and Gottfried, lay elsewhere. When Gottfried describes Tristan and Isolde together at the court of Ireland, they are splendid figures: "The girl glided gently forward . . . shaped in her attire as if love had formed her to be her own falcon, an ultimate, unsurpassable perfection," while he is "marvelously blessed with every grace that goes to make a knight . . . His figure and attire went in delightful harmony to make a picture of chivalrous manhood." On all sides, the courtiers exclaim, "Wherever did God shape a figure more apt for the order of chivalry?" Gottfried uses all the subtlety of his baroque art to heighten the magnificence, the superb decorum, the elegance of the pair, until like two gods they radiate their influence over the entire assembly. But he is preparing us for a brutal change. For the love potion will soon wrench them out of this world of which they are the brightest graces. It will set them careening through an adventure of love and destruction that will entirely corrupt the purity of Gottfried's portrait.

Before her time is over, Isolde will lie, betray, attempt murder, and deceive God. Tristan will use every dishonesty to get his way. He will betray his uncle, lie unscrupulously, torture an innocent girl whom he has tricked into becoming his wife. He and Isolde will suffer terribly as they wander half-naked through forests, and use the grossest ruses with a calm conscience. "Thus Love instructs honest minds to practice perfidy," comments Gottfried. Yet throughout their adventures they will never cease to be glorified and justified.

There is, indeed, a strange contradiction running through the story. Tristan never quite abandons the knightly ideal. Late in the poem, when the fate of his love has long been decided, he travels to England with his friend Caerdin, "to win fortune and adventure." Again, to enhance his "name," he accompanies the dwarf Tristan in battle against a giant. Yet he has nonetheless sworn fealty to a ruthless master, Love, who commands him to transgress the rules of knightly decorum in a fever of anarchy, erotic pleasure, and finally death. Tristan continues to pursue his first ambition—that of a traditional knight, hungry for renown—even as he advances further and further along the road of love.

The two opposing ambitions have more in common, however, than first appears. The key lies in the love experience itself. While Tristan and Isolde remain faithful to their passion, they cannot sin, for everything they do will be "justified" by Love. As the episodes succeed each other, the lovers are immersed more and more deeply in the bittersweet excess of their emotions; they grow to an almost mystical purity, while their calumniators— who in fact only tell the truth—are described as dwarfs, fools, and sensual weaklings. A new ethic of Love has replaced the rule of society. In the name of Love, evil and anarchy break loose, but those who are the cause of it remain pure. Tristan's exploits against Mark are as astounding as any that Lancelot or Gawain accomplish in a more legitimate cause; and Isolde equals her lover in cunning. To this extent, Tristan has simply carried over the knightly ideal into the service of a new lord. The mirror-trick has preserved its power to glorify, but the applause has changed. King Arthur's court would have been horrified by such behavior, but Marie de Champagne's "Court of Love" was delighted and the poet Thomas honored for his powers of invention.

We have considered so far only the surface of the Tristan legend: its outer movement of heroism and adventure. Nothing in the rules of either court prepares us for the sudden ground-swell of emotion, the strange poetry of love and death which takes possession of the lovers, transporting them into a world beyond all decorum, where their intense loneliness and passion will be the only rule. If Tristan and Isolde continue to move us, it is because of this unruly fate which has projected them from a life of grace and moderation into the farthest reaches of the abyss.

The main theme of the story begins to unfold when Tristan, by his wit and courage, wins Isolde for the hand of his uncle, King Mark. Before the pair can leave the court of Ireland, Isolde's mother, fearing an unhappy marriage for her daughter, prepares a love-philter which she entrusts to Brangane, Isolde's lady-in-waiting. This fatal act will destroy all right order and felicity for the two, who are not yet in love, nor would ever have been, were it not for the magic reversal of the love-philter. As they sail the high seas—symbol of the chaotic element soon to overcome them—Tristan and Isolde discover the secret philter, mistake it for a flacon of wine, and drink it together. In some versions of the story, the philter is not discovered until they have reached Cornwall, enabling Mark also to partake of its love folly. A later English rendering even allows Tristan's dog to drink some of the magic liquid. But Gottfried, whose version we are following here, will have none of this. He is less interested in the potency of the magic than in the love it inspires. He wants no third character to distract him, or the reader, as he describes the ambiguous fatality that will pursue the pair to their deaths.

Tristan and Isolde become lovers on the boat that carries them toward Mark: "The yearning that fetters thoughts was stilled. Whenever the occasion suited they had their fill of what lovers long for . . . And so they passed the voyage in a life of rapture, yet not altogether freely, for they were haunted by fear of the future." The ecstasy is rooted as much in desperation as it is in joy, marking the character of their fate from the very first. When the boat reaches Cornwall, Tristan, bound by the laws of chivalry, will surrender Isolde to King Mark, his uncle and second father. But now Tristan will be torn by a double allegiance, to Love and to his honor. And this double allegiance will cause the story to proceed through a series of rising and falling tensions, as one or the other gains the upper hand. Faithful to his honor, Tristan abandons Isolde to her marriage with King Mark. But nothing can withstand the passion of the two lovers, and soon their grief projects them into an underhanded life of ruses, tricks, and hidden rendezvous, as they nourish their love in secret, despite all care for honor and the court. It is not long before they are suspected and forced once more to separate. Again and again the pattern is repeated: the lovers come together, are separated by Mark's suspicions, overcome the worst of obstacles, only to yield to them again.

We have here, in outline, one of those elementary stories that will be repeated without end, as Denis de Rougemont has pointed out, from Heloise and Abelard until its final resting place in *True Confessions* magazine. Yet, on second thought, even this simple story seems too complicated. Why, for example, does Tristan not carry off Isolde to his own kingdom of Parmenie, where they could live happily ever after. The decorum of knighthood made it perfectly honorable to fight for a lady, and then to take her as prize from the defeated hero. Gottfried has already made clear that Tristan is irresistible in battle, if only he would choose that alternative. We have, of course, seen him torn between two duties, one to Mark and the other to Love, for "the loyal man was afflicted by a double pain . . . Honour and loyalty pressed him hard: these two, who had lost the battle to Love when Tristan had decided in [Isolde's] favor, this vanquished pair now vanquished Love in turn." Yet once he has surrendered Isolde to his uncle, Tristan continues to make a fool out of the old king, almost to his face. Surely it would have been simpler for Love, and more honorable for Duty, to have cut the Gordian knot instead of toying with it in this half-decided and ultimately fatal way.

Denis de Rougemont has analyzed this tension between love and the obstacles that prevent its full flowering. The fact, according to De Rougemont, is that Tristan and Isolde need their despair. It is true that no material obstacle can prevent Tristan from carrying off Isolde to Parmenie; but some hidden resistance in his own love will not allow him to do so. The material obstacles—the plot of Marjodoc and Melot, for example— crystallize some inner requirements of his passion, and that is why Tristan is forced to remain trapped among them, battling endlessly with his pain. As Gottfried himself comments: "Love has a way which has entangled her more than all else, namely, that when things are to her liking she refuses to remain steadfast and very easily lets go . . . [She] goes to greater pains to discover her mortal sorrow than she will take for the joy that she can find and possess there."

One conclusion is that Tristan and Isolde do not in fact love each other, no matter how deeply "in love" they appear to be. But, if that is the case, then what do they love? De Rougemont answers that they are in love with their own passions. Love has placed them outside the world of common events, beyond the reach of applause and secular admiration; for they have discovered, in the energy of their desires, a wilder, more unreasonable ambition: "They were burdened by the pleasing malady that works such miracles as changing honey to gall, turning sweetness sour, setting fire to moisture, converting balm into pain; that robs hearts of their natures and stands the world on its head." The lovers are enveloped in a tide of contrary emotions which is further emphasized by Isolde's play on the word "lamier," with its three meanings of love, bitterness, and the sea. Their passion leads them through pain and bitterness, into a communion with that source of all life and love, the chaotic element of the sea. Each is a lever by which the other is lifted upward into a mystical purity; but between the lovers themselves, there is a veil. Tristan "took his heart and soul and searched them for some change: but there was nothing there but Love—and Isolde." "Whatever Isolde thought, whatever came uppermost in her mind, there was nothing there, of one sort or another, but Love and Tristan." First Love comes, and then the beloved. Without entirely knowing it, the two lovers long, not for each other, but for an impassioned solitude in which each can taste, unimpeded, the power of his own emotion. As De Rougemont has commented, "The difficulty lies in the fact that the love which 'maddens' them is not love of the other as he is, in his bodily reality. They are truly in love, but each loves the other only in terms of himself and not of the other. Their unhappiness is thus rooted in a false reciprocation, the mask of a double narcissism."

Many episodes and turns of phrase are thus illuminated.

When Isolde appeared in her father's palace, to the enchantment of the entire court, "there was scarce a pair of eyes to whom her two mirrors were not a marvel and a delight." Her eyes, made above all others for the grace of Love, are described as mirrors: eyes revealing nothing of their own, but only the reflected image of the lover. The real Isolde has disappeared behind her mirrors. The metaphor is repeated later, as Tristan and Isolde drink the magic wine, and already the first signs of their passions are felt: "Love, the reconciler, had purged their hearts of enmity, and so joined them in affection that each was to the other as limpid as a mirror." Gottfried surely did not intend the irony of these lines; but the conventional hyperbole of love has betrayed him here. A mirror is limpid only to one who looks into it in order to discover his own reflected image. But if what he looks for lies behind the mirror's surface, then his frustration will be infinite, for each of the lovers will have become invisible to the other; they will be grasping at phantoms, strange hybrids of presence and absence that only reinforce their solitude.

The image of the mirror is, of course, a complicated one in medieval literature. As a traditional tool in magic and alchemy, it could easily be associated with the enchantment of witches' spells; beyond this, there remains an echo of the primitive fascination with reflected images which we discovered in the Gnostic literature. Indeed magic in one form or another has always explored the mysterious bond between an image and its object. To capture the image meant also to have captured its object-source. In this sense the tragedy of Narcissus is only a special case of the general fascination with the powers of the mirror.

Closer to its immediate place in literary rhetoric, however, is the conventional use of the mirror as a trope signifying the ideal form of whatever is described, as in the title of a famous medieval treatise, *The Mirror of Magistrates,* or in the conventional reference to the Bible as the mirror of truth. All these meanings contribute to the usage in medieval love poetry, where the mirror is employed as a figure of praise for the lady's eyes: those ideal pools of clarity, more beautiful than other eyes, whose magical potency is such that they capture the lover's image, thereby imprisoning him forever in the heart of his enchantress.

Another episode in the Tristan story takes on additional meaning now: the Hall of Statues which Thomas has his hero create when he is exiled in Brittany, married to Isolde of the White Hands, and far from his true beloved. Tristan spends his days dreaming of the first Isolde. But instead of hurrying to her side, he lets the obstacles dissuade him and tries to distract his thoughts by engaging in a series of minor adventures. Then, one day, an idea comes to him. Having overcome a giant in battle, near the boundary of his new home, he accepts the monster's homage: "The following day Tristan commanded him and his minions, who were skilled carpenters and goldsmiths, to make a hall in a cavern and to fashion lifelike statues of Queen Ysolt and Brengvein." When his orders have been carried out, Tristan will have a new focus for his emotions. He will spend long hours in the company of his lifelike but infinitely cold lady: "Whenever Tristan visits the image of Ysolt he kisses it and clasps it in his arms, as if it were alive . . . by means of the image Tristan recalls the delights of their great loves, their troubles and their griefs, their pains and their torments." To be with the statue is like being with Isolde herself, Tristan tells us. And we can almost believe him; but not quite. For this lovely stone Isolde brings to mind all the distant ladies of the courtly ideal: always absent in their presence and present in their absence. Jaufré Rudel will not come any closer to his unknown lady of Tripoli than Tristan to his own Isolde.

"He made the image so that he might tell it what is in his heart." But Tristan is only talking to himself. The Hall of Statues presents us with the image of a couple, and yet of a solitude. It portrays with force the kind of love that Tristan and Isolde feel for each other, each for himself. Later, when Tristan does finally sail to England, he returns without having so much as tried to see Isolde; though upon reaching Brittany, he hurries straightway "to the woods to see the lovely statues."

Gottfried, with his unfathomable irony, has woven a curious word play into his rendering of Tristan's encounter with Isolde of the White Hands. He uses the tradition of the second Isolde to comment, in his way, on the ambivalence of Tristan's love—that bewildering compound of desire and solitude—as the hero thinks of his new wife whose name has brought to mind, so troublingly, the other Isolde:

> "Isolde" laughs and sports in my ears continually, yet I do not know where Isolde is. My eye, which regards Isolde, does not see Isolde. Isolde is far away and nevertheless beside me . . . What a strange thing has happened to me: I have been longing to see Isolde for a great while, and now I have found her; but I am not with Isolde however near I am to her.

The irony is telling, for Gottfried, by this undercurrent of second meanings, allows Tristan to disclose a real insight into his passion.

In another episode, the love-saddened knight, Dwarf Tristan, says to the hero, "Whoever you are, fair friend, in my opinion you have never loved." Again the irony surprises, for Tristan has apparently done little else. He has lost his honor, his kingdom, and soon will lose his life for Love. Yet, if what we say is true, he has, in fact, never loved, and Dwarf Tristan has told more of the truth than is usually recognized.

Thus *Tristan*, the great epic of passion and death in European literature, is not a tale of love as we understand it—as an exchange of emotions and a recognition of the beloved. Gottfried's lovers have been exiled not only from society but from each other. They have been delivered up to the passion which confounds opposites, destroys the limits of earthly decorum, and consecrates them, each apart, as gods of love: solitary lights in a world without grace. They have exchanged the earthly mirror of honor and renown for this other mystical mirror of Love which destroys as it glorifies them.

There is, however, another dimension of the Tristan story which we have touched on so far only in passing: its apology for a life of erotic anarchy, as the two heroes subvert all rules of social behavior in the name of Love. Gottfried's poem is especially interesting in this respect, for the German poet describes what is, in effect, a complete love-religion.

When Tristan and Isolde have at last been driven away by Mark, who can no longer bear the sight of their love, they travel deep into the Cornish forest, accompanied only by Tristan's dog. Unlike other poets of the legend, Gottfried abridges their wandering: he has them make their way toward a place known only to Tristan, a cave surrounded by desperate wilds, where they will be able to live undisturbed. Here, in the Cave of Love, they will have their last happy moments together before they are swept apart, this time to their deaths. But Gottfried's cave is more than a refuge. It is an underground cathedral, gracefully vaulted, encrusted with precious stones; in place of an altar there is a huge bed made of white crystal. Here the erotic ceremony which underlies the lovers' fate will find its fullest expression, far from the court, surrounded by miles of impenetrable forest. Upon entering the cave, the lovers leave behind them the deceit, treachery, and cunning which had been their only resource against a hostile world. The symbolic architecture of the cave, rendered with all the loving detail characteristic of Gottfried's poetry, locates the pair in a paradise entirely fitted to their new religion, surrounding them with Love's Power, Love's Crown of Virtues, Love's Discretion and Understanding, all of which is set over a green marble floor, soothing and firm as Love's Constancy. The bars at the door lock Deceit, Force, and Treachery out of the cave, while three small windows flood the lovers with the pure light of honor. So long as Tristan and Isolde are faithful to Love—though perhaps not to each other, for Tristan will marry another woman while Isolde's duty has brought her often into Mark's bed—they will inhabit this allegorical cave, and have, in fact, inhabited it from the moment the love-philter first took possession of their senses. As long as the "grace" of love is with them, they will be purified; though, in order to remain faithful to its inspiration, they must violate every law of worldly behavior.

The steward Marjodoc, who pursues them with his jealousy, has a dream in which the lovers' crimes are portrayed with great force:

> The steward saw in his dream as he slept a boar, fearsome and dreadful that ran out from the forest. Up to the King's court he came, foaming at the mouth and whetting his tusks, and charging everything in his path. And now a great crowd of courtiers ran up. Many knights leapt hither and thither round the boar, yet none of them dared face him. Thus he plunged grunting through the Palace. Arriving at Mark's chamber he broke in through the doors, tossed the King's appointed bed in all directions, and fouled the royal linen with his foam.

Marjodoc may indeed be a villain, but here he is telling the truth. The boar—the emblem inscribed on Tristan's shield—has betrayed the trust of any man, ungraced by Love, who has obstructed its way. It has dragged down the brilliance of the lovers as they were described at the Irish Court, until nothing remains now of their immaculate "reputations." Yet the Cave of Love has been so conceived that this energy for violence and deceit must be left at the door, for Eros also has his rules. What is permissible toward strangers and the world at large is forbidden between the lovers, who retain for themselves all the harmony they must refuse to others.

Gottfried's erotic anarchy resembles strangely the vision of those wandering Heretics of the Free Spirit who were his contemporaries. The antinomians too preached a religion of erotic "grace," and they too renounced their privilege of transgression only when they were among equals: i.e., among other initiates.

The question has often been raised of heretical influence on Gottfried, and perhaps on Thomas as well, the most frequent accusation being that of Catharism. The religious influences, however, are probably more complicated than that. In the first place, when Gottfried conceived his *Tristan,* the rhetoric of love was already available in a perfectly orthodox form to express mystical elevation, as, for example, in St. Bernard's sermon on the *Song of Songs.* In addition, two heresies at least had made inroads in Strasbourg while Gottfried was writing his poem there, and both of them tended to transform love into a kind of sacrament. We know of the Cathars who were persecuted there during the first years of the thirteenth century—*Tristan* was finished in about 1210. It is less known, however, that the Almoricians, an early version of the Free Spirit, were also active in Strasbourg during the same period.

Nothing is known personally about Gottfried, and this, of course, leaves the field open to all manner of speculation. Still, on the evidence of the poem, he is generally felt to have been well versed in courtly matters, something of a scholar, and sensitive in particular to many questions of religion and theology debated in Europe at the time. It is not at all improbable, therefore, that Gottfried knew of the Almoricians. The idea gains further weight from the fact that the sect seems to have been publicly accused and punished in Strasbourg during the very years when Gottfried was working at his *Tristan.* The poet had every opportunity to become acquainted—even if at a distance—with their erotic individualism, and it would not be surprising if something of this appeared in his work. There is no reason, of course, to claim that Gottfried was himself a heretic. It would be more prudent, and probably more accurate, to surmise that he was confirmed in his doctrine of Love, with its antinomian implications, by a knowledge of this audacious sect of mystics whose principles have an undoubted resemblance to those that guide his heroes through the adventures of the poem.

There is one passage, however, in which the reference may

be more direct. I mean the famous episode of the ordeal by fire, where Isolde manages to fool even God with her love-inspired ruse. Mark finally decides to test Isolde's honor according to an old custom which prescribed that the accused, before witnesses, must hold in his hand a bar of fiery metal. If he is not burned, God is said to have confirmed his innocence; he is immediately acquitted. Isolde, faced with this ordeal, phrases the oath she must take with such cunning that she does not, in fact, perjure herself, though of course she is lying so far as the real issues are concerned. But, as we have seen, Love justifies all the ruses, giving her power even over God's judgment, for she handles the iron and is not burned. The poet then goes on to comment, with his characteristic irony, "Thus was it made manifest and confirmed to all the world that Christ in His great virtue is pliant as a windblown sleeve. He falls into place and clings, whichever way you try Him . . . Be it deadly earnest or a game, He is just as you would have Him." Isolde is so "graced" by Love that she has gained a power even over Christ; just as the Brothers of the Free Spirit were convinced that their mystical purity had made God Himself dependent on their wills. The spiritual pride of the Almoricians may well have inspired this curious episode in Gottfried's poem.

We must not forget, however, that these variations on the theme of Love can also be traced back to a clearly formulated literature of passion and courtship. The inveterate lies, the need to preserve appearances, the evil-minded gossips who tell only the truth, the jealous husband: all these elements in Tristan's scenario belong already to a more or less invariable tradition. We cannot know whether the author of the lost "ur-Tristan"— a French *estoire* probably dating from the mid-twelfth century— was familiar with the Provençal laws of *donnoi*. But Chrétien de Troyes' *Tristan*, which has also been lost, was surely influenced by the spirit of the Midi. As for Thomas and Gottfried, their debt shows on every page—not only in the story itself, but in their sensitive concern with the psychology and the mystical intensity of love. We must therefore be careful in ascribing influences and heretical sympathies. Let us, instead, suppose that somewhere during the twelfth century the traditions of vernacular poetry, the old legends of the *matière de Bretagne,* and the resurgence of mystical religion came together, exchanging their energies, providing each other with the elements of a new rhetoric. One product of this cultural hybrid is the Provençal lyric itself, which precedes *Tristan* and continues to flourish in various forms—stilnovist, Petrarchan, Shakespearean—until the seventeenth century. Another is the mystical literature of the twelfth to sixteenth centuries, with its use of metaphors inspired by the earlier love poetry.

The language of Narcissus will be enriched by these exchanges; for the experience of self-exalting, solitary love will communicate its energy to a whole tradition of European culture. For the moment, however, let us turn to one of the more puzzling offshoots of this erotic individualism in the Middle Ages: the tradition of Provençal love, which runs parallel to the northern literature of chivalry and prolongs its influence far beyond the twelfth and thirteenth centuries.

6 THE MIRRORS OF COURTLY LOVE

I Provence

Even in Gottfried's hands, the *matière de Bretagne* remained close to its pagan sources, darkened by the Northern forest and the passions of the Night which were to inspire Wagner seven hundred years later. But in twelfth-century Provence, the spirit of love moved far from the mystical violence of Tristan and Isolde. On the contrary, the Provençal *canzon* expressed a world of *mesura* and grace. *Lums, clartatz, joi* are at the heart of its conventional language. The power of love—the *fin'amor* of which the troubadours would sing untiringly for a hundred years—could have no better prelude than the harmonious praise of spring, the conventional *début printanier*, which introduces the subject matter of the poem, as in this *canzon* by Guillaume de Poitiers:

> In the sweetness of the early year, leaves grow in the woods and the birds sing, each in its own Latin, to the rhythm of a new song. It is therefore good that each give his heart to what he most desires.

Even the pain of love, the obsessive rhythms of complaint which surround and modulate the praise, has an almost healing gentleness to it: "For it is more touching than a thorn, the pain that cures the joy of love" (Jaufré Rudel).

But the love poetry of Provence contains a mystery of another sort. For one hundred years this tradition of vernacular poetry flourished, expressing a new style of life: a refined attentiveness to the grace of the emotions and to the virtues of individual merit. Then the crusading armies of Simon de Montfort brought to the south the new dispensation of the thirteenth century: the intolerance, bloodshed, and inquisitory vigor which all but destroyed whatever the twelfth century had promised. For the troubadours were not only poets; they had been the spokesmen and arbiters of an entire civilization. By 1220 little of this civilization remained intact; the poetry of the troubadours was already the property of *jongleurs* who sang it from court to court, part of a dead tradition to which nothing could be added.

The real mystery of Provence is that it has come down to us as a civilization with no history. The values of the *joi d'amor*, the graceful language of its poetry, the intricate stanzas and the conventional treatment of its main themes: all this appears full-blown, with unhesitating mastery, in the four love poems by Guillaume IX de Poitiers, which mark the first date in the history of *fin'amor*. Indeed one historian has gone so far as to suggest that Guillaume invented not only this brilliant mode of vernacular poetry (the first in Europe), but the entire concept of "love." He would have done this in order to dissuade the women of his court from entering the convent of Fontevrault (as his two wives and daughter already had done), by giving them another highly serious occupation "in the world": the secular religion of love, which was to mark the history of Provence for a century, and that of Europe ever since. The improbable suggestion that one man—preoccupied, moreover, with the affairs of a kingdom—could have been so complete a creator only serves to emphasize the darkness of our historical insight concerning the origins of *fin'amor*.

The fact remains that the *canzon* (the highest genre practiced by the poets of Provence) can hardly be said to develop or improve after its sudden creation. From the poems of Guillaume IX to those of Guiraut de Riquier more than a century later, it is a brilliant, perfectly achieved genre, practiced by poets whose virtuosity, from the very first, is remarkable. Indeed, in the matter of pure verbal dexterity, they have been acknowledged, from Dante onward, as the greatest masters ever to have written in a European language.

The difficulty of their verse, the amazingly complex stanza forms they chose to use, in particular the enigmas of the *trobar clus* (that all but impenetrable form of poetic expression) appear as part of a courtly game played not with arms but with words. The heroic grace which the *trovères* were to celebrate in the arts of war, the troubadours celebrated in the art of verse. A poem, in the courtly world of Provence, was an "exploit," and the formal difficulty vanquished by the poet heightened the *pretz* and *valor* (the reputation and honor) he commanded in the eyes of his peers. The troubadour's pride in his skill became a subject to which the poems return again and again. When Guillaume IX boasts of his achievement, he gives us the sense of a tournament in which his honor is at stake: "I should like the world to know whether or not this verse is of a good color which I have brought out of my workshop, for in this mastery I bear off the flower."

This joust of poetry, set before an audience of connoisseurs, is nonetheless highly serious. The "sincerity" of the *joi d'amor* has often been questioned because of its accent on formal achievement. But the troubadour saw no difference between the formal "exploit" of the poem and the sincerity of his emotion. To write intricately and well, on the contrary, was proof that his love was sincere; as if the discipline of words had become part of an inner discipline which made the poet not only skillful but also capable of love. It is with these sentiments that Arnaut Daniel begins one of his more celebrated *canzone:* "To this light and graceful air, I write words that I must plane and measure: they will be sincere and true when I have filed them down. For Love in an instant polishes and gilds my songs . . ." The torments and the fugitive satisfactions of *fin'amor* sharpen the poet's love, but also his skill, as Arnaut Daniel points out later in the same poem: "The torment I endure in no way prevents me from loving well, although it keeps me in solitude, for it allows me thus to put my words into verse." Not romantic spontaneity, but patience and discipline lie at the heart of the Provençal ideal in poetry. The love it celebrates is thought to be "authentic" precisely because it is surrounded by a delicate pattern of constraint.

The durable influence of Provence, however, has been due less to the formal innovations of the troubadours than to the story their poems invariably tell of unrequited or half-requited love. The *canzone* express again and again a single emotional dilemma in which the joy of love is mingled with complaint and, above all, with the highly conventional praise of a lady who remains inaccessible though she is, for the poet, an avowed source of grace. Both Dante and Cavalcanti were superb craftsmen, yet they were far more interested in this delicate praise of love than in the virtuosity of the poetic "exploit" itself. Indeed, not until the aesthetic dandyism of Ezra Pound do we find the Provençal poets praised above all for their skill, rather than for their conventional subject matter: the cult of love.

This celebration of the *joi d'amor*, with its intricate pattern of rules for right behavior—those *leys d'amor* decreed by Andreas Capellanus—has a ritual quality which echoes the mood, if not the detail, of Catholic ritual. C. S. Lewis has gone so far as to suggest that the so-called Courts of Love in the twelfth century—if they did exist elsewhere than in the minds of historians—were, in fact, a conscious parody of Church ceremony and opinion, preserving the mood of worship while they pleasantly inverted its object. The general conviction that love was sinful, that sensual pleasure could only be troublesome to the serious life, was reversed in the courts of Provence, much to the scandal of the Roman Church.

The new values proclaimed by the *canzone* have led some specialists to see hidden influences at work under the surface. The humanism of Provence has been interpreted by some as a heroic springtime of free thought in the West, eventually destroyed only by force of arms; while De Rougemont, in a more famous though equally exploded argument, has assimilated *fin'amor* into the widespread dualist heresy of the Cathars. Though neither of these excessive opinions can now be taken seriously, they point to a mood which was undeniably present in twelfth-century Provence: a resistance to the authoritarian civilization of the North; impatience with the cruder spirit of feudalism, and the puritanical morality proclaimed, if not wholly observed, by the Church. In various ways the Midi had always escaped the rigors of the feudal mentality, with its harsh system of obligations and its accent on the military virtues. For one thing, custom had long made the nobles themselves circumspect in exacting service and ceremony from those who were obliged to them by feudal law. From Roman times, large tracts of land had been held according to an unchallenged and wholly independent right: the right of *alleu* which, throughout the Middle Ages, escaped assimilation into the feudal system of dependences. By the twelfth century, the *alleu* had almost entirely disappeared in the north, while in the Midi it not only still flourished but was on the increase. The presence of the *alleu* modified the weight of feudal authority which was modified still further by the early appearance of a lively urban civilization, long before the cities of the north had gained a comparable importance. These and other influences undoubtedly help to explain the readiness of the Midi to honor with something less than awe the obligation of feudal authority; to observe the forms, while often playing with the spirit; to receive the heresy of Catharism, for example, without any great sense of scandal, for the Catholic Church had never, in any case, implanted itself with the same rigor and intolerance as elsewhere in Europe. The values of *fin'amor*, whatever precise historical origin one assigns to them, were perfectly at home in the easygoing civilization of Provence.

Although it is surely far too simple to describe Provençal love as a parody of orthodox ceremony and morality, it is clear that liberties were taken, resistances declared. The religious fervor apparent in the worship of the lady was highly serious and in no way a parody; yet it was a daring inversion of the religious spirit of the age, and of the idea of service, so dear to the feudal mentality. In place of marriage without pleasure, motivated as a rule by political considerations, there was the praise of adultery, as in the famous decree of Andreas Capellanus: "We say, in effect, and declare with great firmness, that love cannot develop its power between two persons united by the yoke of marriage." For love obeys the invisible law of grace, and not the law of society. The *Vidas*, those legendary "lives" of the troubadours, usually end with a terse sentence describing how the poet married, settled down, and died to poetry.

Service to the lord (the eternal father and husband) is thus replaced by service to the lady, usually at the lord's expense; the repressive morality of the "fathers" is replaced by a new, "feminine" concern with the grace of the senses. In the world of *fin'amor*, the seigneur, the source of male authority, no longer leads the dance. Instead he wanders at the edge of the scene, half concealed, a bit ridiculous, though still to be feared. In the role of *gilos*—the jealous husband—he will dramatize the lover's ingenuity in avoiding him. His presence will also justify the clever indirections of the love poetry: the obscurity of the *trobar clus*, the high value placed on secrecy and discretion, the conventional pseudonym—the *Senhal*—given by the poet to his lady.

But the Tristan legend has given us a further insight into the role of the *gilos*. King Mark and the evil-sayers—the *loseigniers* of the Provençal convention—represent more than authority made laughable or hateful. They crystallize an inner necessity of Tristan's love: a need for distance in love, and love at a distance. The purest emotion requires the discipline of solitude, the tantalizing difficulty of obstacles to overcome. The sensual grace of the *joi d'amor* depends on this turmoil of desires partially frustrated, as Arnaut Daniel reminds us in the passage quoted above. The *gilos* is the conventional instrument of this solitude.

He is the obstacle to which the lovers must yield, when their love is burdened with too much presence.

This brings us to another aspect of the Provençal tradition. We have seen that the love praised in the *canzone* is far from a wild display of passion and erotic impulse. Its sensuality depends closely on the decorum which the lovers must observe: on those *leys d'amor* which govern their love as strictly as feudal custom governed the ceremonies and the hierarchical dependencies of the nobility. Indeed, the language of *fin'amor*, as has often been observed, is very much that of the feudal order it tended to subvert: the laws of the Father transposed en masse into the service of love. The inaccessible lady is compared to a lord, and her lover to a vassal; the "service" of love, with its oaths of loyalty, faithfulness, and obedience, is clearly modeled on the feudal service; while the *merci* accorded by the lady to her lover is the fief granted by the lord to his dependent, in return for the service rendered. The troubadour, in his poem, went so far as to address his lady as *midons*, my lord, rather than *midonna*, my lady, recalling the "master mistress" of whom Shakespeare was to write in his sonnets four hundred years later.

This exchange of master for mistress is undoubtedly a trick of language; yet it betrays a strange current of emotion flowing beneath the surface of *fin'amor*: a languorous feminine sensuality not unlike the emotions of homoeroticism. The Arabic poets of the ninth to eleventh centuries, who describe a love experience similar in many ways to that of the troubadours, often addressed their poems to young men. And it is not impossible that this older tradition was familiar to some, at least, of the troubadours. *Fin'amor*, it would seem, aspires to a sensuality which blurs the ordinary distinctions of masculine and feminine, invoking to this purpose the constraining values of the *leys d'amor*. This legalistic spirit, which envelops the passion of the troubadours, transforms and spiritualizes the love experience. Yet we cannot help wondering if it does not perform another, equally important function.

Much has been written about the resurgence, in Europe, during the twelfth and thirteenth centuries, of permissive energies which had long threaded their way among the traditions of European culture, from the Orphic religions of Greece and Rome to the Gnostic cults of the Mother; finding an indirect language in the mystical strain of Christianity but also in the pagan traditions which continued to ferment under the cover of Christian Europe, preserved in legends, folk tales, and obscure customs. In the twelfth century, a new mood is voiced simultaneously in many parts of Europe: a need to reaffirm qualities of experience that had long been neglected. The resurgence of mysticism, the rediscovery of the old Gnostic heresies, the polite rebellion of *fin'amor* in Provence are cited as examples of a new breakthrough of the Great Mother into the mind of authoritarian Europe. As the patristic order weakened in the twelfth century, and the social unbalance of feudalism caused a disruptive mood to prevail on all levels of the society, desires that had been half repressed and half forgotten began to find conscious expression. In keeping with the new spirit, men used and altered the old Celtic forms, as in the case of Tristan and the tales of chivalry; they discovered a favorable ground in the forgotten dualist heresies; they used, and abused, whatever gave them a foothold in Christianity itself. The result in the lower classes was a growing turbulence, a desire for apocalyptic disorder. It was through these "messianic pains" that the masses hoped to solve the despair of their worldly insecurity. We think, inevitably, of Dionysius and his cult of inspired revelers.

But the case of the Brethren of the Free Spirit has shown us that there is a difference between the spiritual anarchy of medieval Europe and that of the Dionysian hordes. The European dissolved the limits of his humanity only to find them again; he was transformed by this chaotic energy which he sought to unleash in himself, only to appropriate it and make it part of his single human willfulness. The heretic aimed beyond anarchy, to a vast projection of self-indulgence made holy, the image of a glorious solitude in which the lineaments of his ego would be transfigured, becoming those of God Himself.

The picture that emerges of the Provençal courts is quite different. Here the only disorder is confined to the heart of the troubadour. There is no question of violence and disruptive anarchy, since the audience as well as the actors in Love were aristocratic and bourgeois. Their interests, but also their deepest sensibility, led them to resist both the violence of the chiliasts and the provoking behavior of the antinomians. They too needed to indulge the energies of the Mother, but they limited the disorder to a sort of game called *damnei:* the *joi* or *jeu d'amor.* The transposition of feudal constraint into the world of *damnei* is understandable. It serves to control the emotions unleashed by love; to turn them away from the kind of expression they receive in *Tristan* or in the violent heresies. This helps to explain the stereotyped plot, and the emphasis on skill—the rigorous laws of versification being, in fact, a transposition into poetry of the *leys d'amor.* The *gilos* may be laughable, but he is alert, assuring the audience, and the lovers themselves, that nothing will get out of hand. He is the other half of the lovers' desire: their patristic moral consciousness—their superego— weakened, perhaps, and ridiculous, but watching nonetheless. The *leys d'amor* are his cleverest subterfuge; they are his stamp of approval, but also his guarantee that the violence of the passions will be turned inward into the hearts of the lovers, rather than outward into the world.

We have seen this dialectic of passion and constraint in the story of Tristan and Isolde, where all its consequences are worked out to their tragic end. We discovered that the constraint had been internalized by the lovers; that King Mark was, in a sense, their own invention. The same is true of the Provençal tradition, where the *gilos* is forever prowling, ready to immobilize the lovers in the pain of separation. He is the reason for their remarkable *mesura;* he justifies their need to describe at great length the power, and pain, of their emotions, while keeping at a goodly distance from the beloved. The same false reciprocation which we discovered in *Tristan* lies at the heart of Provençal love, where the protagonist of the *canzon,* almost always a man, is noted for saying little about the specific qualities of his lady and a great deal about his own feelings.

It is clear, then, that the twelfth and thirteenth centuries witnessed the breakthrough into our culture of powerful desires, once repressed, which now sought an outlet in the available forms of religion, art, and literature. The permissive profile of the Mother rose from its place in the unconscious to invade the central portions of our minds. From now on, the spirit of Europe will be divided between allegiance to the male hierarchies of the Father and a thirst for the obscure pleasures of the Mother. The imagery of our passions will record this split: the heroic strength of the will, enthroned in a clear cold light, will be answered by a fascination with darkness and indolence. The way up into official culture will be echoed, and often challenged, by a way down into the erotic depths.

We must be careful, however, not to systematize too quickly. This division of passions between the eternal Father and the eternal Mother, between authority and permissiveness, is useful. But if we proceed too rapidly, we lose the half-tints of the picture, the details and shifts of color which are not mere accessories to the fact but, on the contrary, are what enable this fact to be grasped as a part of history—not a dull battle of the archetypal family, but a fleshed and changing scene, in which the differences are as important as the sameness.

In the period which concerns us, the differences are especially meaningful. We have already touched on the most important of these differences: the Heresy of the Free Spirit and *Tristan* are not only examples of permissive behavior, both the heresy and the poem are centered around an experience of solitude and self-transfiguration. The permissive energies of the Mother are present in both, but there is also a powerful strain of self-delight and erotic individualism—so much so that Ovid's figure of Narcissus seems at least as accurate a symbol for their deepest experience as the White Goddess herself. Against the patristic order of feudalism stands this strange figure of sensuality and self-indulgence: a mother who is also a lovesick boy, a master who is his own mistress, recalling the hermaphrodite, Narcissus, whose fertility transforms the world itself into a compendium of his emotions.

The courtly lyric confirms this sense of a confusion between the White Goddess and the Self. According to the conventional form of the *canzon,* the poet makes a sensitive analysis of his despair, his expectancy, his *joia,* the alternation of all these. He praises his lady and swears fidelity to her, describing her as the source of all grace and goodness, for himself as for the world. As Bernard de Ventadour was to write, "No man is worth anything without love." Yet something is troubled in this worship of the lady. A curious vagueness comes over the poet when he turns his skill outward toward the beloved, giving the kind of conventional praise that led one critic to wonder, ironically, whether the troubadours were not all in love with the same lady, a rather anonymous lady at that. The best one can say of her is that she is rarely well disposed toward her admirers. Her character is perfectly calculated to complement the dangers of the *gilos* and make her all but invisible to the half-happy suitor. We can sympathize with the poet's vagueness; he seems rarely to approach his lady closely enough to see her. The troubadour Jaufré Rudel epitomized this convention in the moving poems he wrote of his love for the lady of Tripoli, whom he had never seen. But we have already encountered another image of the distant lady and her lover: Tristan embracing the stone figure of his Isolde. The Cave of Statues is doubly appropriate, for it describes how the lover has invented the coldness and the absence of his lady. He needed her coldness, just as he needed the anger of the *gilos* and the decorum of the *leys d'amor,* in order to be alone with his emotions.

The Great Mother must allow a rival in the heart of her admirers: a mirror enshrined in place of the goddess herself. Under these circumstances it is not surprising that the mirror should appear among the conventional tropes of the *canzone*, and with the mirror its most famous lover, Narcissus, as in this poem by Bernard de Ventadour which, in its own day, was sung in all the courts of Europe:

> When I see the lark fly up joyfully in a ray of sunlight, then let herself fall, as if dizzied by the sweetness that comes in her heart, alas, how much I envy all the happy creatures I see! And I wonder that my heart does not instantly melt away with desire.

> Alas! How much I thought I knew of love, and how little I know, since I cannot help but love one who will yield nothing to me. She has taken my heart, she has hidden herself from me, she has taken myself and the whole world, leaving me only my desire and my burning heart.

> I no longer have power over myself since the day she let me look into her eyes, into that mirror which so pleases me. Mirror, since I have seen myself in you, my deep sighs kill me; and I am lost, like the beautiful Narcissus who lost himself in the fountain.

The poem moves between images of freedom and captivity; between the lark, so entirely abandoned to the joy of the sun's rays that it has forgotten itself ("que s'oublid") in the sweetness of its flight, and the poet's heart, held captive by a heat which is the inverse of the sun's heat, the heat of desire. In the second stanza Bernard describes the familiar solitude of the lover: if he too cannot forget self and attain the freedom of those creatures whose happiness he envies, it is because the lady has imprisoned him in his own passions. She has stolen his heart, his self, and the entire world—the air filled with sunlight through which the lark so freely moves—leaving him only the close-fitted walls of his "burning heart."

The third stanza does more than elaborate these themes; it transforms them. Beyond the dramatic reference to Narcissus, the image of the mirror carries with it a halo of aspiration and purity. The "desire" and the "burning heart," which are all the poet has left, represent a paradoxical richness. Because of them he has lost "the world" and his own self, only to find them again, half concealed by the pain, in the ideal beauty of his image, which he loves. We remember the alchemy of the mirror in *Tristan,* and the meanings it awakened in the mind of the medieval audience. Bernard too is transfigured by his love, elevated by the "grace" of his emotions. The image of the mirror renders with a skill that has been justly celebrated, not only the pain of unrequited love, but also an emotion described elsewhere by Arnaut Daniel, when he remembers, "Each day I am improved and refined, for I serve and adore the noblest lady in the world," or by Peiere Vidal: "All pleasing things I have done, and even the thoughts which come from my heart, I owe to her beautiful body filled with grace." The poet has lost all self-control since he was enchanted by this ideal image of himself, toward which he now aspires. He is imprisoned and "lost" in the image, but he is also elevated by it. During all this travail of love the lady remains strangely concealed by the poet's self-preoccupation. She is an unmoved mover, located beyond the world of the poet's spiritual need which she has herself paradoxically created.

These emotions are described even more dramatically in a German poem by Heinrich von Morungen, a minnesinger of the early thirteenth century. In his poem the mirror gains a new complexity and reflects a more tortuous kind of love:

> It has happened to me as to a small child which saw its beautiful reflection in a mirror and reached so hard for its own image that it broke the glass, thus all its joy was turned to bitter sorrow. So did I think I could be happy forever as I saw my dear lady. In loving her I have suffered great sorrow.

Love, who brings increase of joy to all the world, see, she brought my lady to me in a dream as I lay asleep and I was lost in the contemplation of my greatest joy. I saw her wonderful qualities, her bright image, beautiful beyond those of all other women; only her little red mouth, so rich in joys, was a little disturbed.

Because of this I felt great fear, that her mouth, so small, so red, should be pale. So I began a new complaint. My heart was tortured by such misery that my eyes should make me gaze upon such sadness. I was like a child who has not yet learned wisdom and who saw his reflection in a pool and must love it till he dies.

Again the lover is compared to Narcissus, though Heinrich has displaced the mirror from its usual association with the lady's eyes. The poet's sorrow, he tells us, comes from the childish incontinence of his passion which has led him to ruffle the surface of the pool, shattering the ideal beauty he had discovered there. This thought is expressed somewhat differently in the second stanza: the poet has seen his lady in a dream and has been overcome by the joyful presence of her image, until suddenly her mouth, "so rich in joys," appears disturbed, causing him "great fear." In the dream his passion becomes so impetuous that the lady is forced to respond. For a moment her anonymity is torn aside; she surges through the ruffled image of the dream, in all her painful reality. It is this impetuousness, this "natural" energy which must be controlled and transformed if the "truth" of love is to survive. That is the wisdom which the child, in the third stanza, still lacks. He is told to learn the decorum of love if he wants to earn its transfiguring grace. The poem expresses this thought by again referring to the image in the pool which can be loved only at a distance; for to approach the image too closely is to break it; just as to approach the lady too closely is to discover a real woman whose emotions can only disturb the sensual solitude of "true love."

We understand now why the troubadour's lady must be so

evasive. The poet's complaint is that of Narcissus in the *Metamorphoses*, speaking to his image in the water:

> Where are you going? Stay with me;
> O cruelest lover come, nor leave me here;
> It may be fate for me to look at love
> And yet not touch it, but in that deep gaze
> Increase unhappy love to misery.

When Guillaume de Lorris transports "true love" into the dream world of the *Roman de la Rose*, he will remain faithful to the eyes-for-mirrors convention. His dreamer wanders through the garden of Love until he comes to a delightful fountain, "springing in a marble stone," on which is written, in Chaucer's translation: "Here starf the fayre Narcissus." The fountain, we learn, represents the lady's eyes, and it plays an important role in the dreamer's love life, for he sees, reflected in its "mirrour perilous," for the first time, his lady, like "a roser chargid full of roses." Guillaume transforms the conventional trope of the *canzon* into allegory, making it a crucial episode in the lover's progress through the garden. As the play of images over the water captures the dreamer's eye, the mirror gains a power of enchantment; it becomes a miniature world, an ideal form in which all things are reflected, refracted by Love:

> For ther is noon so litil thyng
> So hid, ne closid with shittyng,
> That it ne is sene, as though it were
> Peyntid in the cristall there.

Narcissus, whose pool this is, has become a version of "daun Cupido," son of Venus, and we are told finally what the courtly tradition has hinted all along: that the well of Narcissus is but another name for "the Welle of Love."

II The Sonnets of Shakespeare

Nowhere is the "secret" of Love so thoroughly yet so movingly revealed as in a group of poems which may well be the last and best the tradition has produced. Centuries after Provence and the poetry of the French *trovères;* long after the contributions of Dante, Petrarch, and more recently, Ronsard, Shakespeare's sonnets epitomized the conventional resources of courtly love with new energy. Shakespeare knew the language and the complexity of the genre so well, he believed so firmly in the transfiguring grace of its emotions, that he wrote some of our finest love lyrics. Yet as we read the sonnets, it becomes clear that they contain a strength and clarity which differs in kind as well as in degree from other poems in the tradition. Shakespeare took the conventional themes of Love much as Cervantes took those of chivalry; he was aware of the richness but also of the poverty they contained. In the sonnets, therefore, he not only clarified the conventional emotions, he placed them in a new perspective. The sonnets, like *Don Quixote,* undercut those very responses which they lovingly invoke; they end a tradition from within by mastering it, as they pursue its themes to a limit of absurdity.

The first and most important group of the sonnets (Nos. 1–126) deal with the infatuation felt by an aging poet for a boy of whom we learn very little if not that he is fickle, self-centered, and attractive to men and women alike. The rhetoric of the poems belongs, on the whole, to the courtly convention, that "perfect ceremony of love's rite" (No. 23), in which the boy is described as "Lord of my love," and the poet's "duty" to him as a "vassalage," justified only by the boy's "merit." The poet's very skill is said to come from the purity of his love, or rather from the love-object whose grace, from a distance, irradiates the imagination. Yet the boy remains aloof and vague; he is present, for the most part, only as a negative of the poet's own dilemma which is described in poem after poem, with a power and clarity, but also with a wit, which have rarely been equalled. In all this, the sonnets do, perhaps more skillfully, what the poems of courtly love had always done. Their main originality here lies in the gender of the personal pronoun: a young boy instead of a lady; though we remember the shifting gender of the lady in the Provençal *canzon: midons* for *midona.*

Shakespeare, however, has understood the nature of his love, and his insight is expressed in the poems with a strength that is often painful. What the tradition previously had wrapped in images, or implied by ambiguous turns of phrase, Shakespeare now says openly. The false reciprocation, the solitude, the self-love, all those emotions of Narcissus come to the foreground in the sonnets. Shakespeare not only makes use of them, he talks about them, and makes them into the subject matter of his poetry.

The argument is broached in sonnets 1-17, where the poet pleads with his loved one to forego the adolescent selfishness and the prudery whose only result will be sorrow for others and a life of sterile solitude for himself. The burden of the poet's reproach is the boy's reticence with women, above all his refusal to beget children.

> Is it for feare to wet a widdowe's eye,
> That thou consum'st thy selfe in single life? (No. 9)

To refuse life's responsibility in this way is to lack generosity, but it is also to lack wisdom; for a man so self-contained wastes the most precious part of his own being. The poet exclaims:

> For shame deny that thou bear'st love to any,
> Who for thy selfe art so unprovident. (No. 10)

The boy's reticence, and the sterility to which he succumbs are described eloquently in sonnet 1:

> But thou, contracted to thine owne bright eyes,
> Feed'st thy lights flame with selfe-substantiall fewell,
> Making a famine where aboundance lies,
> Thy selfe thy foe, to thy sweet selfe too cruell.

Shakespeare has traced for us here a delicate portrait of Narcissus. Indeed the verse, "contracted to thine owne bright eyes," seems directly to echo Ovid's lines in *The Metamorphoses:*

> He lay to look deep, deeper
> into two stars that were his eyes.

Nature, the poet argues again, has endowed you with her gifts: a beautiful face, a graceful body, a life made for delight, "which bountious gift thou should'st in bounty cherish" (No. 11). Bounty is the key here; for what has been given should in turn be given. The argument of these first poems is not unfamiliar: they contain nothing less than a plea for generosity; a lover's desire to overcome the self-contained, selfish responses of his beloved. That the plea should be presented as an argument for fatherhood seems, at first glance, unfathomable. The poet's love, on the other hand, although not adulterous, is illicit for other reasons, requiring all the ceremony of discretion, the *mesura,* for which the tradition has prepared us. As the poet himself warns the beloved:

> I may not evermore acknowledge thee,
> Least my bewailed guilt should do thee shame,
> Nor thou with publike kindnesse honour me,
> Unlesse thou take that honour from thy name. (No. 36)

The argument for fatherhood can be thought of as an indirection, a discreet rhetoric whose aim is to awaken the emotions of the young boy and eventually to win his *merci.*

The notion that the first sonnets should be read "indirectly" is confirmed by another turn taken by the argument. As the poet tries to charm his chaste Narcissus, we find that the generosity he has described so amply in terms of abundance and fertility is in fact meant to be only another form of self-love—not the savage timidity of an Adonis, but a warm effusion of self, a natural self-creation, represented in the poems by that living image of one's own flesh: a child.

Shakespeare's argument for generosity and fatherhood is indeed incomplete; not once does he mention the possibility of a girl-child, nor does he make much of the prospective mother. It is the boy who is important, and the child whose role will be to preserve more richly, more generously than mirrors, the precious image of the beloved. The case is clearly put in sonnet 3:

> Looke in thy glasse and tell the face thou vewest
> Now is the time that face should forme another;
> . . . .
> Or who is he so fond will be the tombe
> Of his selfe love, to stop posterity?

Love becomes a way to undo the ravages of time. The self-contained emotions of Narcissus are futile; they embody an ignorance and perhaps even a hatred of oneself:

> For having traffike with thy selfe alone
> Thou of thy selfe thy sweet selfe dost deceave. (No. 4)

Only if he loves will the boy best serve himself, and vanquish death:

> Ten times thy selfe were happier then thou art
> If ten of thine ten times refigur'd thee,
> Then what could death doe if thou shouldst depart,
> Leaving thee living in posterity? (No. 6)

The fertility evoked by Shakespeare in sonnets 1–17 has little
to do, it would seem, with founding a family, i.e., with transforming (sublimating) the infantile solitude of Narcissus. Instead it is described as a ruse, offered by Nature herself; a way
to outwit death and defy corruption through that natural
posterity of the flesh: one's children.

This is, indeed, a curious introduction to a series of love
poems: a poet who begs his beloved to forego chastity and self-
willfulness, not in order that he might love more generously and
accept the precarious life of human exchanges, but only that he
might be surrounded by faithful replicas of his own ever-youth-
ful self. The poet's alternative is not between selfishness and
generosity, as we had first thought, but between different kinds
of self-love. Shakespeare, in writing these poems, seems to have
had in mind something for which the convention of love had
not entirely prepared us. And we need not look far to discover
what it is, for Shakespeare, as we have already suggested, brings
to the surface of his argument themes which had previously
been concealed in the conventional rhetoric. Sonnet 62 is quite
explicit:

> Sinne of selfe love possesseth al mine eie
> And all my soule and al my every part;
> And for this sinne there is no remedie,
> It is so grounded inward in my heart.
> Me thinkes no face so gratious is as mine,
> No shape so true, no truth of such account,
> And for my selfe mine owne worth do define,
> As I all other in all worths surmount.
> But when my glasse shewes me my selfe indeed,
> Beated and chopt with tand antiquitie,
> Mine owne selfe love quite contrary I read
> Selfe so selfe loving were iniquity.
> > T'is thee (my selfe) that for my selfe I praise,
> > Painting my age with beauty to thy daies.

No wonder the poet is so sensitive when he describes the "sinne of selfe love" in a young boy; he knows the "sinne" as well as he knows himself. Though he is "beated and chopt with tand antiquitie," he remains an inveterate self-lover. And the advice he gives to the boy, encouraging him to store up new blood against the time "when fortie Winters shall besiege thy brow," is the advice he himself has followed in the course of his strange infatuation. If the poet loves the boy, we are told, it is because the boy's youth has become a rejuvenating mirror which enables him to roll back the years and conquer the worst enemy of Narcissus: time's encroaching ugliness.

Thus the sonnets introduce us, on the one hand, to an effeminate, self-centered boy, exceedingly responsive, it would seem, to flattery; and on the other, to an aging poet, obsessed by his love as well as by his years, who admits his weakness for the "sinne of self love," as if to explain to us, and perhaps to himself, the strength of his infatuation.

Indeed although the boy appears to be flighty, and even careless of his honor on occasion (see sonnets 41, 42, 70, etc.), he is not entirely unresponsive to the emotions lavished on him by the aging poet. Within the limits imposed by fear of scandal, the boy too loves, as the poet indicates in sonnet 71 ("Noe Longer mourne for me when I am dead"). Yet the boy's response carries less weight in the poems than the poet's own discourse with himself, which fills whole nights and peoples all his thoughts. Is it your love, he asks the boy, that finds me at night and awakens my imagination? "Oh no!" he answers, "thy love though much, is not so great, / It is my love that keepes mine eie awake" (No. 61). Between the two "lovers" an emotion is born which is not quite love, but instead an intricate exchange of self-interests, a sensual companionship enabling each to become closer, not to the beloved, but to himself.

In the first group of sonnets we saw how the poet urged his loved one to make new selves, in order that he might defeat the efforts of "Devouring Time." Soon after this, however, the argument changes ground. It is the poet himself who offers to do what nature, perhaps, cannot be trusted with. Now the skill with which "love" has graced him, the power of the sonnets themselves, will preserve the boy's beauty and renown, as the act of fatherhood was to have done in the first sonnets:

> But thy eternall sommer shall not fade
> Nor loose possession of that faire thou ow'st;
> Nor shall Death brag thou wander'st in his shade,
> When in eternall lines to time thou grow'st. (No. 18)

The poet will dedicate his genius to the task of immortalizing the boy; he will fertilize the boy's youthful beauty in another way, producing, instead of a posterity of children, a posterity of poems. The skill of poetry, he tells us, will enable the boy to live forever, enthroned in the youthful circle of his self-love. In return, the poet will transform his loved one into a flattering mirror; he himself will become young again by loving this image which his emotion has created in the self-made glass. Through the powers of "love" and poetry, the poet has made the boy into his own "child." He has followed the advice the sonnets gave to the boy ("make thee another selfe"), and has indeed made him another self, in return for which he has given birth to the boy's other self: the sonnets. This exchange of love and poetry betrays a strangely sublimated eroticism, in which the lover, through the "skill" of his imagination, becomes both father and mother to the boy, performing in his words a rarefied, but unmistakable, incest.

The sonnets offer us a portrait of two lovers whose most amorous concern is not with the other, enclosed in his irreducible, uncompromising humanity, but with the self: with the lover's own fatality, the pain and corruption attending his own life, and the delicate solitude that allows him whatever recompense love's imagination can offer. The portrait, as we have seen, is not original. The traditions of courtly love had offered us many similar ones since their rise in Provence, four centuries earlier. But never before had the image been drawn with such lucidity. After the sonnets, the formal convention of love tends to become an object of satire, or a vehicle for the kind of rough sensuality that Donne was to praise a few years later. Indeed the savagery and despair of Shakespeare's own sonnets to the dark lady already stand outside the tradition. Here the blindness of love, which in *fin'amor* is also its ennobling grace, has become no more than a prison, a bond of lust mingled with shame and bewilderment. The beloved is turned from a goddess into a devil; from an object of beauty and moral perfection into an object of disgust, made nonetheless desirable by the "wiles" of love. Yet between the "good angel" of the early sonnets and the "bad angel" of the late ones there is a common trait: neither has been seen, nor has either been loved, for what he (or she) is. Both remain exterior to the world of the poems, with its delicate geography of hope and despair, adoration and bitterness. Both have left the poet to himself, unable or unwilling to violate the solitude of his emotions.

There is a meaningful irony in the fact that centuries of lovers have read the "good angel" sonnets to their ladies, ignoring not only the masculine gender of the pronouns but the kind of circular emotion which the poems portray; as if Shakespeare had evoked brilliantly and powerfully the blindness of their own loves: the lovely boy and the mirror concealed in their own passions.

The sonnets have often been read as a prelude to the greater poetry of the plays. In them Shakespeare is said to have tested, perhaps to have discovered, his genius, before embarking on the long effort of tragedy. One can indeed read the poems as a prelude, but not in the sense that is usually meant. Shakespeare, in the sonnets, explores the solitude of Narcissus; he evokes the passions of the mirror and the illusory exchanges of "love," transforming them, and himself, in the crucible of his poetry. When he leaves the sonnets, he will be ready to write great plays, for he will have learned how to love his characters in a way that the boy of the sonnets can never be loved.

The men and women of the plays are described with a clarity and a psychological rightness which remain foreign to the sonnets. For the sonnets are not concerned with dramatic rightness. The convention of love which they follow requires both the vagueness of the beloved and the blindness of the lover. The boy of the sonnets must be blurred by his absence if he is to be properly adored; that, we have discovered, is the secret of "love."

But the characters in the great plays make the poetry serve them; they are unmistakable and alive; their words and gestures radiate from a uniqueness which shapes their personality. The poet never loses sight of their uniqueness, nor of the fate that will exalt or destroy it. Only after the blinders of "self-love" had been removed could the poet truly love the singularity of his characters, displaying for them the same delicate care which, in the sonnets, he had displayed for his own emotions. In this sense, the sonnets represent an exercise in self-knowledge; a moral discipline in which the poet discovered not only his "skill" but a toughness and maturity which needed to accompany the skill, and were, in fact, identical with it.

III *Paradise Lost*

There is another episode in the progress of courtly love which will alter it once again and offer new ramifications of its psychology. Drawing on the allegorical mood of Spenser's *Faerie Queene,* renewing the speculative freedom of the Gnostics, Milton, in *Paradise Lost,* invented images to embody his vision of the Christian fate. In order to justify the ways of God to man, he projected into his poetic space an understanding of man's fallen humanity which echoes curiously the insights of the courtly tradition.

The world we encounter in *Paradise Lost* has been flawed by the adventures of pride. God's angels have divided themselves into opposing armies, and between them, at the very edge of chaos, a new creature, man, dangles precariously. For Milton's Adam is born into a world which has already fallen. His Paradise is an island surrounded by armed legions. Its unconstrained harmony is so remarkable that angels, we are told, fly down from Heaven to admire this museum piece of the order which once prevailed. Meanwhile the world is policed with increasing subtlety. When Eden falls, harmony will be replaced by statutes; the reign of love will become a reign of power: self against self, Abel against Cain. It is a world in which order and constraint have become synonymous.

Milton makes his meaning clear in a passage toward the end of Book Two in which Satan encounters Sin and Death, the allegorical guardians of Hellgate. He is about to engage in combat with Death, who has tried to bar his way, when Sin cries out, "O father, what intends thy hand . . . against thy only son?" Satan is amazed to discover that these hideous monsters are his own daughter and his own incestuous son. Sin reminds him how, in the midst of the conspiracy, he had become strangely dizzy. To the general amazement, flames had leapt out of his head as it gaped open on the left side, revealing a goddess, "Likest to thee in shape and countenance bright." It was she herself, Sin:

> I pleased, and with attractive graces won
> The most averse—thee chiefly, who full oft
> Thyself in me thy perfect image viewing,
> Becamest enamoured; and such joy thou tookest
> With me in secret, that my womb conceived
> A growing burden. . . .

Sin's burden becomes, in turn, a son, Death, whose first impulse is to do what Satan his father had already done. He leaps on his mother, causing her to give birth to a series of monsters who rush in and out of her womb, devouring her entrails.

Satan's unholy family is clearly a deformed reflection of the Divine Family. His revolt was first occasioned by news that God had created a Son; a son who, furthermore, is made in his Father's image, just as Sin is an "image" of Satan. Milton has hit upon a very ancient theme here. The fascination with the mirror, the grotesque figures of incest, the parallel between the upper and the lower creations, the "explanation" of evil with its root in self-love and pride: these are all favorite Gnostic themes. But for Milton the center of gravity is no longer the same. He is far more interested in Eve's frailty and Adam's dilemma than in the difficult matter of cosmology.

It is clear from Milton's account that Adam is destined from the very first to fall from innocence. Even before he sins he has, in a sense, already fallen: his character, his emotions, the quality of his intelligence are only half paradisiac. What is more, he has been born into a fallen universe where any spiritual weakness will be turned against him. From this point of view, Adam's original fall is undoubtedly his inability to remain alone with himself. In the midst of plenitude, he gently conplains to God:

> . . . In solitude
> What happiness? who can enjoy alone,
> Or, all enjoying, what contentment find?

Milton echoes, ever so faintly here, the tradition of an androgynous Paradise, a prelapsarian solitude where Adam, like God, had once lived in pure self-communion. The seventeenth century was fascinated by images of Paradise, and the myth of the androgynous Adam had been used before: by Sir Thomas Browne with his nostalgia for an Eden where man reproduced like trees; above all, by Andrew Marvell's stanzas in "The Garden":

> Such was that happy Garden-state,
> While Man there walk'd without a Mate:
> After a place so pure, and sweet,
> What other help could yet be meet!
> But 'twas beyond a Mortal's share
> To wander solitary there:
> Two Paradises 'twere in one
> To live in Paradise alone.

Milton's Adam, however, is destined to flee himself; his loneliness is only a tarnished replica of God's solitude, of which he says, admiringly,

> Thou, in thy secrecy, although alone,
> [are] Best with Thyself accompanied.

Unlike God, Adam requires a companion, "another self," to complete his happiness. In order to make Paradise better, Adam needs to make it worse. From here on every step will lead Adam and Eve farther from the world of harmony and nearer to the constraints of law.

Eve describes to Adam her first awakening in Paradise. Upon coming to herself, she lay down on the bank of a nearby pond:

> As I bent down to look, just opposite
> A shape within the watery gleam appeared
> Bending to look on me. I started back:
> It started back; but pleased I soon returned:
> Pleased it returned as soon with answering looks
> Of sympathy and love . . .

Eve's first encounter with error duplicates that of Narcissus, and reveals the special frailty that will make her an easy prey for

Satan. Apt to be tricked by an illusion, Eve, like Satan, is inclined to admire her own image. That is why they will come to understand each other so well. On this occasion, however, Adam is still watchful enough to correct his companion:

> . . . There had I fixed
> Mine eyes till now, and pined with vain desire,
> Had not a voice thus warned me: "What thou seest—
> What there thou seest—fair creature, is thyself:
> With thee it came and goes; but follow me,
> And I will bring thee where no shadow stays
> Thy coming and thy soft embraces—he
> Whose image thou art; him thou shalt enjoy
> Inseparably thine; to him shalt bear
> Multitudes like thyself . . ."

The passage reveals Adam as clearly as it does Eve. To wean her away from her own image, Adam offers Eve something more substantial: a living body, his own, which somehow still preserves the intimate likeness of the illusion. Eve, though only half convinced, lets herself be persuaded. She exchanges one image for the other; but her love remains the same. Eve, we discover, learns to love Adam in the same way that Narcissus learned to love his own illusory face. Adam, on the other hand, seems to be satisfied with this arrangement. He too has sought from the first, in Eve, his "best image" and "other self," and is, we suppose, delighted when God tells what is in store for him:

> What next I bring shall please thee, be assured,
> Thy likeness, thy fit help, thy other self,
> Thy wish exactly to thy heart's desire.

Eve's creation allows Adam to satisfy a difficult desire: he can now be both divinely alone and humanly accompanied. With Eve he is still with his "other self," and therefore, though human and imperfect, he can in some measure approach God who is also, we are told, "best with [himself] accompanied." Milton strengthens his meaning at this point with an adroit use of the Genesis story. In order to further convince Eve that she has more to gain with him than with her image in the pond, Adam cries out:

> . . . Return, fair Eve;
> Whom fliest thou? Whom thou fliest, of him thou art,
> His flesh, his bone; to give thee being I lent
> Out of my side to thee, nearest my heart,
> Substantial life, to have thee by my side
> Henceforth, an individual solace dear;
> Part of my soul I seek thee, and thee claim
> My other half . . .

Milton here gives substance to the rhetoric of courtly love. When Adam calls Eve his "other self," he is not using a figure of speech: she is indeed fashioned from his own body, sculpted from his own flesh, blood, and bone. Their love will have a continuity, unlike the poet's troubled infatuation in Shakespeare's sonnets, or the love-ordeal of Tristan and Isolde. Adam and Eve live like happy Narcissi, because each is quite literally an image of the other.

Two allusions seem to be intended here which help to define the emotion of love in Milton's poems. The reference to Ovid in Eve's self-mirroring needs no elaboration. There is, however, a second reference which has not often been noticed. When Adam tells how Eve was fashioned, like a living statue, from his own body, he is surely echoing Ovid's story of Pygmalion: the legendary sculptor who fell in love with his own statue and then persuaded the gods to transform it into a real woman. Milton was surely right in sensing the family resemblance between Narcissus and Pygmalion. Nor was he the only one to do so. A hundred years later Rousseau was to write not only his *Narcisse*, but also a one-act dialogue entitled *Pygmalion et*

Galatée, where he expresses for the first time the romantic theory of art as self-expression.

Both Adam and Eve are built in part upon classical models. Of the two, Adam is the stronger and the more practical: he will not be tempted, as Eve was, by a mere illusion; instead, like Pygmalion, he asks his God for a living statue and gets one. In calling Eve, on several occasions, his "dearer half," or, as above, his "other half," he brings to mind still another classical theme: Plato's theory of the egg in the *Symposium.* The philosopher imagines a time when man and woman were yoked together into a single androgynous being which then was split in two like an egg. Since then, man and woman pursue, and love, each other because their souls are incomplete: they conserve, in their emotions, a nostalgia for their ancient unity. According to Plato's theory, love is, paradoxically, a desire for solitude: a need to cure man's all-too-human loneliness by reviving the perfect self-communion of some prelapsarian experience before time had begun.

The moral drama of *Paradise Lost* turns upon a symmetry in which Adam and Eve occupy the most difficult position. The staging of the poem depends upon this symmetry, with Heaven on the one hand, Hell on the other, and between them the Earth linked upward by a golden chain and downward by a broad highway over chaos. Each of the three worlds springs from an act of creation which, at the same time, is a failure in harmony. God begets his Son, thereby upsetting the balance of order in Heaven; Satan gives birth to Sin and Death, thereby creating the infernal kingdom of Hell. Adam draws Eve from his side, thereby setting in motion the long upward toil of history. God in Heaven embodies the pure pleasure of self-communion, the essential solitude of Godhead which Adam so much admires. Satan, in turn, represents a perversion of God's autonomy: pride, symbolized by the allegorical incest with his own "image." Between these pure limits lies the middle ground: Eden, where

Adam and Eve unravel the strands of their humanity and try to make a life for themselves. Their fate is the hardest because they belong, from the first, to both worlds. By their marriage they reunite, to a degree, the separate halves of the egg, transcending the frailty of their human nature. Yet their love, pure as it is, bears an occult resemblance to that of Satan's unholy family. Both Satan and Adam bring about grave changes in the universe by loving—each in his own way—a woman drawn, by an act of God, from his own body. Knowledge of this parallel between Adam and Satan prepares us for the outcome of the battle. Man, we learn, contains side by side the upward aspiration toward God and the deflected energy of self-love which turns him back into himself.

The couple in Paradise has already slipped a goodly distance toward their fall. True, their felicity remains uppermost until the fatal episode, and Milton must be recognized as the first, and best, poet of the happy marriage. But the balance of their harmony is precarious. Once the heavenly solitude has been dissolved, Adam and Eve move in a delightful but dangerous circle around their inner flaw: the bottomless well of Narcissus concealed in each of them. Paradise offers them a symbol of their danger in the form of the forbidden tree: the constraint impressed by this one law corresponds to an unspoken self-constraint which they have not yet learned to practice; and that, precisely, is their innocence. Eve falls victim to the serpent, not because she has forgotten the interdiction, but because she cannot recognize and act against the flaw in her character to which it corresponds.

Satan, however, will make no mistake about it. The dream he whispers into Eve's ear is troubling indeed, for it plays skilfully on that mixture of innocence, credulity, and self-infatuation which life in Paradise has fostered. Eve dreams of an angel, "shaped and winged like one of those from Heaven," who tastes a fruit from the forbidden tree and then cries out:

> . . . O fruit divine,
> Sweet of thyself, but much more sweet thus cropped,
> Forbidden here, it seems, as only fit
> For gods, yet able to make gods of men!
> And why not gods of men, since good, the more
> Communicated, the more abundant grows,
> The author not impaired, but honoured more?

Satan shrewdly mingles the pleasure of self-glorification (hubris) with the desire to praise and imitate the Divine model, confusing, in Eve's mind, the part of Hell and the part of Heaven. In the dream, Eve gets a preview of her fall; she too tastes the fruit:

> . . . Forthwith up to the clouds
> With him I flew, and underneath beheld
> The Earth stretched out immense . . .

Good and Evil are indeed close neighbors; falling, at first glance, can strangely resemble flying.

When Satan next returns he will strengthen his argument and Eve again will succumb, this time without recourse. When the serpent tells her that she and Adam, by eating the fruit, "shall be as Gods"; that to die means "by putting off human, to put on Gods," the temptation is too great. Eve, inclined already, as we have seen, to take illusion for reality, eats the fruit. The case with Adam, however, is not the same. In a sense, he is the greater sinner, for he knows perfectly what he is about when he accepts Eve's offer:

> . . . He scrupled not to eat
> Against his better knowledge, not deceived,
> But fondly, overcome with female charm.

The usual commentary on this scene tells how Eve fell through her own weak-mindedness; but Adam, generous to the last, fell through love of Eve. We are prepared now to see this in another light. Adam, having once tasted the ennui of loneliness, prefers even death. His first failing remains with him, and now he chooses again to flee into his "other self":

> . . . If death
> Consort with thee, death is to me as life;
> So forcible within my heart I feel
> The bond of Nature draw me to my own—
> My own in thee, for what thou art is mine.
> Our state cannot be severed; we are one,
> One flesh; to lose thee were to lose myself.

The act is done; man has traded the order of consent, the transparency of hearts, for the order of the law. Like Satan before him, Adam has withdrawn from the harmony and fallen into the world of force, statutes, and interdictions. His unruly egotism has destroyed the world in which laws were invisible and lives mutually open. The first thing Adam and Eve will now do is to cover their bodies, hiding first from God and then from each other. Love is replaced by violation, transparency freely consented by a clumsy secret. And God's answer must now be translated into the only language egotists acknowledge: the language of constraint. In a world where each wants to be God, the only true God is the strongest. The chain of being has become an order of military precedence, founded on power.

Part Three

Part Three

7 EACH MAN A PHOENIX: THE SELF AND THE NEW METAPHYSICS

Descartes, in his Third Meditation, gives an unexpected picture of the philosopher. The subject of his meditation is God and the Divine Nature, and the passage in question describes the kind of clear thinking appropriate to such a lofty inquiry: "I will now close my eyes, I will plug my ears, I will turn aside all of my senses . . . in this way, concerned only with myself, looking only at what is inside me, I will try, little by little, to know myself, and to become more familiar to myself." When Plato chose a vehicle for his philosophy, he had also to choose a character and a dramatic voice: those of his mentor, Socrates. But Descartes needed no "character" to present his argument. Philosophy, he felt, was best carried on between a man and himself; only when the doors and windows of the body had been shut could one think clearly and to the point. There is an occult resemblance between Descartes's philosopher gazing at his inward image and Guillaume de Lorris' "dreamer" gazing at his reflection in the pool, where he has discovered, arranged as a halo about his face, the surrounding vastness of the world. Both Descartes and the courtly dreamer must look into, and behind, their own faces in order to discover "things as they are."

Descartes's image of the philosopher is so familiar to us that we find it difficult to imagine another one. Yet the examples of Plato and Socrates are surely from this point of view "uncartesian." Whitehead, acknowledging Descartes as the founder of modern metaphysics, emphasizes this difference. The modern philosopher, he writes, is concerned above all with "a subject receiving experience: in the *Discourse* this subject is always mentioned in the first person, that is to say, as being Descartes himself. The subsequent history of philosophy revolved around the Cartesian formulation of the primary datum." Which is to say that Descartes's philosopher, like the courtly dreamer, though in a different key and for other reasons, speaks to us at length about himself, his thoughts, his experience. Whitehead continues: "The ancient world takes its stand upon the drama of the Universe, the modern world upon the inward drama of the Soul." The novelty and the peculiar strength of the modern vision comes, rather from the amalgamation of these two kinds of "drama" into one, in which the drama of the universe is the inward drama of the soul and vice versa. We saw this to be the case for both Gnostic and Christian mysticism. With the *Meditations* and the *Discourse on Method,* European philosophy adopts a point of view that is not dissimilar. After Descartes it will become difficult to know whether the first person of the philosopher is a mere figure of speech or if he represents the complex inwardness of the man himself. The distinction, indeed, may often become meaningless.

The *Meditations,* however, are by no means a "confession," nor are they the record of an actual philosophical experience. They are above all a work of logic; their argument, from end to end, is presented with the persuasive clarity of a demonstration. The "I" of the *Meditations* casts no shadow; he is entirely without the idiosyncrasy of a Montaigne or an Augustine. Indeed, Descartes had no patience with fantasy or emotion. "The mind," he writes, "must be turned away from the workings of the imagination if it is to know its own nature with perfect distinctness." How surprising, then, for us to discover that this self with no shadows, this purely rhetorical instrument, possesses a strong imagination and, despite its own warning, needs this imagination if it is to think at all to the purpose! Descartes's argument in the *Meditations* depends unexpectedly upon the drama of certain images which erupt into his prose and give new urgency to his ideas.

The best known of these fantasies occurs in the First Meditation, where the reader is asked to imagine that all feeling and perception, everything he knows about the world, including his own body, is a lie. In order to make the fantasy more palpable, Descartes writes:

> I will suppose that . . . a certain evil genius, as crafty and deceptive as he is powerful, has deployed all his efforts to fool me: I will imagine that the sky, the air, the earth, colors, shapes, sounds and everything else that is exterior, are nothing but illusions and daydreams, used by this evil genius to ensnare my belief; I will think of myself as having no hands, eyes, flesh, or blood; as having no senses, but falsely believing that I have all these things.

We are asked to suppose—for the sake of the argument, to be sure—that some powerful demiurge has created the world as we know it; a monster whose only pleasure it is to persecute our intelligence.

We are of course reminded throughout that this *malin génie* is a fiction; an image whose value is above all rhetorical, in an argument whose outcome will never be in doubt. By it, Descartes means only to dramatize the extent of his *doute méthodique*, and that final reversal of thought in which a single truth survives the shipwreck of all knowledge. The *malin génie* can be wholly wicked, Descartes argues, yet one thing remains beyond his power: he cannot destroy the assurance that there is someone who has been betrayed; for if he has fooled me, then I exist. *Cogito, ergo sum.* Let this evil god corrupt my knowledge; there is within me a clear haven, a thought single and unshakable which is immune to his falsehood. This argument precedes the opening of the Third Meditation, and helps us to understand more thoroughly Descartes's image of the philosopher who has closed his eyes, plugged his ears, blocked all his senses, in order to converse with himself in his own mind. In a world whose very nature has become doubtful, the philosopher must look within if he is to discover any sure foundation of knowledge; whatever else he does, he must begin here.

Descartes's figure of the *malin génie* has a curious fascination which remains with us long after the needs of the argument have been satisfied. It evokes in the most unexpected way another scene from a world as unlike Descartes's as can be imagined. Remember the advice of Monoimus concerning the knowledge of first principles: "Do not look for God and the creation and other like things; look for Him by starting in *yourself* and learn who it is in *you* that possesses all things without question . . . If you look for these things correctly, you will find them in yourself." Descartes's advice to the philosopher could have been written in these words. It is precisely this "inward drama of the Soul" which made Gnostic thought so interesting for us.

The Gnostic felt that he had been thrown into a desert, where he was persecuted by the Archons or the Spirits of the Air. But he was not entirely lost, for he could retreat into his mind, to a point he called the "apex" of his soul. That is the meaning of Monoimus' exhortation. Persecuted by the world, the Gnostic found refuge in his "spirit." If we substitute Descartes's *malin génie* for the Gnostic Demiurge, we find that the *Meditations* propose an analogous situation. On the one hand there is the persecuting God who governs over a world of deceit, on the other the individual who discovers in his own thought a source of inalienable freedom.

The limits of the comparison are of course clear. The Gnostics were engaged in a struggle from which there was no escape. The deceitful world, the Archons, the Demiurge formed part of an eschatological drama in which the persecuted self rose upward toward union with the transmundane God. Descartes's *malin génie*, on the other hand, is merely a pawn in an argument. The "salvation" for which the self can hope in the

Meditations consists in clear knowledge of the kind proper to geometry or mathematics. There is nothing mystical here. Indeed, the proposition of the *malin génie* is withdrawn in due time. We are not asked to believe but only to "allow" him for the clarity of argument. Yet these differences allow us to grasp the one point common to them both: their reliance upon the certainties of "inwardness," against a world overwhelmingly hostile and alien to the self.

Descartes's argument expressed in clear language an anxiety which lay close to the surface of Renaissance culture. His *doute méthodique* had been directed ostensibly against the tottering edifice of Scholasticism; its goal, to discredit the old philosophy by attacking its dependence on tradition and authority. In this sense, the *malin génie* became an emblem for those half-sacred authorities (Aquinas, Aristotle, et al.) whose access to right thought is made to appear at the least problematical. Descartes's distrust of authority is part of a general mood of suspicion apparent in sixteenth- and seventeenth-century Europe, a feeling that the old explanations could no longer be relied upon. "New stars" had marred the heavenly spheres. Copernicus, Galileo, Kepler, Harvey had begun to express a more uncertain view of man's location in the world: one based on the senses, on science, on theories which themselves were debated and debatable. It was a world of new explorations, new politics, and new thinking, which had blurred the familiar shapes, making man more and more of a problem to himself. Descartes's *malin génie* is strangely appropriate to this world of uncertainty: it exemplifies the uneasy sense of man betrayed, somehow, by the world he lives in.

Several generations earlier, Montaigne had expressed his bewilderment at a universe he could no longer understand:

> The world is but a perennial movement. All things in it are in constant motion—the earth, the rocks of the Caucasus, the pyramids of Egypt—both with the common motion and with

their own. Stability itself is nothing but a more languid motion. I cannot keep my subject still. It goes along befuddled and staggering, with a natural drunkenness.

The world has become a texture of unforeseeable change; and Montaigne, like Descartes, chose to withdraw into the one haven remaining to him. As he wrote, "I study myself more than any other subject. It is my metaphysics, and my physics." In a world whose outward values were faulty, Montaigne learned to favor an inward attentiveness which became the special subject of his *Essays*. Since "each man bears the entire form of man's estate," to study one man well meant to discover truths common to all men. The certainties which Scholastic philosophy had sought in its intricate reasoning, and in its Christian cosmology, had migrated inward, for Montaigne, making of self-scrutiny the only truly sensitive philosophy. Descartes's argument from the *doute méthodique* echoes, in a calmer, more impersonal mood, this troubled insight of the *Essays*.

We have already remarked the figments of paranoia which erupted in the cosmological poetry of the Gnostics. Their vision of the persecuting Demiurge, of the world as a prison, of the self withdrawing into the "unworldly" refuge of its soul, has indeed the flavor of a psychotic fantasy. Descartes's *malin génie* stands out, in the rarefied argument of the *Meditations*, with a similar density of paranoid insecurity.

The fame of Descartes's argument depends less on this striking image, however, than on the way he develops his argument, once the invitation to doubt has been accepted. In his First Meditation, the philosopher pared away layer after layer of apparent certainty: first the sense perceptions, then abstract thought, then finally even the truths of mathematics and geometry. The estranged self withdrew step by step, until nothing was left but the taste of its own estrangement. This, and only this, could not be taken away from it; for the estrangement itself was seen to be irreducible. Now, in the Second Meditation,

Descartes explores the various elements of this reduced, isolated selfhood: the functions of thought, sense, and imagination; the mobile circle of objects which appears somehow in the mind, produced by the combined efforts of thought and sense, making the self palpable to its own reflection, even as it gives clarity to the objects on which it meditates. Starting with Montaigne's *branloire pérenne*—the "perennial seesaw" of worldly uncertainty—Descartes slowly rediscovers, one might say reinvents, the world. The certainty of the self expands once again, like the concentric rings made by a stone in water, restoring to all objects the density of their existence, in proportion as the mind which knows them learns to know itself. But this world which has been reinvented by the mind has also been reorganized.

Descartes explains this in his passage on the piece of wax. He identifies the wax according to those qualities inherent in it and which the mind, it would seem, passively registers: its smell, color, and shape, the sound it makes when struck, etc. He then proceeds to show that whatever knowledge we have of the wax —and, by extension, of the world at large—is created by the activity of the mind itself: its faculty to discriminate, to reject false appearances, etc. The identity of the wax is sure, because the mind has the power to make it so. The mind shapes the wax, just as it has shaped, and continues to shape, all things. "And thus I understand, by the single power of judgment which resides in my mind, what I thought I had seen with my eyes."

Now every object "seen" becomes a new confirmation of the self; every perception a further strengthening of the mind. For what Descartes remarked concerning the piece of wax is true for men walking in the street, for trees and buildings, and for "all those things which are exterior to me, and are encountered outside myself." Once the firmness of the self has been assured, the philosopher can rebuild the clarities of the world by deepening his knowledge of himself. By acting inwardly, he can impose a new law on the changing mass of reality: the law of his own mind. The power of the *malin génie* recedes while a new maker asserts its prerogative: the thinking self.

Like Antaeus who drew his strength from contact with the earth, the self gains new power from each encounter with the world. Every object, every action known, nourishes it, "for all the reasons which serve to know and conceive the nature of the wax, or of any other object, prove even more conclusively the nature of my own mind." By the end of the Second Meditation, the autonomous, thinking self has become limitless: a kind of beneficent demiurge whose creative energy lies in the power of clear thought.

Once again Descartes echoes that confidence in the estranged spirit which we encountered in the Gnostic religions. His argument has made of the self not only a refuge but a source of power, able to counter the designs of the *malin génie,* just as the Gnostic could overcome the worldly power of the Archons with knowledge (gnosis) of what lay within, at the apex of the soul. Subsequent philosophers, like Kierkegaard and Nietzsche, will amplify the reasoning of the Second Meditation, exploring more thoroughly, and with more subversive designs, the metaphysical resources of the self. Whitehead, in *Science and the Modern World,* describes this vast revolution of sensibilities which occurred during the seventeenth century. According to the new scientists and philosophers, Whitehead writes:

> . . . bodies are perceived as with qualities which in reality do not belong to them, qualities which in fact are purely the offspring of the mind. Thus nature gets credit which should in truth be reserved for ourselves: the rose for its scent; the nightingale for its song; the sun for his radience. The poets are entirely mistaken. They should address their lyrics to themselves, and should turn them into odes of self-congratulation on the excellency of the human mind. Nature is a dull affair, soundless, scentless, colorless; merely the hurrying of material, endlessly, meaninglessly.

Nature, in this sense, became not only dull and meaningless, it became terrifying. And it was against the terror, in order to counter and neutralize it, that Descartes invoked a new god: the inward divinity of the mind; a strangely spiritualized Narcissus, whom the poets eventually will name, no longer making the "mistake" of which Whitehead accuses them.

Descartes, of course, will not follow all the implications of his argument. In the Third Meditation he asks a question which by now we expect: What is to prevent me from believing that I am God? It is, indeed, a reasonable question. Since the mind and its faculties have been able to counter the *malin génie,* since it has "reconstructed" the world in a way that is safe from doubt, why indeed should we not consider it a God? But Descartes reveals here what he has known all along: that the self could not be divine, that the material world does exist, that the "I" is, after all, a mere atom, a minor citizen on God's vast continent. Because he has known this from the first, his style has had the consistency of a glass figure. He has aligned his arguments, and impelled them toward their most radical implications, with no hint of passion or uncertainty, for he knew the perfect, if paradoxical, orthodoxy of his views. In this, Descartes exemplifies a double allegiance typical of his century. Radical thinkers, experimental scientists explored their new vision, while holding firmly to the old religious orthodoxy. Leibnitz and Pascal among the philosophers, Traherne among the poets will describe brilliantly the subversive energies of the self, and yet each will deploy his genius to keep the old Authorities unshaken. Only Spinoza will refuse the double allegiance; and his work will be thoroughly reviled by the philosophical communities of Europe.

"No century," writes Émile Bréhier, "has had so little confidence in the spontaneous forces of Nature." And no century did so much, we might add, to make these forces present to men's minds, whether in literature, science, or philosophy. The anxiety produced by such conflicting attitudes characterized the intellectual life of the century. Images of chaos and disintegration lay close to the surface of thought, as in Donne's *Anniversary Poems,* or Shakespeare's *Troilus.* Nature was an overpowering solvent (the storm in *King Lear*), or a monumental space ruled over by Chaos (Book II of *Paradise Lost*). In it, man was not at home. No one perhaps has described as well as Pascal the terror and the loneliness of such a vision:

> I see those terrible spaces of the universe enclosing me, and discover that I am attached to one corner of this immensity, without knowing why I am placed here rather than elsewhere, nor why this little time that is given me to live has been assigned at this point rather than at any other of the eternity which has gone before or of that which will follow me. I see only infinities on all sides enclosing me like an atom, and like a shadow lasting but an instant with no return.

Pascal's infinite spaces are icily real. They enable us to understand, among other things, the growing popularity of "meditation" during the seventeenth century, with its disciplined attention to the resources of the inner life. In order to neutralize the cold infinities which lurked behind the most familiar objects, men preferred to look inward and discover themselves. As Donne wrote, in his *Anniversary Poems:*

> Every man alone thinkes he has got
> To be a Phoenix, and that then can bee
> None of that kinde, of which he is, but hee.

In a world from which "all coherence (was) gone," men struggled to establish a new center in their own phoenix-like separateness.

This "inward drama of the soul" fired the awareness of poets during the seventeenth century, turning even the old figures of speech—the familiar correspondence between Macrocosm and Microcosm, for example—into a new poetic medium, as in this passage from Sir Thomas Browne's *Religio Medici:* "The World that I regard is my self; it is the Microcosm of my frame that I cast my eyes on; for the other I use it but like my Globe, and turn it round sometimes for my recreation." There is a mobility and a whimsical freedom in Browne's language which the old image did not imply: here the Microcosm is no longer Man but the poet's idiosyncratic self, while the Macrocosm, the twirling globe, becomes a garden of private delights, a mirror for the single energies of the self.

A short poem by the Cavalier poet Lovelace employs the figure of the snail to express, in a more complicated way, the curious pleasures of a self which has become its own object and companion:

> Sage Snayl, within thine own self curl'd,
> Instruct me softly to make hast,
> Whilst these my feet go slowly fast . . .
> Who shall a name for thee create,
> Deep riddle of mysterious state? . . .
> Thou, thine own daughter then, and sire,
> That son and mother art intire,
> That big still with thy self dost go,
> And liv'st an aged embrio.

The snail here embodies the singular perfections of the androgyne. Within its own self curled, it is its own father, daughter, son, and mother, the source and end of its desires. Its very life has become a kind of pregnancy, feeding and breeding upon its own circular energies. This erotic privacy of the snail becomes a source of wisdom in the poem, an envied example for the poet who knows all too well the dislocation and the violence of his times. That this is so is further emphasized by the snail's hard shell which turns away the turbulent world, as it shapes the slow intimacy of the life within. For the snail is its own world; its self-engendered intimacy has taken the place of that other world from which all coherence is gone.

The most remarkable example of this new mood is to be found in the poetry of Thomas Traherne. With Traherne the exalted "inwardness" of meditation has become strangely innocent. Traherne was able to bypass the ritual disciplines of meditation, with their emphasis on self-analysis and their preoccupation with the exemplary sufferings of Christ. Instead he discovered, in and beyond these disciplines, the immediate innocence of his emotions, the "holiness" of his own aggrandized selfhood. We can imagine the horror of St. John of the Cross could he have foreseen the highly unorthodox piety to which "meditation" would lead the young Englishman. Traherne found, in the space of his own existence, an answer to those broken fragments of the Macrocosm which had so frightened Donne and Pascal. Like Descartes, he reinvented the world; unlike Descartes, he worked out his vision to its furthest consequences. For "Dame Nature told me there was endless Space / Within my Soul; I spy'd its very face." We remember the dreamer in the garden of love, who also had spied a face, and beyond the face an expanding universe of trees, sky, and wind. Once Traherne discovered this inner face, he never tired of examining and above all describing it:

> I was an inward Sphere of Light,
> Or an Interminable Orb of Sight,
>   An Endless and a Living Day,
>   A vital Sun that round about did ray
>   All Life, all Sence,
>   A Naked Simple Pure Intelligence. . . .
>
> I felt a Vigour in my Sence
>   That was all SPIRIT. I within did flow
>   With Seas of Life, like Wine. . . .

Freud's account of Primary Narcissism—that "oceanic feeling" of the infinitely extended self—is clearly prefigured in this passage from Traherne's *Centuries of Meditation:*

Infinite is the first thing which is naturally known. Bounds and limits are discerned only in a secondary manner. Suppose a man were born deaf and blind. By the very feeling of his soul, he apprehends *infinite* about him, infinite space, infinite darkness. He thinks not of walls and limits till he feels them and is stopped by them. That things are finite, therefore, we learn by our senses. But *infinity* we know and feel in our souls.

The ecstatic tone recalls that of the Free Spirit, or, among Traherne's own contemporaries, that of the German poet Angelus Silesius. It prefigures the spiritual exuberance of Emerson, Whitman, or Nietzsche. Traherne is a new Narcissus who has learned that the "infinite spaces" which so terrified Pascal will yield their secret, if only one can unleash this first of all infinities: the complex, inexhaustible delight of self with self:

> No more shall Walls, no more shall Walls confine
> That glorious Soul which in my Flesh doth shine:
> > No more shall Walls of Clay or Mud
> > > Nor Ceilings made of Wood,
> > Nor Crystal Windows bound my Sight,
> > But rather shall admit Delight.

The seventeenth century has been called the century of genius. Its distrust of the old realities, the clean slate proposed by Descartes's radical doubt, the uneasy sense that familiar values could no longer be relied upon to give shape and location to one's life: these, in addition to other, more political upheavals, created a sense of urgency to which the best minds responded in some of the ways we have described. That English poetry reached the height it did during this period must be ascribed not only to the freshness of a young language but to the urgency of the demands made on the poet's imagination: the need for a wholeness of experience which had become more and more openly problematical in the world. There is a sense in which the poetry of men like Donne, Herbert, Vaughan, not to mention Shakespeare, can be said to answer T. S. Eliot's description of much nineteenth-century romantic verse: it is "spilt religion," an attempt to center the most familiar "religious" responses on the poet's own continually reinvented sensibility.

There was however another, more "philosophical" response to these dilemmas of the "modern" sensibility. Much in the work of Spinoza and Leibnitz, for example, must be understood as an attempt to answer the subversions of Descartes's *Malin Génie*. Both philosophers inherited from the rationalism of the Schools a conviction which Descartes had tried to erase once and for all with his *doute methodique*. Both were convinced that God's universe had essentially to be "reasonable," accessible therefore to some form of complete knowledge. The philosopher's task, they felt, was to find a language that would express this ultimate order of all things. Spinoza and Leibnitz were the first systematic philosophers in the modern tradition. Yet there is something troubling in their sense that all is explicable and well with the world. Their arguments are strangely insistent and extreme, as if the structure of their thought were being guarded at every moment against the possibility of some failure, some intrusion of the ambient chaos they so distrusted. As George Friedman has written:

> The whole subtle construction of Leibnitz's optimism, so carefully polished, decorated, and rounded, gives off, from the very first, a hidden resonance of anxiety and pain, [which makes us wonder if this unfaltering optimism isn't] in reality one of the first forms of the modern philosophies of anguish and despair.

Friedman's insight is perhaps even truer of Spinoza thàn it is of Leibnitz.

The method and style of the *Ethics* are surely "reasonable" beyond anything ever before attempted in philosophy. Spinoza's argument has the relentlessness and the austerity of a demonstration in mathematics. Axioms, propositions, corollaries, detailed cross-references are built page by page into a massive

pyramid the pinnacle of which is "the intellectual love of God."
Yet Leibnitz easily pointed out the obscurity of certain demon-
strations, the clumsiness of the geometrical procedure. Indeed if
today we are fascinated by Spinoza's genius, it is less because of
his geometrical method than because of certain insights to which
his argument led him: his attempt to resolve the Cartesian
dualism, his philosophical praise of the body, his defense of
tolerance.

Spinoza's geometrical "certainties" are arrayed against an
enemy whose name we are never told. The ponderous machines
of his logic must account for every shadow of the reality; they
must be relentless and irresistible. For if a single thought escapes
the machine, if one shadow of experience refuses to be ac-
counted for, then all is lost. Spinoza shuts out the disorder, the
"natural" infinities—the world from which "all coherence is
gone"—refusing even to name it. In his *Ethics* we see only the
vast system of walls and trenches meant to keep the enemy at
bay, thrust away beneath the sill of consciousness.

Neither Spinoza nor Leibnitz could accept the corrosive
principle of a *malin génie*. A method which depended on such
radical doubt was questionable, they felt, and finally dangerous.
In their eyes, Descartes, if only for this brief hypothetical
moment, had opened his mind to the enemy. He had organized
his philosophy around the principle of a worldly insecurity so
radical that, if taken seriously, it could provoke only terror: that
Pascalian terror against which both Spinoza and Leibnitz were
to erect their insistent barriers of reason.

The key to Spinoza's vision in the *Ethics* lies in a single axiom,
the consequences of which he develops and explores in a number of contexts, until it has become the principle of a harmony
encompassing all the orders of our experience. "Each thing," he
writes, "insofar as it is in itself, endeavors to persevere in its
being." Each group of particles in nature, from the simplest to
the most complex, strives, before all else, to maintain itself, and
to preserve its identity: men, animals, trees, stones, even the

remote emptiness of the heavens can be known in their identity because the energies which compose them are devoted above all toward this effort of self-preservation. The universe, in turn, is but the pattern of these energies, interlocked and impinging on one another, but each directed, as much as its degree of "perfection" will allow, toward this end of self-maintenance. The perfection of an object must be measured, therefore, by the degree of its resistance to change—i.e., by the success or failure of its self-directed energies. An object which fails of perfection will yield to the general mutability. It will eventually lose its drive toward singularity and die.

Not only the world of things is governed in this way. Man too is driven by the complex need for survival which, in his life, takes the form of *appetite, will, desire*. The physical pressures of the universe, and those which shape man's life, psychologically as well as physically, belong to a single category; and therefore a single language must be used to describe them. Spinoza thus repudiates the Cartesian, Pascalian dualism, for which only the spirit is free—as divine spark, or as *cogito*—in a world governed by alien forces. On the contrary, the *Ethics* describes a universe swarming with life, animated from top to bottom by the interlocking drives toward self-preservation. The self which Descartes had sought to maintain through doubt and negation, Spinoza redefines according to this insight into what he took to be a universal harmony: a great chain of life-energies—akin to the traditional Chain of Being—in which the self was not alien but merely a member, an individuality among others.

If man, therefore, is to act in accordance with nature, if he is to be guided by the universal law of reason which asserts that each thing pursues its own best interest, then he too must look to himself. To do otherwise would be out of keeping with the general decorum of the universe, would indeed be "irrational": "Since reason demands nothing which is opposed to nature, it demands, therefore, that every person should love himself." The man who acts in the spirit of this love is "virtuous"; when he is successful he is "happy." Conversely, whatever distracts him from this "reasonable" self-love will cause unhappiness, whether the influence be that of some established "morality," the blindness of the passions, or the impingement of some unmasterable event or object.

There is a spirit of quiet pessimism in the *Ethics,* for Spinoza knew that man's self-love—his desire for the "autonomy" of the existentialists—could never be entirely satisfied. Like Narcissus, man too had to lose his love, for so much of his life escaped him: his ignorance could never be entirely cured, nor could his dependence on forces beyond his control. As Spinoza writes, "Our sorrows and misfortunes mainly proceed from too much love toward an object which is subject to many changes, and which we can never possess." At best, man could approximate the conditions of the good life through "reason" and correct discipline. By perfecting mind and body, by controlling his passions, he could lift himself part of the way toward the goal of immutable self-communion embodied for Spinoza in the idea of God.

Spinoza's God is devoid of passion and constraint, loving "Himself with an infinite intellectual love." All perfections in the universe, the moral success of the individual as well as the permanence to which each thing may aspire, contribute to the vast energy of this self-love. The individual who gains wisdom has learned, by this very wisdom, that the power of his own mind is derived from God; it is natural, therefore, that he lift his thoughts progressively toward the source and cause of his intelligence in a mood analogous to that of mystical contemplation. This mood Spinoza calls the "intellectual love of God." As a man becomes capable of this "intellectual love"—the summit of his moral and intellectual progress—he learns to resemble God, becoming as much "like" Him as is possible for man. Each day he finds fewer obstacles, either within him or in the world, which resist the energies of his thought. In this way he learns, in Spinoza's sense, to love himself. But at the same time his very life becomes like a clear mirror, holding up to God a portion of His own perfections to contemplate. For "the intellectual love of the mind toward God is part of the infinite love with which God loves Himself."

Despite the geometry and the cold logic of its method, we find at the heart of the *Ethics* the same metaphysical mirror invoked by the mystic. God, we are told, lives with His universe as did Narcissus with his mirror. Spinoza goes on, however, in a way that is profoundly unchristian. It is here, undoubtedly, that he provoked the righteous anger of his century. For he insists that everything in the universe—and man foremost—is "reasonably" devoted to the same act of self-admiration and self-maintenance. The Christian morality of selflessness and humility is, for Spinoza, no morality at all. It is, in fact, the opposite of morality; it is contrary to reason, to Nature, and therefore to God. On the contrary, it is the man who has loved himself well, the man who has wisely cultivated the energies of his mind and body, who can properly hold up the mirror to God. For Spinoza, "self-satisfaction . . . is the highest thing for which a man can hope." To increase a man's contentment is to bring him closer to God:

> It is the part of a wise man . . . to refresh and invigorate himself with moderate and pleasant eating and drinking, with sweet scents and the beauty of green plants, with ornaments, with music, with sports, with the theater, and with all things of this kind which one man can enjoy without hurting another.

The more capable we become of joy and laughter, "the more do we necessarily partake of the divine nature." By allowing to man the luminous privilege of self-love, Spinoza sweeps aside the Christian obsession with humility and self-punishment, giving us a foretaste of the moral vision which will predominate in Nietzsche's philosophy two hundred years later.

Between Descartes and Spinoza the philosophical mood has shifted. Cartesian dualism had divided matter and soul, knowledge and faith; its vision of the self was highly unreligious. The clear thinking mind of the *Meditations* is interested above all in knowledge of the kind appropriate to science. Once his ontological proof had assured the existence of God, Descartes delivered his soul up to the Church with no second thoughts. For "salvation" and the good life, he felt, were of no concern to the philosopher as philosopher. Spinoza's system in the *Ethics,* however, leads to the opposite conclusion that knowledge is inseparable from the good life. Ethics, for Spinoza, becomes a version of science or philosophy. As was the case with the Gnostics, and the various occult traditions which are said to have influenced Spinoza, the function of knowledge, in the *Ethics,* is to make "salvation" possible. Indeed knowledge and salvation— the ability to lead a good life, rising thereby to the "intellectual love of God"—are the same thing.

This helps us to understand the interest shown in Spinoza by one of his most brilliant contemporaries: Gottfried Wilhelm Leibnitz. Leibnitz too was convinced that the world was entirely knowable, and that the goal of philosophy was to express the hidden coherence of all things, enabling man to live in harmony with himself in the light of this revealed knowledge. At first glance the differences between the two philosophers are overpowering: Spinoza, the austere, ungraceful thinker, contradicting the oldest habits of Christian morality; Leibnitz, the facile courtier, defending Christianity with all his talents. Yet at the heart of Leibnitz' system, there is a sense of radical individuality which is perhaps even more extreme than that of Spinoza.

The cornerstone of Leibnitz' philosophy, from his early notations as a young man to the mature "system," lay in his sense of the self-contained individual drawing the threads of his identity out of his own inward possibilities. The young Leibnitz described the individual as a "microcosm," whose inner complexities "mirrored" the infinite richness of God. Later he was to generalize this sense of individuality, endowing every substance, place, and event in the universe with a similar self-enclosed identity. The Monodology may indeed be described as a generalized theory of the self, according to which the universe is composed of an infinite number of spiritual units called Monads, each entirely closed and isolated—"windowless," to use Leibnitz' expression. The Monads in no way impinge upon one another. All change and development come from within, so that each Monad works out its destiny in perfect solitude.

This theory of universal individuality, however, made difficulties for Leibnitz. If the Monad was "windowless," how could any larger order be maintained; how could this universe of Monads display a harmony in which the parts were somehow appropriate to the whole? For Leibnitz then goes on to describe each Monad as a kind of "mirror" from whose single viewpoint the entire complex life of the universe may be descried. And this life, he maintains, is that of a harmony consonant with Christian wisdom, making this "the best of all possible worlds."

Leibnitz reconciled his contradictory vision by a device which today has almost an air of comedy about it. He declared that when Monads seem to affect one another—when, for example, two people are in love, or when the wind blows down apples from a tree—we mistakenly interpret what we see. For God, when He created the infinity of Monads, enclosed in each a pattern of fate, harmonized in advance with all other Monads. This is Leibnitz' famous law of the "pre-established harmony." His own image is that of a clockmaker who has wound up all his clocks so that they go on ticking, each for itself, though appearing always to agree with one another. Thus when people exchange words or share emotions, when a man or an object influences another, they are merely working out the mechanism of their destinies. At no moment do they violate their true solitude. Leibnitz' universe is the network of these "windowless" selves which have been attuned to one another before life itself began.

Beneath the glittering, highly political piety of the courtier, we discover a hidden desolation and a solitude which are all the more startling for the apparent optimism of language. A universe wound up like clocks, going through the motions of cause and effect, love and decay—if this is harmony, then surely it is a deadly one. Leibnitz describes tellingly the imprisoned energies of the individual whose grace and value rise from a source within himself, and yet who can talk no language that will be heard, evoke no response that will be properly his. In order to bar the very shadow of disorder, in order to avoid the risk of an irrational world, Leibnitz' philosophy encloses life in a mechanical solitude beyond anything his century had devised.

8 THE INNOCENCE OF JEAN JACQUES ROUSSEAU

The language of self-love has served often in the West to characterize our deepest experience. The isolated, inwardly regarding self stands at the heart of our spiritual life: in the strained elevation of the mystic, in the "grace" of the courtly lover, in the insistent reasoning of the philosopher. Yet there is a curious lack which the reader may have noticed. Among all these glorified selves we have yet to encounter a unique recognizable individual. As with the self of Descartes's *Meditations*, their singularity casts no shadow. Dean Inge once remarked, of the many mystical treatises he had read, that they might all have been written by a single person, so much did the unity of their language and experience give a sense of impersonality to their ecstasies. When Eckhart or Plotinus wrote "I," nothing remained of their singleness. They leapt abruptly, and with no emotional residue, from the particular into the universal. Even the antinomians are strangely repetitive. Their extravagant sexuality, their self-deification, the marvelous excess of their emotions are described in the same way by fourteenth-century Germans as by seventeenth-century Englishmen. Is it not surprising that these thoroughgoing subversives, enclosed in the pure grace of their emotions, should be as interchangeable as the conventional characters of the mystery plays, or the lovesick lords of Provence? Even Shakespeare's sonnets owe more to literary convention than to the singular experience of the poet. The selves we have encountered lack a dimension of character and personality. Before we come to know them, they have discarded all but what is "essential"—the love emotion, the capacity for thought, the mirror in the soul. Thus purified, they stand in the empyrean of our culture with the exemplary permanence and the universality of a myth.

With Jean Jacques Rousseau we enter a different world. His style reveals no conventional literary self, no rhetorical "I," but rather the involvements and obsessions of the man himself. Little that he wrote, after the first *Discourses,* is not closely concerned with the separate, idiosyncratic character of Jean Jacques. Even the *Social Contract* is curiously rooted in autobiography. As the Vicaire Savoyard is made to say, "I will never reason, even about the nature of God, until I am forced to do so by the feeling of his involvements with me." For Rousseau, nothing had interest in itself. Philosophy began only when his emotions impelled him to wonderment and thought. There could be no permanent distinctions between his reflective work, his fiction, and his autobiography. From the vantage point of old age, it seemed to Rousseau that "all [his] life [had] been nothing but a long reverie." It seemed that all he had written, thought, and suffered had been part of a single effort from which nothing personal, no detail of the emotions, could be omitted.

On the first page of the *Confessions,* he imagines the trumpets on Judgment Day and himself, Jean Jacques, rising up before the judge with this book in his hand. "I will say in a loud voice: This is what I have done, what I thought, what I was . . . I have shown myself as I was; despicable and low when I was so, good, generous, sublime when I was so: I have bared my inner self as you yourself have seen it." Like Homer's epic warriors, declining their interminable genealogies, like Don Quixote and the reluctant lion, concerned with gaining witnesses for his "deeds," Rousseau never tired of telling what he had done: in the autobiographical letters to Malesherbes, in the *Confessions,* in the *Dialogues,* and in the *Rêveries,* there are different versions of the same incident, and he told still more at the end of his life to friends like Bernardin de Saint-Pierre.

The need to "remember" was identical, in Rousseau's mind, with the need to write about himself. Repeatedly he announced his decision to give up "literature," though he could never bring himself to do so. In the end, his story was interrupted only by death, as if living and "telling" had become a single, inextricable act. Even when he had abandoned the hope of being listened to, the need to recompose himself upon the page remained. In the *Rêveries du Promeneur Solitaire,* Rousseau at last is speaking alone, but he is still speaking. He tells how he has abandoned the world of the living, which has abandoned him; yet even here he needs an audience if his reverie is to gain shape and consistency: he becomes his own audience, as he did once before in the *Dialogues* in which Rousseau and his imaginary double, Jean Jacques, carry on endless conversation. But once he begins, the show is as before: beneath the conventional surface of his acts, Jean Jacques reveals himself "as he is," according to "nature." He gives eloquence to that private energy of the emotions which, during his entire life, had been more real to him than the acts they led him to commit.

Rousseau was an exhibitionist. After announcing in the *Confessions* that he has "unveiled" his true self once and for all, he addresses God: "Eternal Being, gather round me the vast crowd of my fellow beings, so that they may hear my confessions . . ." In the presence of all humanity, Rousseau will be strangely, passively heroic. Instead of doing, he will tell; he will strip away the covering and exhibit himself to the world in all his privacy. An incident early in the *Confessions* suggests how deeply anchored in Rousseau's character was this need to show himself *d'après nature,* with a nakedness that was not always figurative. He tells how the boy Jean Jacques would often stand in the shadow of a building in Turin, exposing himself to passersby of the opposite sex: "I looked for dark alleys and hidden places, where I could exhibit myself from afar to women, in the state in which I would have liked to have been when with them." This act of sexual confusion and passiveness reveals

Rousseau in more ways than one. The inspired moral nakedness of the *Confessions* is adumbrated here in an incident described by those very *Confessions*. Between one and the other, between the youthful exhibitionist and the mature moralist, intervene years of sublimation, increased self-awareness, and a growing need to conceptualize the impulses of his character. Yet they are clearly the acts of a single sensibility, and one must qualify the other in our minds, in a way unprecedented in literature: "In this project I have made to reveal myself to the public, nothing of me must remain obscure or hidden from them, I must keep myself constantly before their eyes . . ." Rousseau's gesture toward the world is somehow not a gesture, for it returns to its source in the privacy of his emotions.

It was Rousseau's genius to have revealed himself copiously and yet always to have told more than he knew. Some years after the Turin episode, he wrote a play in the manner of Marivaux, entitled *Narcisse ou l'Amant de Lui-même*. Valère, the play's central character, is an effeminate dandy who is tricked by his fiancée into falling in love with his own portrait disguised as a woman. Already, in this work of his adolescence, Rousseau has guessed the affinity between his passive, feminine character and the obsession of Narcissus.

By the time he wrote his *Confessions*, Rousseau had come to feel an elusive barrier, a "difference," which separated him, he felt, from other men, locking him more and more into a life of painful isolation. The words he heard spoken fell short of the inward energy which mattered most to him; they described only the surface of his life, the acts and the artifice, but not the intimate center. Years later, in the *Dialogues* (subtitled *Rousseau juge de Jean Jacques*), this atmosphere of stifled language became, with Rousseau's growing paranoia, a vast conspiracy of silence, "a deep, universal silence, no less inconceivable than the mystery it conceals . . . a frightful and terrible silence." In the *Confessions*, one already feels the encroachment of the silence, turning each misunderstanding into a betrayal, strengthening the corrupt surfaces which, for Rousseau, had come to characterize his society. The *Confessions* were initially directed against the silence; their task was to find a unique language to unlock the differences, shedding light on what had been so painfully obscured. This was the singularity Rousseau claimed for his enterprise, declaring, "I undertake a project which has had no precedent." Rousseau insisted often upon the uniqueness of his character and his fate, claiming to be, if not better, at least different from his fellows. We shall see how paradoxical this claim was in Rousseau's own terms. Yet the *Confessions* are in their way more unusual than at first appears; for Montaigne comes immediately to mind as an example and precedent. Well on into middle age, he too had discovered his own problematical self at the heart of the moral universe, and had developed a sensitive exploratory language which he turned inward rather than outward. By comparing these two great confessors, we may get a clearer sense of what was indeed unique in Rousseau's enterprise.

Like Rousseau, Montaigne two centuries before had set out to reveal himself as he was, "a life low and without glitter," hiding none of his faults, yet faithful also to his qualities. This psychological realism is embodied in the style of the *Essays*. The images, the earthy humor, the solemnity are artfully interwoven until they have become the voice of a truly great character. Yet we are not tempted to confuse the man on the page with the man who is telling about him. The real Montaigne moves in and out of his words; he handles his literary self with an art which gives the impression of being artless.

This psychological realism is absent from the *Confessions*, for Rousseau's language obeys a more ideal rhythm. His periods throughout are delicate and harmonious. Whereas Montaigne can change his voice several times on the same page, Rousseau has only one voice which we recognize alike in the *Confessions*, in *Émile*, in the *Nouvelle Héloïse*. The limpid musicality of the style gives one the impression that his words are on the point of vanishing into their own music, and into the lyrical "reality" which they embody. Rousseau comes out from behind the words, to "expose" himself: a Rousseau who has been transformed, made limpid as crystal, harmonious as music. Between Montaigne and his words there is a distance and a decorum which he never violates, yet the "realism" of the style is unexampled. Between Rousseau and his words there is no distance at all; he has become his text, and yet his style cares nothing for psychological realism. Rousseau, in being "true," had in mind something far different from being "real." What this was we will see shortly.

For the moment we are concerned with a trait of Rousseau's self-exploration which marked his personality and shaped the insight of his social philosophy as well. In the Second Dialogue he writes, "Our most pleasant existence is relative and collective, our true *self* is not placed entirely within us. For such is the nature of man in this life, that he can never truly enjoy his selfhood without the help of others." For Rousseau, this "help" had become a problem. He felt more and more strongly that it had been denied him for reasons he could not fathom, and that, if he were not to remain helpless, he would have in some way to help himself. The *Confessions* were the form his answer took. He wrote in order to dissolve his "absolute solitude," a state of being which he qualified as "sad and unnatural." By "exposing" himself in this way Rousseau formed a society of his readers. He withdrew from sight, as in his retreat to the Hermitage, in order to be more completely present in his words.

At the same time, the words became his best and only life. "In general," he admits, "things make less of an impression on me than does the memory of them." But the *Confessions*, the *Dialogues*, the *Reveries*, much in the *Nouvelle Héloïse* and in *Émile*, are largely exercises in memory. And the memories were not only meant to be a recollection of experience; they were the experiences themselves relived:

> Among the situations in which I've been, some have been marked by such a sense of well-being, that in remembering them they affect me as if I were there once more. Not only do I recall the weather, the places, the people, but all the surrounding objects, the temperature of the air, its smell and color, a certain local impression felt only in that place, and whose lively memory transports me there again.

When he wrote, he recomposed these "fantasies" and relived them in imagination. If, in the *Confessions,* Rousseau becomes the text, it is because without his words he fears that he will not have lived at all.

There is a paradox in Rousseau's passion to confess, which reveals once again the involvement of the man with his philosophy. "Confession," for Rousseau, was a way of shaping the old selves into a flow of self-delighting images: "Wanting to recall so many sweet reveries, instead of describing them, I lived through them once more." As in the practice of meditation, the images deepen until they have become another life. These exercises in memory become a veritable composition of place, reshaping past experience almost to the point of hallucination. We have indeed come a long way from Augustine's account of the sinful mind. According to Augustine, the man who dwelled too much upon the phantasms of past delight fell into the sin of pride, preferring himself to the better presence of God. But according to Rousseau, there was no question of sin. As with Spinoza, to prefer and love oneself was the most "natural," most "necessary" pleasure known to man.

Marcel Raymond has written, "The objects whose thoughtful images Rousseau welcomes within him have lost their 'objective' quality; they have become a part of him, surrounded by a flame endowing all existence with the charm of a subjective magic. . . ." We see now how the difference in style between Montaigne and Rousseau corresponds to a vastly different intention. Whereas Montaigne meant to philosophize with truculence, in a spirit of psychological realism, Rousseau was concerned with the "fictive" inner surface of the events. Because Montaigne was "realistic," he found it hard to confess the worst in himself; he spoke of his faults but was careful, as Rousseau commented, to give himself only "lovable" ones. Rousseau, on the other hand, was enflamed with a sense of his own harmony: what he thought of as his innocence. He did not care to be "realistic" and therefore could exhibit everything: the worst indignities, the sexual strangeness, the dishonesties. For these formed only the periphery, the outer surface of an energy which entirely transformed them. Rousseau evoked and wrote about the real events, only so that he could recompose them in the spirit of this inner "truth" of the emotions.

We know that the *Confessions,* the *Dialogues,* the *Reveries* were largely works of self-justification. By an unlikely concourse of circumstances, Rousseau had become the "pariah" of modern Europe: distrusted by his fellow *philosophes,* harried by governments, mocked and even stoned on occasion by the populace. The somber egotism and the paranoia of the *Dialogues* reflect disconcertingly not only the fantasies of a haunted man but a world which acted out those fantasies. Between the paranoia and the reality the lines are blurred. Rousseau in the *Dialogues* saw himself at the heart of a vast conspiracy, guilty before the world, hemmed in by a myriad of conspiring eyes which had immured him in his guilt without appeal: "They have raised around him walls of shadow impenetrable to his eyes; they have buried him alive among the living. It is perhaps the most unusual, the most astounding enterprise ever accomplished." This is pure fantasy, and yet how closely it resembles the reality of his persecution. It is perhaps this resemblance which makes the later books of the *Confessions,* and all of the *Dialogues,* so compelling. The words have not been launched into a sealed space of fantasy; they are spoken aloud to real people who act in all too real ways. For all his isolation, Rousseau is never abandoned to himself. By a strange economy of pain, his persecution saved his sanity. And the confessional works gain, from this curious exchange, an incisiveness, a power of clarity which enables them, in a sense, to accomplish their purpose: they convince us, and explain to us, with unexampled power, if not Rousseau's "innocence," then at least what he means by that innocence.

For Rousseau chose a revolutionary method in order to justify himself. He did not deny the acts, but instead he reversed them and showed their concealed inner surface. The acts, he tells us and demonstrates to us by the elevation of his style, are justified not according to their effect, which may indeed be unfortunate, but according to that pure "natural" energy which brought them to completion. "To the pure all is pure," and Rousseau sets out, in his confessional works, to demonstrate this "grace" at the core of his being: a grace not of God but of nature, of pure intentions and impulsive energies. By thus proving his "innocence" Rousseau recomposes his life in terms of the until-then-ineffable purity, and delights in it.

Between Rousseau's character and his social philosophy there is an exchange of insights which is apparent as early as the first *Discourses*, where the governing virtue of the "natural man" is made to lie in what Rousseau calls *amour de soi,* an expression rendered variously as "self-esteem," "self-love," or "self-respect." In the *Discours sur l'Inégalité,* we read, "Self-love is a natural feeling which leads all animals to care for their own preservation; when governed, in man, by reason and modified by pity, it produces humanity and virtue." In the "state of nature" which had long since been obscured, for Rousseau, by the overlying constraint of civilization, "each single man considers himself to be the only spectator of his acts, the only being in the universe to be interested in him, the only judge of his merit." Throughout his life Rousseau was to argue that man's best nature lay, as he wrote in *Émile,* in "the only natural passion of man . . . self-love"; years after writing *Émile,* harried by paranoia, he still insisted, "All positive feeling derives immediately from self-love. It is quite natural that a man who loves himself should try to extend his being and his pleasures, and to possess by attachment whatever he feels to be good for him: it is a simple question of the emotions . . ." Rousseau contradicts the orthodox opinion that human nature is corrupt because man has lost sight of God and loves himself. Instead he sets the energy of *amour de soi* at the center of our humanity. For Rousseau, as for Leibnitz and Spinoza, our best experience grows out of this central passion, which is then deflected—sublimated—and most often perverted by life in society. In the *Profession de Foi* Rousseau reverses the traditional relationship between piety and self-love, asking finally of man's love for God, "Isn't it a natural consequence of self-love, to honor what protects us, and to love whatever is well intentioned toward us?" The words are almost those of Spinoza, describing the "intellectual love of God." On this point, the rationalist and the sentimental "romantic" find themselves in agreement.

But Rousseau, as we have seen, went on from here. "Such is the nature of man in this life," he wrote, "that he can never fully enjoy his own selfhood, without the help of others." Man, obedient to his *amour de soi*, must complicate his solitude. He must include others in the life of his emotions. His alternative is the sad prison of isolation, or the subhuman simplicity of the animals. In his *Discours sur l'Inégalité*, Rousseau begins by describing what he calls the "infancy of the world," in which men have not yet founded even the rudiments of a society. In this state of primitive solitude, *l'homme sauvage* is closer to the simplicity of the animals than he is to man. He lives in a world of blurred contentment, filled with the "overwhelming sense of his present existence." He is happy and "natural"—i.e., good— yet he can hardly be called human. His nature is incomplete and this draws him onward toward the more complicated life of society. Once the elements of community are established, however, the old balance is destroyed. The simplicities of animal solitude give way, and something new stirs in the minds of *l'homme naturel*: "[Men] get used to looking at different objects, making comparisons; slowly they acquire the notions of merit and beauty which induce feelings of preference. Through the habit of seeing one another, they will soon need still more to see one another." It is here that man—*l'homme de l'homme*—is created, for better and for worse. For "each began to look at the others, and wanted to be looked at in turn." Mankind was born, for Rousseau, out of the desire to be seen and "recognized." It was in this most elementary sense that man's self-love required him to seek the help of others. And with this need began the painful, erratic climb which, for Rousseau, characterized the history of civilization.

This logic, however, reflects a more personal predicament. Rousseau's "exhibitionism" in the *Confessions,* as well as the curious episode in Turin, show clearly how the need to be seen shaped his emotional life. Repeatedly Rousseau holds up his solitude to be recognized, forever treading the delicate line which separated *l'homme naturel,* which he needed to reveal beneath his acts, and *l'homme de l'homme,* who needed so desperately to be "seen" and justified. On one side of the line is the "sad prison" of his loneliness, a life of stifled recognition, closer to death than to life; for "someone who gathers all his emotions inside him, finally loves nothing but his own self . . . his frozen heart no longer trembles with joy . . . he is already dead." On the other side of the line, however, lie the corrupt energies of society, where the natural self has been sacrificed to the passion for appearances, for comparison, and finally for vain pretense. Here, the natural *amour de soi* has been twisted into a simulacrum; it has become *amour propre,* vanity, which for Rousseau was the source of all "negative sensibility" and all aggressiveness:

> As soon as we get into the habit of measuring ourselves against each other, and moving outside of ourselves in order to be sure of getting the first and best place, then it is impossible not to dislike everything that surpasses us, everything that makes us smaller, everything that hems us in, everything that by being something prevents us from being everything.

It was between these two kinds of death—between the living coffin of isolation and the social nemesis of *amour propre*—that Rousseau tried to lead his sensibility.

The distinction between *amour de soi* and *amour propre* renews an insight which had long been obscured by the traditional Christian distrust of the self. We remember the two Narcissi of Gnostic cosmology: the self-delighting God who creates only to converse with himself and admire his beauty; and His creature, Primal Man, filled with restless curiosity, who engenders sin and death out of his jealousy of the Demiurge. For Rousseau, however, this distinction has become a purely human one. *Amour de soi* and *amour propre,* self-love and vanity, share a single source in man's undifferentiated passions. It is out of the unsteady concourse between man and man that the passions later separate and turn against one another. Yet the "evil," as we have seen, turns out to have been necessary. Our world of human understanding and self-understanding was born out of the same need to be seen which engendered the deviousness of *amour propre.*

This interdependence of good and bad, of historical "progress" and moral suffering, resembles the Hegelian dialectic of history in the *Phenomenology.* There too it is through the sufferings and betrayals of history that man leaves behind him the emptiness of his origins, as he is shaped and lifted toward progressively greater mastery of himself and of the world. Although this kinship with Hegel has often been pointed out, it is, in the end, a limited one. For Rousseau had little patience with history. For all his dialectical insight, he seemed rarely to trust the kind of logical, historical synthesis which was to characterize Hegel. Rousseau could develop the contradictions—between *amour de soi* and *amour propre,* for example—with great logical and emotional power; he could present with all the genius of his style the dilemma of irreconcilable needs. But, as Jean Starobinski has suggested, the synthesis of these opposites could not for Rousseau be a work of history or logic. His temperament drove him to a more personal, more impassioned solution. It was in the work of imagination—in the lived "fiction" of his words— that Rousseau sought to reconcile the opposites and resolve the deceptions. Between the historical philosophy of the *Discourses* and the personal adventure of the *Confessions,* there is an impassioned continuity, foreshadowing both Hegel and his bitter enemy Kierkegaard—as Starobinski describes them, those "two opposite currents of modern thought: the progress of reason in history, and the tragic quest for individual salvation."

From this point of view, the *Confessions* represent a tragic attempt to reconcile in imagination the natural virtue of self-love with the civilizing vice of vanity; to close the gap, somehow, between *l'enfance du monde,* when man lived in harmony with himself, and *la jeunesse du monde,* when men had already begun the perilous effort to live in harmony with others. Rousseau often dreamed of a society where the healthful solitude of *amour de soi* would be preserved, uncorrupted by the passion to see and be seen, and yet enriched by it. In such a society, to *be* and to *seem* would be one, and the need for recognition would give rise, not to pretense and hostile vanities, but to a truly open revelation of self, a mutual transparency between souls schooled in the only true morality: self-love.

How differently now one sees the scene, so painful and yet so strangely symbolic, in which Rousseau describes how he read his *Confessions* aloud one day at the home of the Comtesse d'Egmont. He read from morning till night, exhibiting his moral nakedness to this circle of friends. It was an extraordinary moment: here were the man and his words together; the defensive, distrustful Jean Jacques enacting with his own voice the generous ritual of his *Confessions.* How terrible it must have been for him, and yet how commonplace, that when he finished there was no illuminating transformation, but only a few moments of embarrassed silence and some disconnected remarks from the more polite of those present. The *Confessions* had been written for such a moment of revelation; they were to have reversed the current of "betrayal" and "misunderstanding" which had isolated Rousseau, by allowing others to recognize now what Rousseau had always known, or thought he knew: the pure, self-delighting energy inside his acts, the "natural" man whose *amour de soi* contained no vanity. For years Rousseau had been haunted by fantasies of persecution. Then the persecution had become real, forcing him to flee from country to country, accused by his enemies of being a veritable monster: *l'ennemi du genre humain*. Here at the home of the Comtesse d'Egmont, Rousseau made a last, desperate attempt to bridge the gap, to restore, at least among friends, a semblance of the harmonious community—the *transparence des coeurs*—of which he had so often dreamed. For a moment the buried self would destroy its prison and Jean Jacques would become the man of his words: he would be seen, not in his vanity, but "as he is."

What Rousseau desired, at this moment, was not the idiosyncratic disclosure which the romantics were to see in his behavior, but a true meeting between the personal and the general, an act of exhibitionism which would at the same time be an act of philosophy. To his audience he would present a man "drawn exactly according to nature, in all his truth . . . who may serve as the first model for comparison in the study of men." This man was himself, the impersonal energy shining through the personal acts. But he was also a mirror held up to the world of men, in which they could recognize not only the true, and thus the innocent, Jean Jacques, but also an image of the undiscovered self in each of them.

The *Discours sur l'Inégalité* tells how Diogenes spent his life in a vain search because he looked "among his contemporaries for the man of a time that no longer was." Rousseau would heed this warning. He would look, instead, beneath the deceptions of his own life to discover the honest man, the truly natural man. For, as he was to write in the *Dialogues,* "Where can the painter and apologist of nature today have taken his model, if not from his own heart . . . it was necessary that one man should fully describe himself, in order to reveal to us, in this way, the primitive man." For a moment the harmony of seeing and being seen would pass from the words into the living community of his audience. Jean Jacques would show to his friends a man engaged in the pure delight of "being himself"; and this show would be, in turn, a mirror in which each could admire his own true self. In this way Narcissus would create a society of brothers from which loneliness and vanity were banished. As the Spanish poet Antonio Machado has described it:

> This Narcissus of yours
> Cannot look in the mirror now
> Because he is the mirror himself.

On that painful day at the home of the Comtesse d'Egmont, Rousseau felt the doors of incomprehension close upon him once and for all. But this imagined "help of others" which he invoked in the *Confessions* continued to shape his fantasy in other ways. The harmony that escaped him in his life became a theme to which his words aspired again and again. He never tired of sketching models for the perfect society, communities where a rhythm of openness and love prevailed:

> What if someone told you that a mortal, who was otherwise very unhappy, regularly spent five or six hours a day in the most agreeable company, made up of men who were just, true, gay, lovable, simple though with great intelligence, gentle though with great virtues . . . that this mortal was known, esteemed, loved by this company of elite spirits, living among them in an exchange of confidence, friendship and familiarity; that he found there, at his choice, sure friends, faithful mistresses, tender women friends . . .

It was here that Rousseau spent his best hours, in a world like the one he had described years earlier in the *Nouvelle Héloïse*: a place of perfect agreement where Julie Wolmar like Rousseau himself could radiate the natural magic of her emotions, for "everything which comes near her must resemble her; everything around her must become Julie." If through self-love we express our truest nature, then the citizens of Clarens are entirely natural. The old evil of seeing and being seen has been purified for them by the power of Julie's and Rousseau's example.

The most remarkable fantasy of this kind is found in the First Dialogue. It describes so well the link between Rousseau's utopian imagination and the solitary impulse of his self-love that it deserves to be quoted at length:

> Imagine a world exactly like ours, and yet completely different. Nature there is the same as on our earth, but its economy is more visible, its order more accentuated, the spectacle it reveals more beautiful; the forms are more elegant, the colors livelier, the odors more suave, all objects more interesting. All of nature there is so beautiful that to contemplate it enflames souls with love for such a moving scene, and inspires them with a desire to contribute to this beautiful system, along with fear of troubling its harmony; from this fact, a delicate sensibility is born, allowing those who possess it to have immediate pleasures unknown to hearts which are unenlivened by such contemplations . . .
>
> The inhabitants of this ideal world have the good fortune of being maintained by nature, to which they are more closely attached, in that happy state of being to which we all once belonged, and by this fact alone their souls still possess their original character. The primitive passions all tend directly toward our happiness; they occupy us only with objects related to this goal; since their only principle is self-love, they are all essentially gentle and loving . . .
>
> Beings so constituted must necessarily express themselves differently from ordinary men. It is impossible that with souls so differently composed they would not carry the mark of these changes into the expression of their feelings and ideas. This mark may be invisible to those who have no idea that such a life can exist, but it cannot escape those who know it, and who are themselves affected by it. It is a characteristic sign by

which those who have been initiated can recognize each other; and what makes this sign so valuable, so little known and even less employed, is that it cannot be imitated . . . when it doesn't come from the heart of the person who imitates it, it cannot reach the hearts of those who are made to recognize it; but when it does reach the heart, no mistake is possible; it is true as soon as it is felt.

Rousseau's world is a place of natural equality. It is governed by no written laws, for the style of "recognition" and the exchanges of feeling which govern its humanity are inscribed in the hearts of its citizens. Equality here is not legal because it is natural. But this harmony of the emotions—a utopian balance between self-love and the "help of others"—is only a special case of the general harmony. Rousseau has imagined a secular Parousie, where fruit drops from the trees, the lion lies down with the lamb, and men live in the paradoxical purity of their natures. Even the language of this world is not the same. It has an instinctive music which can immediately be recognized, for it speaks not to the mind but to the heart. It is much like Rousseau's own language: that single, supple voice we recognize in all his more personal writings. In fact, as we learn a few pages further on, Jean Jacques is a citizen of this utopian world. Those who listen to him hear the voice of a purer nature, translated into language they can understand. To a citizen of this ideal earth, "democracy" was no political theory, it was a pure expression of the law of hearts; that unwritten balance between *amour de soi* and *amour propre*, between self-love and the necessary help of others.

The connection between Rousseau's fantasy world and his political vision in the *Social Contract* is clear. The problem he faced in constructing his ideal model was that of translating into the medium of practical law something which he knew to be ineffable, of giving political shape and consistency to a law of natural sentiment: "To find a form of association which defends and protects with all the force of the community the person and possessions of each member, and according to which each individual, uniting with all, still obeys only his own self." The members of Rousseau's ideal community could not be asked to give up what they already possessed: their privilege of solitude, the "animal" mood of peacefulness characteristic of the state of nature. "Adam was sovereign of the world, like Robinson on his island, as long as he was its only inhabitant; and this empire was most convenient, for the monarch was perfectly sure of his throne, and had to fear neither rebellion, war, nor conspirators." In the world of democracy, each man retained the privilege of Adam, even though he now was bound into the framework of the written law.

This condition implies still another, with more immediate political consequences. The very notion of a pact supposes that those who enter into it are responsible, sovereign beings. If the society they form is to be rooted in "nature," the sovereignty and self-love at the heart of their political commitment must remain active. Rousseau insists, therefore, on the right of all citizens to withdraw from the pact when they wish to do so. For if this right to withdraw were violated, then the pact would lose its natural basis in individuality. Conversely, if for any reason the pact itself were violated, then each citizen would automatically "return to his primitive rights, and take possession again of his natural freedom." The community of the *Social Contract* is rooted in the sense of a solitary kingdom which, for each man, is inviolable: in order to be with others, a man must retain that zone of privacy which allows, and indeed obliges, him to be with himself.

Another basis for democracy is contained in that first of all public acts: the contractual vote itself which creates a public arena, a space of political exchanges. The founding vote is more than a legality. It expresses an exchange of sovereignties, a simultaneous giving and receiving, endowing Rousseau's law of hearts with a permanent shape and a language. As such, it differs from all subsequent votes, which will be no more than legal conventions, validated by this founding act of generosity. Of the contractual vote, Rousseau writes:

> There is only one law which, by its very nature, needs unanimous consent: it is the social pact itself; for civil association is the most voluntary act in the world; each man is born free and master of himself, therefore no one, under any pretext, can oblige him without his consent.

The balance between self-love and the "help of others," between sovereign individuality and the pressures of the common life, is expressed politically by the unanimous vote, the agreement of all with all. Any subsequent failure of agreement impairs the ideal balance, clouding the mutual harmony which, for Rousseau, was the goal of society. Majority rule is no more than a law of expediency, a convention made necessary by the failures of human nature. Without it, no society would be possible. Yet it is clear that "the more agreement reigns in assemblies—i.e., the more opinions approach unanimity—the more dominant also is the general will," and the closer the society comes to composing nature and artifice into a pure exchange of individualities, a veritable *transparence des coeurs*.

The task of the law, for Rousseau, will be to preserve this ineffable balance, so that "each one, giving to all, gives himself to no one; and since there is no partner who has not yielded to us exactly the same right that we ceded to him, we get back the equivalent of what we have lost, along with more power to conserve what we still have." The community of the *Social Contract* is a community of natural selves, for whom being and seeming need not differ, for what each gives is returned to him in a single, harmonious gesture of exchange.

There is nonetheless a troubled note in the *Social Contract*. Rousseau, unlike the utopian dreamer he is often accused of being, could not forget that "all things . . . wholly outside nature have their shortcomings, and civil society more than all the rest of them put together." Democracy was a fine ideal, yet it was clearly beyond the capacity of men to make it work. "If there were a people of gods," he wrote, "it would govern itself democratically. Such a perfect government is not possible among men." A community must inevitably reflect the inner balance, or unbalance, of those—the mere mortals—who compose it. Rousseau knew that his *transparence des coeurs* was a utopian ideal, that the balance he spoke of between self-love and vanity was too infinitely delicate to be preserved in human society. Only gods could do it, and Jean Jacques, who thought he was better than most men, knew he was not a god. Even the community of Clarens, in the *Nouvelle Héloïse,* contained a secret failure; in the end, Julie Wolmar had to die in order to find her personal salvation. The final reconciliation was beyond the scope of even the most perfect community.

Despite the rigor and the agility of his social imagination, Rousseau was not at ease in society. The early pessimism of the *Discours sur l'Inégalité* was never entirely reversed in his mind. It was only during flashes of utopian fantasy, or in the strangely theatrical gesture of his *Confessions,* that he could solve the impenetrable distance between self-love and vanity. Again and again he insists that he is no misanthrope, that his greatest desire has ever been to live happily among men. Even in the *Dialogues,* where he is moved to the point of delirium with paranoid distrust, he repeats that he would "willingly leave the company of plants for that of men, if only [he] could find any." Yet here, as elsewhere, Rousseau is telling a half-truth. For the only companion he ever loved, wholeheartedly, without the blustering reticence which characterized him, was made of his own solitary images. His life had to be transposed into a play of memory and meditation in order to be truly livable. When, in the *Dialogues,* he comes to imagine the kind of honest friendship he has never known in real life, it is no accident that the two friends are named "Jean Jacques" and "Rousseau."

Even the dream of community which shaped Rousseau's politi-

cal philosophy is described, in the *Social Contract,* as a con-
cession made to human frailty. In agreement here with the
Christian tradition of politics and the state—which he otherwise
thoroughly contradicts—Rousseau asserts that if man were better
he would have less need for the difficult project of community.
Each of us, like Adam before the Fall, would be sole sovereign
of his kingdom. It is true, Rousseau agrees, that we need the
"help of others" in order to complete our self-delight; but that
is so, he adds, only "in this life." If man were more perfectly
conceived, he could do without this "help of others"; he would
be autonomous and self-delighting, like God Himself. This
dream of autonomy runs parallel, in Rousseau's imagination, to
the dream of the ideal community, and finally conquers it. In
describing his own character, he writes:

> Jean Jacques did not always run away from men; but he has
> always loved solitude. He loved to be with the friends he
> thought he had, but he liked it even more when he was alone
> with himself. He cherished their company; but sometimes he
> needed to gather his thoughts together in solitude, and perhaps
> would have preferred living always alone than always with
> others. His predilection for the novel *Robinson Crusoe* has
> made me think that he would not have been as unhappy as
> Robinson to be confined to his desert island.

At the end of his life, in the *Rêveries du Promeneur Solitaire,*
Rousseau embraces the logic of his thirst for solitude. Years of
half-real, half-imagined persecution had weakened the utopian
longing in his character. The distrust expressed by Julie's death
in the *Nouvelle Héloïse* prefigures what was to become Rousseau's own experience of life in death. The First Promenade
begins, "Here I am, alone on the earth, with no brother, neigh-
bor, friend, or company other than myself." After a lifetime
spent at the edge of society, treading the fine line between
"seeing" and "being seen," Rousseau at last makes the decisive
break. He arrogates the right proclaimed in the *Social Contract*

and abandons his citizenship in the human race. Henri Roddier is perhaps right, in his introduction to the *Rêveries,* in seeing a link between this abrupt declaration and the incident described by Rousseau several pages farther on.

Rousseau tells how he had been knocked over in the street by a huge dog and forced to remain in bed for some days afterward. When he is finally well enough to resume his daily walks, he discovers that all of Paris is filled with talk of his death. Obituary notices have appeared in the newspapers, the king and queen have been informed. One afternoon he appears in the Tuilleries, and people stare at him as if he were a ghost. Rousseau has enough humor to be amused by the incident. At the same time he reads into it a sign of the fate prepared for him. Was it this final misunderstanding that convinced Rousseau to abandon the living? Buffeted by isolation, disappointed in his dream of companionship and love, he could not ignore an event so roundly symbolic. Now that he had been declared dead, Rousseau could at last turn his back on the world; he could embrace the singular mood of tranquillity and self-delight so well described by the *Rêveries.* "Having lost all hope in this life, finding no further nourishment on earth for my heart, little by little I learned to feed it on my own substance, looking within me for all its pasturage."

In the Fifth Promenade, Rousseau describes the profound peace of his confinement on the Isle Saint Pierre. During such periods of reverie, the mind became like crystal, emptied of all disturbing images. The boundaries of the self expanded, until the entire world became a delicate rhythm, a gentle interpretation of thought and object, seer and seen: "What do we enjoy at such a moment? Nothing outside us, nothing if not ourselves and our own existence; as long as this feeling continues, we are self-sufficient, like God." Self and world were so profoundly intermingled as to have become synonymous. The formal anthropomorphism of the Renaissance finds a parallel in Rousseau's imagination. The correspondence between Macrocosm and Microcosm, exploded by seventeenth-century science and skepticism is re-established in the emotional experience of the *Rêveries,* though on a completely different scale. For Rousseau, the center of the world is no longer man but me. The chaotic infinities of Donne and Pascal, the disorder and the hostility of man's newly "natural" world, are solved, for Rousseau, in this harmony of revealed emotion. The *Rêveries* describe a world that has once again been shaped with and by humanity; a world that is neither hostile nor formal and hierarchical. It is an "ego-morphic" world, shaped by the pleasures and the character of a single imagination.

Part Four

9 THE HERO
AND THE POET

There is no society of heroes. The exceptional man whose fate it has become, in some measure, to change the world, discovers that his task leads him into a region of experience from which all companions are banished. His path is strewn with enemies, tricks of the gods, oceans to be crossed; and it may be that the most difficult obstacle he encounters will be his own all too human emotions. In order to equal his fate, the hero, the man of exceptional powers, must change the rhythm of his life. He must overcome that segment of his character which finds its contentment in a middle range of the emotions: the common zone of language and responsibilities composing life in society. The hero myth, in all of its many forms, does not allow its protagonist to come to grips with his task—the creation of a world, the founding of a society, the rescue of a sacred object—until he has undertaken a dark journey away from his own humanity: across oceans as in the case of Gilgamesh or Hercules, down to the underworld like Orpheus, or into death itself like Dionysius. In order to master the demonic forces, the hero must first uncover those elements in his own nature which are permanent and "godlike."

It will be objected that a certain kind of hero, closer perhaps to our own sensibilities, undertakes no heroic journey. Carlyle, in *Heroes and Hero Worship*, describes Luther's conversion as "his deliverance from darkness, his final triumph over darkness." Before becoming the father of a new religion, Luther, he tells us, had to fall "into the blackest wretchedness; had to wander staggering as on the verge of bottomless despair." The spiritual hero must also undergo the ordeal of initiation; he must travel outside all the known countries, thereby transforming his life. As Kierkegaard wrote, "Only he who descends into the underworld rescues the beloved." In Kierkegaard's mind, this reference to Orpheus expressed very well the kind of journey beyond society which prepared the hero of faith—Kierkegaard was later to call him the "Isolated One"—for his task. In the case of Martin Luther, it is not difficult to see that the obstacles he vanquished were, above all, interior obstacles. In order to change the world, he had first to change his life.

In primitive hero myths, the work of heroic transformation is done through a series of perilous adventures; in the case of more "modern" heroes, the ordeal is one of inward suffering and purification, a journey into, and beyond, their own attachments. This is perhaps what is meant by those hard verses from Luke, in which Jesus is made to say: "If any man cometh unto me, and hateth not his own father and mother and wife and children and brethren and sisters, yea, and his own life also, he cannot be my disciple." Christ, we are told, is speaking to the meek, who will inherit the earth. What is extraordinary about His revelation is that it is meant for every man. Yet the condition He proposes in these few words goes far toward making the common life impossible. Among heroes, Odysseus or Agamemnon had done worse; other "great men" had betrayed the bonds of society in order to gain access to a higher strength. The New Testament seems to be saying, however, that all men, and especially the "meek," must become heroes—that the human condition itself, when seen in the light of Christian insight, requires a continual act of heroism. No longer is the exceptional man asked to perform his duty toward the closed world of his community; no longer need he act out the precarious adventure that estranges him from his society in order to allow each one of its members to remain comfortably human—i.e., social—because he alone, the hero, has been delegated by them to visit the underworld and mingle with the gods. Now, according to Luke, every man must make the journey for himself.

This is the insight which will be inherited by Kierkegaard, and which undoubtedly lies behind Ortega's understanding of human life as "radical solitude," a perpetual estrangement best described as loneliness. From this point of view, the hero's greatest task has always been to solve his loneliness. By carrying his own case to the gods, he somehow bought for his fellow citizens the right to choose an easier solution: that of the common life, the community. The number of spiritual heroes canonized by the Church makes it clear that the difficulty contained in this text from Luke was eventually solved by being ignored. In the spiritual economy of Catholicism, the saints performed the role of heroes whose ordeal and triumph allowed them to serve as intercessors for those of their fellows who couldn't, and shouldn't, be asked to do the same thing.

This brings us to another of the hero's faces. Although by definition there can be no society of heroes, although the exceptional man journeys toward his great deed by peeling away layer after layer of his common humanity until he has become the most solitary of men, still his adventure is not complete until he has returned home, or has at least seen to it that his deed becomes known to those who remained behind. Agamemnon's sacrifice of Iphigenia would have been meaningless if, later, he was not acclaimed and recognized by all of Greece. The heroic ordeal requires recognition. What the hero has done for himself, by changing his life, is truly done only if it is also done for others. After his journey into "bottomless despair," and his moment of illumination, Luther returned to tell about it, and to found a church. We have already remarked a similar requirement among heroes of a completely different order. When the fictional knight of chivalry has undergone his ordeal, accomplished his adventure, he still must return to Arthur's castle to tell what he has done. The deed needs the word. Don Quixote needs the certificate from the keeper of the reluctant lion. The exceptional deed is solitary; the hero must conquer his loneliness—in the chivalric tradition he is inevitably lovelorn—while he conquers the enemy; but the final word must exhibit his victory to those who caused him to leave in the first place. The tales of chivalry echo ever so faintly in this respect the original force of the hero myth, which also requires that society benefit from the solitary energy of the hero. The mythical hero founded a civilization; Christ, suffering the exemplary loneliness of the Cross, is seen by all of Jerusalem and then by two thousand years of Western history. If we are right to understand the heroic act itself as a kind of revelation—a turning point, as in Rilke's concept of *Umschlag*, which transforms the pain of the hero's ordeal into an abundance of power—then we will perhaps be allowed a further analogy to strengthen our argument.

There is a decided resemblance between the traditional career of the hero and that of most religious mystics. Like the hero, the mystic must undo his attachments to the common life by going into the desert, by sexual abstinence, or by intensive solitary meditation. He must overcome the sense of utter abandonment which St. John of the Cross named the Dark Night of the Soul. Only then is he capable of illumination. That is the end of his journey; and yet, according to a need which now becomes clear, he is still only at the midpoint of the way. His illumination is momentary; he glimpses "eternity" and then, returned into the flesh among men, remembers what he has seen. His life has been changed, but the change is not complete until, once more simply a man, he can allow others to witness what he has gone through. Most of the great mystics—Eckhart, John of the Cross, St. Theresa—left long descriptions of their experiences, in the form of poems, sermons, or autobiographical essays. In order for their intense glory to be meaningful, it must be shared and recognized—as if the mystic were an emissary whose illuminating message had, afterward, to be recomposed in words familiar to all. Most Christian mystics devoted their lives, after their moment or moments of illumination, to doing good works, to organizing monasteries, to preaching, etc. After obtaining for themselves, in isolation, what was most precious, they returned to face the hazards of human frailty, as if they now had become living guarantees of some higher dispensation. The same tendency is to be found, in even clearer terms, in Buddhist mysticism. Though the path of individual salvation is the central mystery expounded by Buddhism, and though the techniques of concentration are, in fact, a kind of heroic ordeal, still the doctrine of universal compassion makes it a sin for the initiate to leave the world behind, once victory—nirvana—has been achieved. The Bodhisattva's enthusiasm, writes Dasgupta in his *Hindu Mysticism*, "is not for the egotistical calm of the saint who is anxious for his own deliverance; he is moved by the most altruistic of all motives, viz. compassion for all creatures."

Whatever immediate reason they may give, the mystic and the hero must return from their journey out of the common world. For a moment they were more than men; now they must consent to be men once more, exposing themselves to the general eye, talking about themselves and above all, translating their glimpse of Permanence into the language of men.

From the point of view of those energies which the hero and the mystic have released, the community is a middle ground whose tranquillity depends upon its keeping the fences mended. This is the fragile balance Rilke saw when he suddenly became afraid that all the fences had crumbled: "Could we but find a pure, reserved, narrow humanity; a strip of fertile fruit-land of our own between the rock and the river." A narrow strip of humanity between the rock and the river; a place, circumscribed and tranquil, fitted for the business of life—neither the hero nor the mystic is gifted for this life of moderation and decorum. Their ambitions are excessive, their lives contain a grain of folly. Yet the men of moderation have always suspected that something in their own circumscribed world depended on these excessive

men. The proof is the universal worship of heroes, the venera-
tion of saints, the awe felt for men—yogis, shamans, magicians,
monks, hermits—whose lives are made of separateness. Their
separateness is understood as a guarantee, a sign from the gods,
that life will continue to be meaningful.

The hero and the hero's story; the deed and the words that
perpetuate it; the illumination and the spiritual biography that
make it known and admired—both halves of the adventure
need to be completed. The man whose life is an ordeal of self-
exclusion needs, in the end, to be included once again. This is
the meaning of a passage from Kierkegaard's *Fear and Trembling* which could serve as an epigraph for this entire discussion:

> If there were no eternal consciousness in a man, if at the foun-
> dation of all there lay only a wildly seething power which
> writhing with obscure passions produced everything that is
> great and everything that is insignificant, if a bottomless void
> never satiated lay hidden beneath all—what then would life be
> but despair? . . . If an eternal oblivion were always lurking
> hungrily for its prey and there was no power strong enough
> to wrest it from its maw—how empty then and comfortless
> life would be! But therefore it is not thus, but as God created
> man and woman, so too He fashioned the hero and the poet
> or orator. The poet cannot do what that other does, he can only
> admire, love, and rejoice in the hero. Yet he too is happy, and
> not less so, for the hero is as it were his better nature, with
> which he is in love, rejoicing in the fact that this after all is
> not himself, that his love can be admiration. He is the genius of
> recollection, can do nothing except call to mind what has been
> done . . . If he thus remains true to his love, he strives day
> and night against the cunning of oblivion which would trick
> him out of his hero . . . for the poet is as it were the hero's bet-
> ter nature, powerless it may be as a memory is, but also trans-
> figured as a memory is.

The poet is the hero's memory; he is the permanence concealed
in the act; the witness that a spark of "eternal consciousness" has

come down into the hero's passing triumph and preserved, in the eyes of all those who need to know it, that narrow strip of humanity from the energies which threaten to engulf it.

Little that Kierkegaard wrote was not closely tied to the difficulties of his own life. No philosopher, perhaps, has talked so exclusively about his own problems, and the bizarre sensitivity that made his life all but unbearable to others as well as to himself. The greatness of a book like *Fear and Trembling* lies in the author's power to find a common language, and a common ground of sensibility, into which he translates the rather doubtful episode of his engagement to Regina. Few philosophers have been able to generalize so powerfully from such narrow and unpromising grounds. In the passage from Kierkegaard quoted above, the hero and the poet form a necessary couple: the "eternal consciousness" which is revealed by the hero's act is not complete until it has been transformed by one whose gift is not to do but to say. The poet's words give the heroic deed that permanence which enables it to go on outside of time, preserved in the memories of those who need to remember it. It is possible, we have seen, for the hero to be his own poet. The knights of chivalry were under that obligation. The great mystics were also great poets. In this passage from *Fear and Trembling* the hero is ostensibly Abraham, and the poet Kierkegaard. Yet it takes little effort to discover that Kierkegaard means himself to be both poet and hero. Speaking of Abraham's enigma, he wrote in his *Journal*, "To explain this enigma is to explain my life." Through the poet's gift he has entered into Abraham's parable and become, more or less openly, the hero he is writing about. Kierkegaard was to note, with remarkable insight, several years later in the *Journal*, "One day not only my writing, but my life itself, all the intriguing secrecy of its mechanisms, will be studied again and again."

When Kierkegaard wrote about Abraham he was interested not in his whole life but in that short moment of it which made a hero of him. If we hold to the analogy discussed above, however, we must conclude that Kierkegaard, hero and poet, understood his entire life as an act of heroism, and his gift for language as a means of preserving, for the permanence of all memories, that "eternal consciousness" which made his life, and thereby all lives, unshakably meaningful—i.e., rooted in, and transformed by, what Kierkegaard later called "the Idea." He himself quotes the passage from Luke and obviously applies it to his own case.

With these remarks on Kierkegaard our discussion has, in fact, shifted ground. The hero and the poet have not only been merged into a single person, but they have become, in a sense, exact contemporaries. The act which the poet celebrates can no longer be separated from the act of celebration itself. The poet is "the genius of recollection," who admires, loves, and rejoices in what he calls to mind. But what he calls to mind, in the case of Kierkegaard, is the secret event of his own life. He must "be his own contemporary," and this, for Kierkegaard, meant to become "transparent to oneself in a spirit of calm"; to transform "the obscure passions" and the "bottomless void" into a calm transparency, assured of its meaning.

Without the power of love and reflection embodied in the poet's words, his life would be obscure, disorganized; it would be no life at all but simply a monotonous rhythm in the "surge of fruitless activity" which is Nature left to herself. In order to be his own contemporary, as Kierkegaard puts it, the hero must at every moment be capable of thinking his life, of raising his every gesture into the transparency of the word—Rilke was to describe this as the terrible genius of "praise"; the poet, in turn, must be able at every moment to live his thought, to descend from his words into the life now illuminated by the simultaneous effort of his "poem." Living and writing, closely intermingled, become a single, intensely moral act.

This shift in the ground of poetic recollection belongs largely to the nineteenth century. And the literary sensibility which translates it most directly is that which gave rise to the *journal intime:* that unending, formless attempt on the part of some men to pursue a phantom of spiritual certainty through the freshly lived confusion of their acts. During the dozen or so years of his enormous productivity, Kierkegaard not only turned out book after book—the volume of his collected works is staggering—he also kept a journal which runs to several thousand pages. In it he performs the task of "poetic" transmutation, converting the base metal of his life into the Idea; searching through the labyrinth of his "unlikeness," his eccentricity, his absurd melancholy, for the "true self," the calm self-transparency which the ordeal of his life seemed to conceal, yet almost to reveal.

Toward the end of the eighteenth century it had become fashionable to keep a daily record of one's moral temperature, in printed "barometric" diaries sold widely for that purpose. The models for the new fashion were Montaigne and Rousseau, though neither had in fact ever kept such a record. Still they had undertaken to see clearly into the hidden movements of their lives, to bare as much as possible their "veritable" selves, in order, so they said, to further mankind's understanding of its own soul. "Each man bears the entire form of man's estate," Montaigne had written. The philosophical basis for Rousseau's *Confessions* is similar, despite obvious differences between the two writers which we have already pointed out. Rousseau had gone so far as to conceive the project for what he called a *Morale Sensitive:* a system of correspondences between the moral condition of an individual—his *états d'âme*—and the minutely analyzed circumstances of his physical life—his personal climate, so to speak. The way to establish the barometer for such a *Morale Sensitive* would be, he wrote, to keep a detailed account of all the movements of one's inner life, along with the immediate circumstances which accompanied them. This meant, in fact, an exhaustive record of one's daily existence, kept with a view toward advancing "scientifically" man's knowledge of himself. It is significant that Rousseau left his project unapplied. The kind of inward concern that drew him into autobiography was not tempted by the uncertain struggles of a journal, even a "scientific" one. Rousseau's idea, however, was enormously influential. Fifty years later, in order to excuse his own *Souvenirs d'Égotism,* Stendhal was to note, "Egotism, if it is *sincere,* is a way to describe this human heart of which we have gained so much knowledge since . . . Montesquieu."

Stendhal goes on to develop this idea, giving it an extension which would have made it more familiar to Kierkegaard, or to some of Stendhal's contemporaries: men like Maine de Biran in France or Emerson in America: "If I truly desired something, it was to gain a knowledge of men. Each month I remembered this idea, but the tastes and passions, the hundred follies that fill my life, would have had to leave the surface of the water in peace if that image were to appear there." The psychological penetration of which Stendhal speaks, that close intermingling of action and self-reflection, requires a "spirit of calm," a mood of inward transparency as Kierkegaard would have said; only then will he be able to see past the confused gestures of his life, into that other self reflected by the water. As long as the life and the word have not succeeded in embracing one another, the water will be ruffled by *cent folies,* until it resembles a "bottomless void," a deformed and crippled selfhood. Yet, if the water could be calmed, if the hero and the poet could be truly contemporary, then Narcissus looking into the water would find a self made of permanence, a faithful image of what is truest not only in himself but in all men.

Stendhal has moved quite a distance from the fashionable idea of a "barometer" composed for purely scientific reasons. By keeping this record of his life, he was trying to penetrate beyond the *cent folies,* beyond the confused layer of emotions imposed on him by his character, in order to grasp another image, one that hovered just out of reach, half obscured by life itself. In his early journals as well as in his late autobiographical writings, Stendhal, fascinated by the secrets of *"le coeur humain,"* is not merely keeping a register of his inward acts; he is searching for something behind the acts, something which the acts of his life tend to hide or deform. Narcissus, gazing into the water, is engaged in a painful vigil; the image he is looking for escapes him. The more he looks, the more he is filled with the sense of a painful lack. From the point of view of this inward vigil, no act he accomplishes "in the world" can give him satisfaction if it doesn't also point beyond itself to the obscured image in the water. And yet that is the one thing it cannot do, for every life-movement ruffles the water, making the image less recognizable than before. The man who has given himself up to this inward expectation undergoes from minute to minute the ordeal of seeing the sought-for image betrayed, not by some enemy who might, with effort, be defeated, but by the needs and passions of his own life. He is himself the enemy, and the only meaningful victory must be over himself.

It is not difficult to understand now why Rousseau never followed up on his project for a *Morale Sensitive,* or why those like Stendhal and Maine de Biran who did, found themselves involved more and more in a process of self-understanding which was scarcely "scientific." A man who follows the secret movements of his life from day to day and minute to minute is apt to find the firm groundwork of his character continually dissolving. As he follows his own words into the confusion of his daily experience, he finds not a confident progress of motivations, ideas, intentions but instead those *cent folies* of which Stendhal speaks. The more he tries to shape the energies of his life, and to transcribe them "in a spirit of calm"—i.e., the more he tries to be "his own contemporary"—the more those energies escape him, appear disorganized, meaningless. The self he is most familiar with appears to be no self at all; he is led to question everything about his existence, his ambitions, his life in society. The mood of the *journal intime* is one of self-doubt and isolation. As the writer pushes forward, mingling words and acts, life and reflection, in a way unprecedented in literature, his existence appears more and more clearly to him as a painful ordeal. He is destined to pursue a tenuous image through a world of isolation, melancholy, and physical discomfort, in which all the social satisfactions must slip through his fingers. The goal of his life becomes, not social success—though he may, like Benjamin Constant or Delacroix, become immensely successful—but victory over this sense of inner formlessness. In order to discover himself, he must vanquish himself; he must change his life. Maine de Biran writes in his journal, "I am always concerned with what is happening inside me," for only by this continual self-preoccupation can he give shape to the inner life and create a semblance of order out of unreason:

> I believe the only man who is on the road to wisdom or happiness. . . is one who is ever concerned with the analysis of his emotions; he has scarcely a feeling or thought of which he is not aware, careful to exclude everything which might contradict the model of perfection he has given himself.

The shift in mood which we discovered in Kierkegaard and Stendhal has brought about an entirely new relation between the hero and the poet. Not only must they be exact "contemporaries"; the heroic ordeal now lies precisely in the never-ending effort of self-reflection, the attempt to put aside the common goals of men and society, passing through loneliness and self-doubt, in order to grasp in the net of the poem the clear features of another self. Along the way the hero becomes, in his own eyes, a kind of failure—an "anti-hero," to anticipate Dostoevski's underground man—for his announced goal always escapes him. In addition his poem has become a veritable anti-poem: a formless magma of words, organized only by the dates at the top of each entry, the opposite of a work of art. A hero who cannot act, or whose acts appear meaningless to him, is rendered into permanence by a poet who cannot create. We couldn't be further from the mood of Rousseau's *Confessions*. At no moment in the *Confessions* do we feel Rousseau fumbling for a truth which escapes him. On the contrary, his only effort throughout is to convince the reader of what he, Rousseau, already knows: his own luminous innocence. Rousseau is celebrating himself, justifying himself. Unlike Stendhal, he does not peer anxiously through the *cent folies* of his character in search of something which fades as he advances toward it. The subject of Rousseau's autobiography is precisely those *cent folies* which he describes lovingly, convinced, and convincing us, that each one of them is transparent and meaningful. In his own eyes Rousseau's persecution, the supposed betrayal of his friends, appear undeserved. They are an absurd accident which could be solved in a minute if only a few self-evident truths could be made known. That is the goal of his *Confessions:* to tell the truth about himself. But neither Stendhal nor Maine de Biran knows the truth about himself. Their journals and autobiographical writings are a tortuous effort to pursue this truth. The difficulty that makes their lives so painful is, to them, no accident. They never doubt that it is entirely "deserved," for it is the one constant theme they find rooted in their experience. Maine repeats often in his journal the sad recognition that "My physical and moral condition, with which I am less and less happy, is an inner cross compared to which all outer crosses are nothing . . . How to cure that inner discouragement which is the true cross, the one which makes all the others so hard to bear?" Yet Maine's reaction to his inward cross, like Stendhal's and above all like Kierkegaard's of whom we will speak in a moment, is not to turn his back on it, nor even to cure it. Instead he chooses to enter more and more fully into the suffering and the discontent caused him by the sense of inward dissolution. Kierkegaard was later to write, "To keep a wound open is sometimes not at all unhealthy; yes, a healthy, open wound; the worst, often, is when it closes over." The entire effort of Maine's life is to keep the wound open; to scrutinize, dissect, record every twinge of his clouded selfhood. His suffering becomes a kind of mirror, in which all the inner movements are clearly marked: "When a man doesn't suffer, he hardly thinks of himself. Sickness or the habit of reflection must force us to descend into ourselves. Only those who are ill feel themselves to exist . . . health inclines us to the outside world, illness returns us to ourselves."

The analogy of the hero and the poet is useful in helping us to understand this inward-turning vision of experience. The new hero embarks on his ordeal of solitary self-inspection; his life, directed toward a goal of spiritual perfection which fades continually out of reach, becomes a tissue of lonely failures. Yet the point of his ordeal is to welcome the failures, the *cent folies,* the loneliness; to raise them into the clear medium of thought, to record them, hoping little by little to discover the pure image that underlies them, the "true self," and to transpose his entire life into the permanence of that image.

10 KIERKEGAARD, THE ISOLATED ONE

The analogy of the hero and the poet appears exaggerated when applied to Stendhal, Emerson, or Maine de Biran. They were such mild, unspectacular men whose lives, apart from the daily adventure of their journals, can hardly be called excessive. In the case of the Danish philosopher and theologian Sören Kierkegaard however, the analogy remains scrupulously exact. Few men have devoted themselves so entirely to the task of transforming their lives into a continuous act of heroism. Kierkegaard expended all his genius in pursuit of this goal, deepening the web of misunderstandings which surrounded him, willfully increasing the hostility and isolation which never ceased being painful to him.

In order to become his own "contemporary," Kierkegaard had compulsively to undo all the links of sympathy and understanding which attached him to the common life. In 1842, during the first months of the frenzy of literary activity which was to last until his death, Kierkegaard noted in his *Journal,* "It is my peculiar malediction that I never can dare allow any human being to become deeply attached to me." Isolation of the most painful kind was the climate in which his permanent self-revelation flourished; and he chose to pursue this isolation with increasing energy. The unhappy poet in *Repetition,* whose story is obviously a version of Kierkegaard's own, writes of his ambition in a letter: "Thus to be a hero, not in the eyes of the world, but within oneself, to have no plea to present before a human tribunal, but living immured within one's own personality, to be one's own witness, one's own judge, one's own prosecutor, to be in oneself the one and only." Though Kierkegaard placed this ambition in the mind of a character meant to be doubly fictional—*Repetition* is one of the philosopher's pseudonymous works—it expresses a thought about life which in Kierkegaard's eyes was not at all literary, for it never ceased to govern his every gesture. It is no wonder that he was so intrigued by the theater—his *Journal* is full of theatrical references, and *Repetition* itself contains brilliant pages analyzing the fascination for those parallel lives which the actor can put on and off again like so many well-thought-out daydreams—for Kierkegaard devoted all his life to the task of transforming the painful fate imposed upon him by his character into a rigorously exact scenario, all of whose effects were expected and necessary. Nothing in his life was foreign to this effort. His published works, both signed and pseudonymous; his *Journal;* the decisions leading to his rupture with Regina and later to his refusal of a pastorship in the Danish Church; his violent polemic against the Church, ending only with his death; and woven among these greater events, the texture of his smallest daily choices: all this was part of an increasingly simple plan whose result was a life of rigorous, almost unbearable solitude, led in a city whose hostility he had willfully aroused. None of these actions could be omitted if Kierkegaard was to embody, in the most literal way, the "Category of Isolation": the true category of the Christian life, according to the theology he evolved in the late 1840s.

The two faces of the hero require that he follow his adventure into regions of privacy unsuspected by the ordinary man, and yet nothing of his ordeal must be kept from the community. Kierkegaard exemplifies this double requirement in a new way, and to the letter. Unlike Stendhal, Maine de Biran, or even Delacroix —all of whom kept journals—Kierkegaard forced his private self into the shape of a public figure; the very talents and anxieties he reveals in his *Journal* are ones that require at every moment his appearance before the public. The heroism which he describes in *Repetition* converts him, paradoxically, into an actor on the stage of Copenhagen. His solitude, in order to be meaningful, had to maintain him in a restless and contradictory relationship with others:

> While I continue to keep others away from me, and can boast of no material success, I still find myself in an intense relationship with men . . . They are busy insulting me, and making fun of me, but without realizing that they are caught in my plan, and when all is finished they will be marked by me once and for all.

During the Middle Ages spiritual solitude was respected, he writes; it belonged to the very fabric of the religious life, and its expression was the institution of monasteries. Today, Kierkegaard notes ironically, the only place where we have a use for solitude is in prison. Therefore the Category of Isolation can be served only by his remaining at the center of the mindless, characterless masses, as a kind of spiritual gadfly, reminding them by the spectacle of his victimization and his loneliness that another dispensation is needed if they are to survive:

> There has not until now been the least false step, not the slightest error, and I hope to make none until my death, so that it will be entirely clear that I served the idea of Isolation, and for that reason only, lived wholly alone, though observed by almost everyone. That is the point. To live alone, out of sight, with the idea of Isolation is neither a logical nor the most exact expression of the idea. But to be alone and then to have all others against one, that is, in the dialectical sense, to have them all for one; for to have them all ranged on the other side helps to make it apparent that one is alone: that is what it means to be dialectical, and that is the victory.

As we read through the *Journal,* it becomes clear that the "idea" of isolation which he chose to serve belonged to a category of reflective truths which he read in the book of his character. If character is fate, then Kierkegaard dealt with his fate in a unique way: he neither accepted it nor turned his back on it; instead he chose to build it willfully, changing himself into what he already was, an isolated, singular personality, but with a difference. It is in the light of this final "Idea" that we must try to understand Kierkegaard's career and his influence. All the resources of his imagination, his dialectical skill, and his simple stubborn will power are devoted to it. In order to be "immured within [his] own personality," Kierkegaard performed a constant exchange, making "ideas" out of his most ineradicable obsessions, and making, in turn, from the ideas a plan for action which would transform the living man and his writings into a single, unified performance.

The early pages of the *Journal* give us an insight into the shape Kierkegaard was later to impose upon his life. Beneath the surface of his "melancholy"—the feeling of aimless insecurity which he was later, in the language of his theology, to call "anxiety"—we find the young man painfully conscious of a lack in his inward organization: "That's the trouble with me: my whole life is an interjection, nothing is nailed down (everything is in movement—no stillness, nothing stable)." He is troubled by these broken ends of thought that make him feel continually at sea within himself: "How often does it happen that just as we think we have at last grasped ourselves, we find that we have hugged only a cloud for Juno?" What the cloud hides—what Stendhal had described as the image in the water—escapes him.

Kierkegaard knows, however, that his melancholy conceals an authentic inwardness. He writes, "My present life is like a deformed counterfeit of an original edition of my true self." The melancholy and the feeling of self-betrayal—they are undoubtedly one and the same thing—give new urgency to the familiar romantic "nostalgia" for a spiritual homeland: "Terrible, the complete spiritual impotence from which I've been suffering these days, for the very reason that it is accompanied by an all-consuming nostalgia, almost as if the mind itself were in heat—and yet so formless that I don't even know what it is I'm lacking." Already, as a student, Kierkegaard knew that nothing could be done until he had accomplished what he called "the work of inwardness." "Only after having so understood himself is a man able to exist independently, and thus avoid losing his selfhood." The *Journal*, which he began keeping almost ten years before the publication of his first important work, *Either-Or*, is in more ways than one the groundwork for this painful search. In it he hoped to grasp his thoughts in the act of birth, fresh from their origin behind the cloud. As his problem became clearer, he realized the need to work more exclusively at the *Journal*, "by more frequent notes, letting the thoughts appear with the umbilical cord of their first enthusiasm . . ."

Earlier Kierkegaard had used another image to describe the kind of effort that awaited him. In a letter to a friend he described the soothing effect of his isolation in the Danish countryside, away from the obligations of friendship:

> As for the silence of our friends, it is beneficial to me inasmuch as it teaches me to fix my attention on myself; it impels me to grasp this self, and to keep it steady in the midst of the infinite changeability; to turn toward myself the concave mirror in which I previously had sought to embrace life outside myself; this silence pleases me because I see that I am equal to the effort, and that I feel strong enough to hold the mirror.

By holding up the mirror to himself, he hoped to reinforce the "interior action" which he already thought of as the "divine side of man," thereby cultivating his "unknown god," his individuality. This meant also to cultivate a means for grasping the peculiar rhythms of "inwardness." Kierkegaard's first reflections on literary style show clearly that he knew how much of his struggle was to be lived in words, and by means of words, "for isn't the primary virtue of a writer always to have a style of his own, that is to say, a means of expression and exposition modeled on his very individuality?"

The road which, a dozen years later, was to lead to the

Category of Isolation, begins in another, vaguer solitude: that of his initial "melancholy," as he decides to brush aside the wisps of deformed selfhood in order to see down through his own words onto the surface of the water: "I am going to try now to direct my eyes calmly into myself, and begin to act from within; for, like the child whose first effort of consciousness teaches him to use the 'I,' that is the only thing which will enable me to use it less superficially." Reaching inward, through the "cloud for Juno," Kierkegaard tried to embrace himself, to find the permanent form concealed in his own acts. But all he grasped was an echo inhabiting his thoughts; it was the echo of his own mind coming back to him as a voice, almost unrecognized: "Every time I'm going to say something, there's someone at the same time who says it. I have the impression of being a spiritual double; it seems as if this other me always started first . . ." "How strange this feeling I've often had that the life I led, instead of being mine, was detail for detail that of some other person . . ." Here again Kierkegaard is very much of his century. The intimacy of a man with his own double was a familiar romantic fantasy. Out of the unrelenting effort to see and be seen in a single intense moment, to become both object and subject of his own sensibility, the poet found that his imagination took possession of the inward split, as if to resolve the two halves with the logic of fantasy into two separate personalities. In the case of Kierkegaard, the *Doppelgänger* is an involuntary fiction, a phantasm soon to be replaced by a series of more elaborate fictions. He muses somewhere over the project for a novel in which the protagonist would slowly lose his mind; the novel would end in the first person. This is exactly the path his imagination did take countless times, though in the opposite direction. His *Journal*, as well as his early published works, is filled with fictional sketches, third-person autobiographies, or simply anecdotes, all of them obvious transpositions of his own life. In *Fear and Trembling* alone three of these sketches organize the entire philosophical development: the parable of Abraham, Agnes and the Mer-man, the story of the bridegroom and the oracle: all dealing with his own dilemma over Regina. In the effort to discover a shape for his confused emotions, Kierkegaard brought forth image after image, as if by trying on these forms one after another he might find one that fit. Each of these ephemeral fictions is a kind of double, projected briefly onto the screen of the imagination, whose soothing power over their creator consists in the shapeliness of the story they tell. We have mentioned Kierkegaard's fascination for another mode of fiction, the theater. One has the impression that his *Journal* becomes, in these sketches, a kind of private theater. The spectator need only choose among the characters on his stage; better still there was no need to choose, for any character would do; all that was required was the momentary illusion of a form, a living reminder that somewhere in the sea of broken thoughts a continuity was to be found.

Kierkegaard had a weakness for self-dramatization. A role well acted gave body to the idea that lay behind it. It mingled, in a way that evoked life itself, the thought and the act. A "character" was, by definition, his own contemporary. "This was also why I wanted to be an *Actor;* by entering into someone else's role to gain a substitute for my own existence, and by this superficial change to find a certain distraction." He liked to summarize himself and his melancholy in aphorisms that were slightly melodramatic; images sparking into life out of the tense effort to coincide with himself, which gave pleasure through their very simplicity, born of exaggeration: "A strange desire comes to me sometimes, to do a dance step, snapping my fingers, and then . . . to die." "I am Janus *bifrons:* one of my faces laughs, the other cries." More curious than the number and variety of these imaginary scenes, however, is their sketchiness. Never do they take on the complexity and the independence of good fiction; as if Kierkegaard were not sufficiently interested in these substitute lives to follow them through, to truly "create" them. Later, when he divided the progress of the spiritual life into three stages, he placed the work of imagination in the first stage: the "aestheti-

cal," thereby making clear that the pleasures of fiction were perhaps admirable but had to be left behind if one were to undertake the hard task of self-understanding. As early as 1835, when
the passage quoted above was written, he considered his desire
to be an actor as a kind of self-indulgence. His behavior during
the rupture of his engagement to Regina indicates that the self-
indulgence, in his eyes, lay not so much in the talent for invent-
ing roles as in the aesthetic illusion of the stage. If one needed
to act a part, the only stage was life itself; and if the "illusion"
was to have any value in this larger theater, it had to be entirely
convincing. Let a single person detect the premeditation, and
the whole enterprise would fall out of life back into the aesthetical; worse, it would become nothing but a vulgar lie. Secrecy, a
complete rupture between the inward life and the outward
appearance, was necessary if the role was to be effective.

The great event in Kierkegaard's life was the episode of his
engagement to Regina Olsen. He loved Regina intensely yet
because of a blemish in his character—he was later to call it
his "thorn in the flesh"—he felt that it would be impossible for
him to lead a normal married life. His only choice then was to
break the engagement. In order to detach Regina from him entirely, Kierkegaard decided to play the part of a seducer in the
eyes of all Copenhagen. For months he loitered in theaters and
let it be generally understood that he was a man of doubtful
morals. To Regina he explained that he had merely been toying
with her, and now needed to pass on to fresh interests; that one
day perhaps when he was tired and older he might take some
young girl and settle down, but that was in the distant future.
His behavior in this affair is almost unbearable. The passages in
the *Journal* which refer to Regina are painful to read, they are
so filled with self-justification, annoyance at Regina's "sentimen-
tality," and a kind of fascination at the power over the girl his
"plan" had given him. And yet he suffered greatly because of his
decision, for in his own eyes he had chosen the only way to

remain truly faithful to a woman he continued to love until the end of his life.

The story would have no more than biographical interest, if Kierkegaard had not made it the scarcely veiled subject of all those works he later called his aesthetical writings. He knew that his fate hinged upon this inability to lead a normal life—to "express the general," as he put it in *Fear and Trembling*. The spiritual quest undertaken years earlier in the *Journal* would be consolidated not by words and imagination but by the act of life itself. In his case this meant an act of deepening isolation. His affair with Regina made this clear to him once and for all. Looking back on it, he recognized that if he had managed to "become something, it was because of that step."

The parable of Abraham in *Fear and Trembling* gives, for the first time, a public voice to the conflicts that overwhelmed Kierkegaard at this moment of painful self-confrontation. Abraham received from God a sign intelligible only to himself, commanding him to offer up in sacrifice the source of his only earthly happiness, Isaac, the son of his late years. Abraham's love for Isaac was inexpressible; equally inexpressible was the certainty which invaded him at the recognition of this inward sign from God. There was no common ground on which these certainties could meet; no judge to whom Abraham could appeal. He could not hint even a word of his conflict, since the very notion of a sign from God, entirely private, ordering him to transgress the most elementary law of earthly happiness, could be understood by no one but himself. Still, Abraham knew what he must do. His love for Isaac could scarcely be greater. Obedience to the inward sign—to his *magister interior*—did not replace the earthly love; yet Abraham did not hesitate, and from this moment on his life, for Kierkegaard, was a pure expression of the "Idea." His acts coincided with a pure inward determination; he set out with his son on the road to Mt. Moriah.

The pages that tell and retell this simple parable are among the most beautiful Kierkegaard wrote. They movingly express the double allegiance which for Kierkegaard lay at the heart of our earthly fate. He "sacrificed" Regina to his "thorn in the flesh," thereby stepping beyond the private absurdity of his existence. Like Abraham with Isaac, he loved Regina, in whom resided his one chance for earthly happiness. Yet he sacrificed her, in accordance with a sign which he took to be from God.

When we read the *Journal*, we are aware of a discrepancy between the highly moral lyricism of many passages in *Fear and Trembling* and *Repetition*, and those pathological bits of the reality which he transcribed privately, for his own use. Into the gap of this discrepancy have been fitted, at one time or another, various diagnoses based on the categories of abnormal psychology, which characterize Kierkegaard as a schizophrenic, a latent homosexual, a cyclothymic, a masochist, etc. Kierkegaard himself would not have disagreed with the verdict of abnormality. It was this abnormality he called his "thorn in the flesh"; and despite obsessive reticence about such matters, he went so far as to consult a doctor about it. In the private conversation of the *Journal*, he had for years acknowledged signs of his illness; he had analyzed them unflinchingly, and come to a verdict of what, in more recent language, we would describe as narcissism: obsessive self-preoccupation:

> Like a solitary pine tree, egotistically hugging itself and growing only upward, I stand without casting any shadow . . .

> How horrible it is when all of history dissolves before the morbid preoccupation of our own tiny history . . . one seems to be the only person ever to have existed past, present, or future.

> Is there a worse danger, a worse paralysis, than to isolate yourself, endlessly gazing only on your own self? The history of the world, the life of men, in short everything, disappears; and, like the Omphalopsychites sitting in an egotistical circle, you end up seeing nothing but your own belly button.

Kierkegaard knew that he had been born on the extreme edge of sanity, and that all his life he would run "the danger of isolation," the danger of "withdrawing too completely from the bonds of society." He was fascinated by the relationship between "genius" and "madness," for he was aware both of his own genius and of the fragile limits of his sanity.

Like Abraham, who received a son when it would have been reasonable to have given up hope, Kierkegaard had also been given a reprieve, a momentary hope. He had met Regina, and discovered, against every possibility of his illness, that he loved her. Then a secret premonition intervened warning him that he had been mistaken. He broke the engagement, in the manner already described, and abandoned himself once and for all to the danger of his self-preoccupation. Having lost the only real person he could have loved, he writes:

> I have still one intimate confidant, just one . . . my melancholy; in the midst of my pleasure, my work, she makes signs at me, and calls me aside, though my body doesn't move; she is truly the most faithful mistress I have known. Is it surprising then that I must always be ready to follow her?

Kierkegaard notes somewhere that he would have given anything to lead a normal life, even if only for six months. Here, in the *Journal,* he sadly reports the failure of his hope; there will be no respite, not for six months nor even for a minute.

It is the other side of the discrepancy, however, which has given Kierkegaard a permanent voice in the development of modern philosophy—not the private failure, but his translation of the failure into a thought about "existence," and above all into a plan for action. To Kierkegaard, the break with Regina was important, not because it marked a failure, but because it made a writer of him: it gave permanent contours to his "melancholy," allowing him to grasp the values of "inwardness" in a way that shaped not only his own life but all lives. Regina in this sense was not his love but his muse. As the young man in *Repetition* was to say: he hadn't loved her, he had only "longed for her." Her absence was the only means by which she could be truly present to him, and so marriage was impossible. This recalls the courtly *leys d'amor*, in which the lover weaves poems out of his own emotion, praising a lady he longs for but cannot love. In *Repetition*, Kierkegaard goes even further: "The girl is not a reality but a reflection of the movements within him and their exciting cause . . . her existence or nonexistence was in a certain sense of no importance to him."

What, then, was important to him? Years earlier Kierkegaard had described "inward action" as "the divine side of man." Now, in *Fear and Trembling,* he expresses a thought that will lead him year by year to the Category of Isolation. "Faith is the paradox that inwardness is higher than outwardness." More pressing than the obligations of the world are "the inward determinants of feelings, mood, etc." What Kierkegaard before had described as a danger—the danger of narcissism—now becomes a secret language of the spirit: the way God has chosen to make Himself known to men. The image in the water, the true self for which Kierkegaard had expressed a nameless, almost erotic nostalgia, is now discovered to lie where no one had thought to look for it. Stendhal had tried to brush aside the moods and feelings (his *cent folies*) in order to grasp the clear shape of an image they had spoiled. Rousseau, convinced by the natural harmony of his "innocence," knew that the moods and feelings were themselves innocent; for a man sufficiently "natural," they presented no problem. But the moods and feelings of "inwardness" have value for Kierkegaard only *because* they present a problem. A man's true self is not obscured by the idiosyncrasy of his emotions; on the contrary, it is to be found in a certain way of experiencing those idiosyncrasies. For Kierkegaard, this was the way of faith. God is not revealed to "man" but to individuals. Individuality—the irreducible, incommunicable "unlikeness" that isolates one man from another—is the vessel of revelation. This is the paradox which, for Kierkegaard, can be accepted only through faith. A man must embrace the full storm of his existence, "for the conclusions of passion are the only reliable ones."

Like Pythagoras and Socrates, to whom he refers, Kierkegaard knew the dangers of the Greek "Know Thyself"; he knew that "by delving deep into oneself one would first of all discover the disposition to evil." This is one of the perils which the inward-looking hero must undergo if he is to transpose even this disposition for evil into the transparency of his self-communion. He obtains certainty, not by curing the Unlikeness or by hiding it—in Kierkegaard's vision there is no difference—but by accepting the loneliness and the suffering, the unsavory impulses, the idiosyncrasies which *are* the Unlikeness. Only by advancing farther and farther into the storm does one discover the eye of the storm. Without the storm, there is no eye: no seeing.

Abraham became a "hero of faith" because he allowed the full range of his individuality to play within him: he refused nothing, neither his love for Isaac nor his confidence in the invisible sign which required that he sacrifice Isaac. Every step on the road to Mt. Moriah sharpened the paradox of these irreconcilable demands. If he, at any point, renounced his love for Isaac, he would become an impersonal agent, a selfless moment in the flow of transcendence; if he refused the inner sign, he would become a victim of his own worldliness. Instead, according to Kierkegaard, he did the impossible: he fully accepted both demands, even as he was about to raise the knife. This was the miracle, for Kierkegaard. And this was why he could receive Isaac back again, when the ram was seen in a nearby bush. The miracle of the "absurd" lies in this reconciliation between opposing terms of our experience, neither of which can be ignored: on the one hand the demands of society, the public requirements of speech and morality; on the other, the private demands of "inwardness."

Kierkegaard makes it clear that Abraham underwent a heroic ordeal; he did battle in himself and conquered his terrible solitude. In doing so, he changed his life. By confiding "absurdly"—i.e., through faith—in his inward nature, by listening to the *magister interior*, the interior God, he found an immovable center which confirmed his individuality. On this subject Kierkegaard notes, "It is only the lower natures which find in other people the law for their actions, which find the premises for their actions outside themselves." The antinomian consequences of such a vision are clear, and Kierkegaard is aware of them, especially in those passages where he meditates on the difference between Abraham, the hero of faith, and a common infanticide. "People are afraid," he acknowledges, "that the worst will happen as soon as the individual takes it into his head to comport himself as the individual."

On this point there are no simple distinctions. In the final analysis, he writes, "Whether the individual is in temptation or is a knight of faith, only the individual can decide." The originality of *Fear and Trembling* lies in the solution to this problem which Kierkegaard discovered inscribed in his own character. The true hero of faith expresses his inward autonomy paradoxically. He does not act in any extraordinary way; on the contrary, he appears from the outside to be entirely, even excessively, "normal." Like the hero, he has given up all the common pleasures; all his worldly desires have been "bent inward." But then, "by virtue of the absurd," he receives those things he had abandoned, as Abraham received Isaac again, and as Kierkegaard, when he wrote *Fear and Trembling*, still hoped to receive Regina. The "knight of faith" lives in the world, a perfect image of the normal self Kierkegaard dreamed of becoming. But the new insight he has obtained into his individuality changes the quality of this worldliness. Kierkegaard borrows an idea from Leibnitz to express the apparent harmony between the knight of faith and the world: the idea of the *harmonia praestablita*, the pre-established harmony. Leibnitz' Monads only seem to interact. In reality they are folded into themselves, generating the course of their existence from a purely inward necessity. The knight of faith is similarly self-generating, but the self he generates has acquired a new dimension. By descending "into the underworld"—into the hidden recesses of his privacy— he has "obtained the beloved"; but he is himself the beloved. He has obtained himself. A few lines farther on, Kierkegaard expresses this in another way: "He who does the work gives birth to his own father."

There are many ways of reading this strange aphorism which might find its place among Blake's Proverbs of Hell. He who does the work earns the self-enlacing plenitude of the hermaphrodite, begetting out of himself the principle of his own being and pleasure; he becomes, thereby, his own father. He who does the work becomes his own "authority," his own witness, judge, and prosecutor. Kierkegaard has been accused, with some justice, of advocating an extreme form of authoritarian religion. He himself insists that obedience, submission to absolute authority, must lie at the heart of the religious life: "In case a son were to say, 'I obey my father, not because he is my father but because . . . his commands are always profound and clever' —then . . . the son accentuates something which is entirely beside the point . . . (and) undermines obedience." A contradiction between this sense of obedience and Kierkegaard's lifelong refusal to submit to any authority whatsoever is often indicated. The contradiction, however, is only apparent. For "he who does the work," gives birth to the only authority worthy of absolute obedience: the inward father, the *magister interior*, God.

Transposed into the language of theology, Kierkegaard's "proverb" becomes even more curious. He who does the work does not discover God within him, he "gives birth" to God, building Him by the labor of his work. This is far from the traditional scope of authoritarian religion. It recalls the poetry of Angelus Silesius, the seventeenth-century German mystic, who wrote, "I know God cannot live a moment without me: / If I should come to nothing God shall cease to be." It also looks forward rather unexpectedly to Rilke's unchristian sense of spiritual labor, as in these lines from the *Book of Hours:* "We are all workingmen: prentice, journeyman, / Or master, building you—you towering nave." Or these:

> What will you do, God, when I die?
> When I your pitcher broken lie?
> When I, your drink, go stale or dry?
> I am your garb, the trade you ply,
> You lose your meaning, losing me.

Kierkegaard's religion is authoritarian only because the son, through the work of his "inward action," must become the father, owing obedience to this new dimension of his own selfhood.

Rarely has religion been grounded so entirely in subjectivity. And this is precisely the insight which has made Kierkegaard one of the fathers of modern existentialism. Even in *Fear and Trembling,* where the accent is on a paradoxical harmony with the common life, the Category of Isolation governs Kierkegaard's vision. In a world of change, where illusion and doubt predominate—a brief autobiographical sketch in the *Journal* is entitled *de omnibus dubitandum*—the only meaningful center of authority lies in a man's inward life. To be one's own contemporary, in Kierkegaard's language, is to coincide at all times with this source of unimpeachable authority. In the language of modern existentialism, this means to have become "authentic," "autonomous," freed from servitude to all outward constraint.

The knight of faith, as Kierkegaard describes him in *Fear and Trembling,* does not reappear in the subsequent works. The paradox of harmony with the common life—and its personal reference to the hope that Regina will one day be his "by virtue of the absurd"—fades from Kierkegaard's immediate interests, largely because of two events which fixed the pattern of his life. Regina, finally convinced by Kierkegaard's behavior, decides not to die of chagrin; instead she becomes engaged to a respectable schoolmaster and marries him. This unexpectedly embittered Kierkegaard, unleashing a number of unfortunate reflections in his *Journal*. In any case, it closed the one gap he had left open in the thickening isolation of his life. He writes bitterly that if he had had faith, he could have married Regina. This goal now is closed to him forever.

The other event, several years later, is typically woven of malice, misunderstanding, and almost comical willfulness. By this time, Kierkegaard had acquired a reputation in the small intellectual world of Copenhagen. His polemical skills were feared. His brilliance and verbal grace were widely recognized. Through a series of foolish incidents, involving a dispute with some minor literary figure, Kierkegaard managed to provide a coarse attack against himself in a widely read scandal sheet, the *Corsaire*. What made the attack even more improbable is the fact that the director of the sheet had great respect for the man his paper smeared day after day and almost begged him to make some gesture to end the conflict. This Kierkegaard refused to do. When the episode ended the director was so unsettled by his success that he closed the paper and left Copenhagen. The immediate result of the *Corsaire* incident was to make Kierkegaard a notorious public figure. Everyone in Copenhagen, children, delivery boys, respected councilmen, recognized him and laughed with the *Corsaire* at his ridiculous toothpick legs, his flapping trousers, his clumsy gait.

Kierkegaard's polemical nature had always led him, in conversation, to provoke those around him. Now circumstances, at least half due to his own inclination, had plunged him into an atmosphere of vulgar hostility. A revealing passage in the *Journal*, dated several years earlier, helps to explain this provocative strain in Kierkegaard's character:

> I have the courage, I think, to doubt everything; to fight, I
> think, against everything. But the courage to recognize nothing,
> to possess nothing: that I lack. Most people complain that life
> is too prosaic, that life is not at all like those novels where lovers

are lucky; as for me, I complain that life is not like those novels where one has hardened fathers to fight against, virgins' bed-rooms to force open, convent walls to leap over. I have only the pale figures of the night, stubborn and bloodless, to battle with, and I am the one who gives them life and being.

In order to overcome his inward enemies—the fear, the anxiety, the melancholy—Kierkegaard needed to transform them, pro-jecting them into identifiable outward shapes, which he could then confront. Victory or defeat had less importance in this enterprise than the daily reality of the struggle itself. In fact defeat was preferable if the struggle was to endure.

In Kierkegaard's final understanding, the enemy would be vanquished only through his own daily defeat. This was the meaning Kierkegaard gave to his progress, both personal and theological, toward absolute, heroical solitude: the Category of Isolation. His unshakable model in this was no longer Abraham, who retained his worldly happiness, but Christ, who had to be defeated in the eyes of all Jerusalem for his message to become permanent in men. Christ's ordeal, for Kierkegaard, did not lie in the Passion, or in the pain of being nailed to the Cross:

> It is not that in death he was nailed on the cross, but that alive he bore the hard cross of incomprehension; an incomprehension so complete that his entire life seemed to have been in vain, that he seemed to have come into the world for nothing. . . . So he passed, solitary, abandoned, in the abandonment of men, who abandoned him by the very fact that they clamored curiously all around him. . . .

From here on Kierkegaard's "plan" is clear: by maintaining the barriers of incomprehension, by leading his painful solitude into the midst of hostility, he was to embody, as Christ himself had done, the heroic ordeal of solitude. His obsessive fear and secrecy had allowed him to confide in no one, if not in his own melancholy. Now, he notes ironically, by becoming an author—

and, even more, a controversial public figure—he has confided in the public. Through his own choice he has been surrounded by a city of witnesses and adversaries, all of whom are necessary if he is to fulfill his role. Isolation is no longer a danger for Kierkegaard. It is a role played out on the public stage of his life.

His "thorn in the flesh" had crippled his hopes for a normal existence, converting his every moment into an ordeal. Yet this very "thorn in the flesh" had opened the gates of the "underworld," and allowed Kierkegaard to "obtain the beloved." The way down into anxiety had become a way up toward possession of the beloved: possession of his "true self." Kierkegaard explains this clearly in many passages of the *Journal:*

> I threw myself into life with a leak in my hull from the first—and the very effort to keep afloat by endless pumping has made it possible for me to develop a spiritual existence which has rarely been equaled. My effort has succeeded. I've interpreted that suffering as a thorn in my flesh, and I've recognized the spiritual strength by the pain of the thorn, and the pain of the thorn by the spiritual strength. That is how I have understood myself.

> My thorn in the flesh has broken me forever as far as earthly life is concerned—but in the infinite I leap only the higher.

Yet, as we have seen, what the hero does for himself must also be done for others. By excluding himself from the common life the hero obtains a power to act on those who still lead that life. Thus the logic of Kierkegaard's ordeal required that he return toward those he had left behind. This was his justification for becoming an author and a public figure. He increasingly interprets the entire movement of his life in terms of this "plan" to convert the willfully thickened web of his "failures" into a heroic redemption of the general failure of his times. He writes, "The literary, social, and political situation having need of someone extraordinary, the question is to know whether there is anyone in Denmark capable of assuming this role, aside from myself."

Before judging too severely the self-exaggeration of passages like this one, we should remember that the man who wrote it was already a public figure whose genius was widely recognized, even if it was also feared and ridiculed. Indeed the effect he hoped to obtain was a complicated one. The message of his writings had to be hammered home, but in such a way that their author would never constitute an "authority." He himself, by living as an outcast in the midst of Copenhagen, would discourage all disciples. For the only authority a man needed to comply with lay within him, and it was not to be discovered but rather to be created by the discipline of isolation. Like Nietzsche after him, Kierkegaard knew the absurdity of discipleship: "As long as I live, I cannot be recognized, for only a few people can understand me; and if I begin to be recognized, I would have to use all my energy, through the use of other ruses, in order to prevent it." Thus Kierkegaard arrives at his final isolation. The barriers have been carried into place. The melancholy has become first a thorn in the flesh and then a doorway down into the private ordeal of the hero. Individuality has been proclaimed as the paradoxical vessel of God on earth: not the "spiritual impatience" of the mystic, who aims at transcending the self, but the heightened selfhood of isolation, lived day after day by the exemplary hero, the Isolated One.

Kierkegaard never forgot the dangers of "narcissism" which hung over his early manhood. Even later he was aware that his exemplary life, and his theology, continued to resemble some extreme illness of the self. The difference, he knew, was all but invisible; it could be seen only by those who were themselves sensitive to the transformations of "inwardness." He expressed this idea in a passage in the *Journal* which is a fitting close to our discussion:

> The relationship of the Isolated One to God is, in the eyes of the world, only egotism. Since the world, deep down, does not

believe in God, the one who fears God must, in the final analysis, love only himself—the one who fears God does not, in fact, love what the world loves; then what is there left? God and himself: but the world eliminates God: thus the one who fears God loves only himself. The world considers the fear of God to be egotism.

11 MELVILLE'S WORLD OF CHANGE IN *MOBY DICK*

Moby Dick describes a world of continual movement, as if Melville saw the objects of his world only as they changed into one another and then changed again, inscrutably, often murderously. The sailors of the *Pequod* are like wrestlers who turn nervously from side to side to keep an adversary at bay. A false step, one relapse into stillness, and the next wave will bury them. Melville is a great poet of movement. His descriptions of the whale hunt—the tense skill of the harpooners, the foam and thunder of the caught whales, the death flurries, the sudden squalls—all reveal a sense of violent action which has rarely been equaled.

These epitomes of violence, however, are only the more jagged curves on a background of still further movement. In *Moby Dick* nothing twice occurs in the same place. Even stillness is but a steadier form of change. The rocking of the waves on a calm day, the slow sparkling sunlight stretching as far as the eye can see—this is as close as Melville approaches to the fixed shapes that inspire confidence and convince us that one moment will resemble another. After having been dragged through a herd of hunting whales, one of the *Pequod's* boats glides into a sudden calm:

> Here the storms in the roaring glens between the outermost whales were heard but not felt. In this central expanse the sea presented that smooth, satin-like surface, called a sleek, produced

by the subtle moisture thrown off by the whale in one of his calmer moods. Yes, we were now in that enchanted calm which they say lurks at the heart of every commotion.

The stillness emanates from the very churning of the outermost whales; it is the eye of the storm, the inner side of the surrounding violence. At a signal it will dissolve into a flurry of waves and stray fish.

In this world of water and flux, made to the measure of both Thales and Heraclitus, the points of reference have been thrust out of sight. The shores are treacherous; the land is less a haven than a failed freedom, an energy that has been repressed. Bulkington's brief "epitaph" is meant to tell us this:

> Know ye, now, Bulkington? Glimpses do ye seem to see of that mortally intolerable truth; that all deep, earnest thinking is but the intrepid effort of the soul to keep the open independence of her sea; while the wildest winds of heaven and earth conspire to cast her on the treacherous, slavish shore?
>
> But as in landlessness alone resides the highest truth, shoreless, indefinite as God—so, better is it to perish in that howling infinite, than be ingloriously dashed upon the lee, even if that were safety! For worm-like, then, oh! who would craven crawl to land!

The whaler, more than any other boat, has renounced the stable continent. Men-o'-war are merely floating fortresses; merchantmen are movable bits of land, connecting one shore to another. Their souls are land-bound. But the whaler has no destination; it follows the natural rhythm of the sea and wanders with the season. It leaves port equipped for years of landlessness, a self-contained, single-minded creature whose business is part of the very heartlessness of the sea itself: the business of murder, for which it is even more gifted than the sharks that always accompany it. We are perhaps all "killers," as Melville says, but some of us, it seems, are more so than others. And the sea is the element of this perpetual alteration; it embodies a kind of moral liquidity, in which the most familiar gesture contains a mystery. The most alluring scene has a "dark hindoo half" that will flow out of it in an instant: "Consider the subtleness of the sea; how its most dreaded creatures glide under the water, unapparent for the most part, and treacherously hidden beneath the loveliest tints of azure."

Not since Montaigne, or since the Shakespeare of *Troilus and Cressida,* has a writer advanced so deeply into this realm of "ungraspable phantoms." For Melville was convinced that this dangerous liquidity of all things was more than a special condition of the world at sea; it described all earthly experience. "Panting and snorting like a mad battle steed that has lost its rider, the masterless ocean overruns the globe." Like the ocean rising and falling on all sides of them, the men of the *Pequod* race in one direction and then another, "not so much bound to any haven ahead as rushing from all havens astern." In the end, Bulkington's epitaph becomes their own; when land can no longer be a haven, the only haven that remains is at the bottom of the sea. The ocean becomes a murderous solvent, and the universe itself, when seen from a slippery deck, resembles "a vast practical joke." The horizon shows nothing firm enough to hold on to, and the heavens are no more revealing. The sounding whale becomes a symbol of the general collapse of one thing into another, the highest into the lowest: "Out of the bottomless profundities, the gigantic tail seems spasmodically snatching at the highest heaven." The very notion of a goal, of a finished achievement, becomes impossible. The *Bachelor,* loaded with oil, its voyage delightfully ended, is a scandal in the world of *Moby Dick,* and Ahab is understandably scornful. Even the idea of a finished book, a work of art, becomes a dishonesty, and Melville interjects: "God keep me from ever completing anything. This whole book is but a draught—nay but the draught of a draught."

The author, the men of the *Pequod,* Captain Ahab in whose shadow they are all driven, travel on this sea of unfinishable forms, surrounded "by all the horrors of the half-known life."

They are pursued by the very thing which causes Pip, the cabin boy, to go mad: the indeterminate, changing vastness of their element. The day Pip was left floating in miles of "shoreless ocean" the water was calm, as easy to ride in as "a spring carriage ashore": But "the awful lonesomeness [was] intolerable. The intense concentration of self in the middle of such a heartless immensity, my God! who can tell it?" Several hours later the *Pequod* rescued him; but Pip had been driven so deeply into himself by the terrible shorelessness that he never found his way out again. There are more ways of drowning than one. Pip, "jeeringly" kept afloat by the sea, was drowned in his own self. "Not drowned entirely, though. Rather carried down alive to wondrous depths . . ." Pip was driven mad by fear, loneliness, uncertainty: so the verdict goes. But the inner side of his madness tells another story; it is a side which Ahab, though he senses and sympathizes with it, will never entirely grasp. Pip, radically abandoned, forced to look squarely at the unveiled heartlessness of his sea world, discovers an ambiguous haven: the "one insular Tahiti" in the soul. His mind is cut loose from the world that everyone sees; it is driven inward and upward, until he glimpses, far inside himself, something of "heaven's sense":

> He saw God's foot upon the treadle of the loom, and spoke it; and therefore his shipmates called him mad. So man's insanity is heaven's sense; and wandering from all mortal reason, man comes at last to that celestial thought, which, to reason, is absurd and frantic; and weal or woe, feels then uncompromised, indifferent as his God.

Pip's madness and Ahab's are meant to reflect on one another. They are parts of a single madness. Melville's model here is undoubtedly Shakespeare, especially those scenes in *King Lear* where Lear and his fool interwine their different insanities as they huddle together against the storm. In *Moby Dick* the storm has become the sea, half physical, half spiritual, that plays with man's half-mad intentions as do wanton boys with flies. Ahab, like Pip, has been locked into himself by his encounter with the sea. He has fastened his grip on the one firm thing he knows: not the shore, but his own self, his will, his "inner spaciousness." He is less "mad" than Pip, because he is more earthly: his deformed will is aimed at the world and is guided by a very earthly intelligence (Ahab is a good whaling captain). But he is also less "wise"; what Pip sees clearly, Ahab battles to get a glimpse of. Where Pip is madly lucid—the fool's role!—Ahab is a heroic fool. Melville tells us that all earthly greatness "is but disease": "all men tragically great are made so through a certain morbidness." Ahab's greatness is demonic, but it is an earthly greatness, founded on his "monomaniac" will to measure up to what the world has thrust upon him: his life can only resolve itself in action. But spiritually Ahab is a failure, and that is where his tragedy lies. He will never have an inkling of that "celestial thought" which lies at the root of Pip's folly: the uncompromised, godlike "indifference"; the condition of inner self-sufficiency named *ataraxy* by the stoics.

One of the fascinations of *Moby Dick* has always been its elusiveness. Melville prepares our imagination for great symbolic meanings; his rhetoric links every detail of the sea adventure into a net of spiritual cross-references. Yet, as we proceed, the symbols glide out of reach. The white whale above all refuses to yield to any simple or single understanding. This is perhaps the kind of complication we expect from any good symbolic language. But *Moby Dick* breaks all the rules. Its symbols are more elusive than most, to the point of confusion. The line of thought we have taken up, however, allows us to shift the basis of the enigma. The multi-meaningful symbols of the book do not come together easily, precisely because the mood of their adventure is one of disrupted meanings, of forms shifting dangerously into each other until they defy all human understanding. Ahab's heroism comes from his relentless insistence on making things clear: on reducing the flux to some recognizable shape. This meant, perhaps, turning Moby Dick into a mere whale, accessible as other whales, killable, and finally even useful because of his harvest of barrelable oil. Ahab failed because he attempted the impossible; also because he never understood just what it was he was looking for.

Melville inserts a passage at the beginning of his book which can be read as a comment on Ahab's tragedy:

> Why did the old Persians hold the sea holy? Why did the Greeks give it a separate deity, and own brother of Jove? Surely all this is not without meaning. And still deeper the meaning of that story of Narcissus, who because he could not grasp the tormenting, mild image he saw in the fountain, plunged into it and was drowned. But that same image, we ourselves see in all rivers and oceans. It is the image of the ungraspable phantom of life; and this is the key to it all.

We know, at this point, that Moby Dick has no "key." The above passage, however, sheds an interesting light on Ahab's "monomania": the one fixed energy in a world of change. Ahab, like Pip, has been driven into himself by his encounter with the sea. And now, with the "pride" and the deluded energy of a demiurge, he tries to grasp the ungraspable, to mold the chaotic waters into his own image; to reduce the unknowable to what he knows best. Pip, maddened and made wise by his glimpse through the veil, rises into himself; he abandons the world which has abandoned him. Ahab, made of more familiar mettle, more earthly strong and, finally, more "human," reaches after the murderous images and the elusive gliding fins in order to make them answer to his own inwardness. Unlike Empedocles, he will not leap into the volcano until he himself has become the volcano.

Close to the center of all human experience, for Melville, is a painful separateness which can never be fully accepted by those who become aware of it. The intense solitude can force a man to surpass himself if he is endowed with spiritual heroism;

or he can be defeated by the solitude and retreat into a half-aware humanity which is not without honor though it has the mark of defeat on it. The latter case describes Starbuck, the *Pequod's* first mate, who is tempted by his insight into Ahab's ambition, though he never ceases to erect barriers of "prudence" between himself and his captain.

The *Pequod's* crew reflect this separateness of human experience: they are all islanders, Isolatoes: "Isolatoes too, I call such, not acknowledging the common continent of men, but each Isolatoe living on a separate continent of his own." Yet they are bound together, "federated along one keel," by a solitude more powerful than theirs: they all swear allegiance to Ahab's insanity, thereby verifying Emerson's opinion that all institutions are but the "lengthened shadow" of one man. Only Ahab refuses this, or any other form of brotherhood. Though he casts the shadow, he will swear no allegiance to it, or indeed to anything but his own will. In order to obey himself, he refuses all other obedience and, like Narcissus, turns away from men, so as to see more clearly the shape in the water:

> Though nominally included in the census of Christendom, he was still an alien to it. He lived in the world as the last of the Grisly Bears lived in settled Missouri. And as when Spring and Summer had departed, the wild Logan of the woods, burying himself in the hollow of a tree, lived out the winter there, sucking his own paws, so, in his inclement, howling old age, Ahab's soul, shut up in the caved trunk of his body, there fed upon the sullen paws of its gloom.

Ahab has resigned from humanity, and now his only companion is the image mirrored back to him by his own pain: "Ahab and anguish lay stretched together in one hammock." "He sleeps with clenched hands; and wakes with his own bloody nails in his palms." The terrible "concentration of self" which accompanies suffering has made Ahab more than a man. He is strangely self-sufficient, feeding on himself, nourishing his will out of his own pain: "God help thee, old man, thy thoughts have created a creature in thee; and he whose intense thinking thus makes him a Prometheus; a vulture feeds upon that heart forever; that vulture the very creature he creates."

Melville's Narcissus pays for his single-minded folly. He reaches after the ungraspable and drowns. Ahab also discovers that the inwardness he seeks to transfigure by the sheer power of his will is made of no firmer stuff than the elusive world around him. The more he grasps at it, the more it sinks away from him. He too, like Narcissus, is engaged in the "tormented chase of that demon phantom that some time or other swims before all human hearts," "the gliding great demon of the seas of life." But whenever he reaches toward it, it eludes him, as he eludes himself, only to reach out more frantically than before. What he finds dissolves before his eyes; the haven of the self yields finally to the same murderous changefulness that governs the sea world: "Ahab leaned over the side and watched how his shadow in the water sank and sank to his gaze, the more and the more that he strove to pierce the profundity."

Ahab's obsession forces him to pursue the sinking shadow; it forces him also to refuse any gentle, more human image that the mirror might reflect back. Locked into his pain, transfigured by it, Ahab looks for the image of himself that is least recognizable: the image of his monomania. When the time comes, he will look down at the water and find the shape, not floating on an illusory surface, but rising up from the very bottom of the waters:

> Ahab could discover no sign in the sea. But suddenly as he peered down and down into its depths, he profoundly saw a white, living spot no bigger than a white weasel, with wonderful celerity uprising, and magnifying as it rose, till it turned, and then there were plainly revealed two long crooked rows of white, glistening teeth, floating up from the undiscoverable bottom.

It is his sinking shadow, coming back to meet him in the form of Moby Dick. Before the fatal encounter, however, Ahab must work to simplify his elusive self, to make it hard and unyielding, like the perfect man he dreams of ordering from his blacksmith, equipped with "no heart at all, brass forehead, and about a quarter of an acre of fine brains." Above all, he must avoid the softening brotherhood of friendship and compassion; the mutual transparency of hearts that mirrors each man back to himself in a style of perfect understanding. Starbuck is a danger not because he might weaken the crew's allegiance to Ahab with his all too human dissension, but because he might weaken Ahab's allegiance to himself, or at least to that pain-transfigured image of himself which he has chosen.

In a moment of weakness, Ahab looks into the eyes of his first mate and cries out, "This is the magic glass, man; I see my wife and child in thine eye." The mirror contains all the images; to be drowned in it means to be confronted with more selves than one. Goethe's Mephistopheles knew the secret that man is twofold. Ahab must unravel this secret and then throw away one of the strands. After the painful recognition which Starbuck thrusts upon him, Ahab is troubled, he looks over the side of the boat and finds this time something firmer than a sinking shadow: he sees "two reflected fixed eyes in the water there. Fedallah was motionlessly leaning over the same rail."

It is a singular fact that when Ahab looks into himself, he never finds quite what he expected. Here he discovers not his own reflected eyes but those of his shadowy double, Fedallah: the dark twin common to the mythology of the heroic quest. Fedallah glides through the book, more like a shadow than a full-blown character. He strengthens the dark side of Ahab's will, having "some sort of half-hinted influence" and even a kind of "authority" over him. Melville sows many hints through the book which tend to blend the two men into each other, linking their inmost characters. On one occasion "Ahab chanced so to stand, that the Parsee occupied his shadow; while, if the Parsee's shadow was there at all it seemed only to blend with and lengthen Ahab's." As the final chase approaches, Ahab gives himself over more and more completely to the demonic reflection he finds in Fedallah. When, for the last time, Ahab weakens at the image in Starbuck's eyes, Fedallah's reflected eyes bring him back to his other, chosen self.

In the end Ahab dies because he cannot reach deeper than this image floating on the surface of his life: his own image, or rather that of his inner affliction, his outrage at the world's absurd cruelty toward him. Ahab cannot or will not see that Moby Dick is a whale, a huge animal with a brain the size of a cantaloupe; in D. H. Lawrence's words: a lonely, warm-blooded leviathan; even lovable, and not at all of the "Hobbes sort." Instead, the "white whale swam before him as the monomaniac incarnation of all those malicious agencies which some deep men feel eating in them, till they are left living on with half a heart and half a lung." Wherever he looks, it is Ahab and anguish lashed together until his pride, bred on suffering, gives him nothing less than the world as his mirror. During one of his nightly turns on the quarterdeck, Ahab stops to look at the gold doubloon he has nailed to the mast, offered to the first who sights the white whale. Seeing the design of three mountain peaks stamped on it, topped, one by a flame, one by a tower, and one by a crowing cock, he meditates:

> There's something ever egotistical in mountain-tops and towers, and all other grand and lofty things; look here,—three peaks as proud as Lucifer. The firm tower, that is Ahab; the volcano, that is Ahab; the courageous, the undaunted, and victorious fowl, that, too, is Ahab; all are Ahab; and this round gold is but the image of the rounder globe, which, like a magician's glass, to each and every man in turn but mirrors back his own mysterious self.

When, at the end of the passage on Narcissus, Melville concludes, "This is the key to it all," the words are not meant as a rhetorical flourish. There are perhaps no "keys" to the elusiveness of Melville's sea world; but there is a truth about human experience which takes form as the book proceeds. Ahab's madness has raised walls about him; it has sealed him into himself and made a prisoner of him. This Promethean isolation gives Ahab the stature of a hero, for his monomaniac will becomes a challenge to the gods: in a world of impenetrable change, only Ahab chooses to stand firm. "How can the prisoner reach outside except by thrusting through the wall? To me the white whale is that wall, shoved near me." Ahab doesn't understand that his own self-bound emotions have erected the wall. The source of his strength is also the reason for his failure. He looks at the emblematic world of the doubloon and sees only Ahab; just as God, in the mystical metaphor, looks at the world He has created and sees His own image reflected in it. Ahab, however, has not created the world; what he sees is a delusion. He has, in fact, become blind to what the world, in Melville's vision, really is: a dangerous, inscrutable, sometimes beautiful wave.

Ahab is, finally, earthly and not spiritual; but he is also blind. And his, in Melville's opinion, is a blindness common to all men; it belongs to the very nature of our experience, since the round globe, we are told, is like a "magician's glass," mirroring back to each man his own half-familiar image. Melville would undoubtedly have echoed Nietzsche's and Freud's definition of man as the sick animal. For Ahab's madness lies at the extreme limit of that madness from which all men suffer: the madness of the self. This is dramatized by the succession of brief monologues following Ahab's meditation on the doubloon. Starbuck, Stubb, Flask, Queequeg all gaze at the coin, each reading into it an image of his own preoccupation. Pip, who has followed all this from in hiding, echoes Ahab's first insight: "I look, you look, he looks; we look, ye look, they look." His fool's chorus underscores the self-bound vision of each man. Between the "inner spaciousness" which Melville tells us to cultivate, and that other spaciousness which surrounds each one of us, the lines have been cut. We are afloat in ourselves, Melville writes, and our hard fate will be to drown, like Pip, in the inner sea, or like Ahab in the outer one.

12 BAUDELAIRE, THE WAY OF THE ALCHEMIST

"He who does the work becomes his own father." For Kierke-gaard, this meant to immure himself in his personality, trans-forming the base metal of his character into a pure selfhood. The alchemical metaphor may appear exotic in reference to so austere a Christian as Sören Kierkegaard; yet it is accurate on more than one count. The alchemist embraces the "imperfect" metals; by entering the secret of their imperfection, he allows them to be-come what, potentially, they already are: pure gold. To obtain the gold, he must know the metals intimately; he must become sensitive to their most imperceptible rhythms. His intimacy with all that is base in the metals enables the alchemist to gain power over them. By "doing the work," he creates the father of all metals: gold. The alchemist, however, is not interested only in gold. The goal of Chinese alchemy, for example, was immor-tality: to transmute the imperfect metal of the body into a sub-stance more durable than human limitation could allow. By applying the science and the personal discipline of his craft, the alchemist transformed his own humanity.

The language of Western alchemy also has a double mean-ing: what is said about the metals may be applied, esoterically, to the initiate himself. The chemicals, the shifts in color and temperature, the alembics, become symbols for an invisible operation: that by which the alchemist converts his imperfect nature into a pure spiritual element. Like Kierkegaard, he does this not by turning away from his fragmented self but by transmuting it, with all its imperfections, into a purer, more permanent form. This moral alchemy, which was popular among occultists in the nineteenth century, resembles the traditions of high magic popularized by men like Eliphas Levi, who wrote of the Magus that his "Great Work" is none other than the regeneration of the ego. The resemblance between Eliphas Levi's "Great Work" and Kierkegaard's, by which a man creates his own father, is striking.

We must not forget, of course, that Kierkegaard was a Christian. The *magister interior* to whom he owed allegiance resembles the harsh God of the Old Testament: the God who tried Job and Abraham. The Great Work, for Kierkegaard, was to regenerate the ego, but only because the ego opened inward toward its center—i.e., toward the Authority whose word must be obeyed. The Isolated One only seems to be an "egotist"; in reality he adores a God whose difference from the ego is infinitely subtle, yet unmistakable for one who sees correctly.

The *philosophia perennis* seeks also to regenerate the ego; yet it introduces us to a mood of discovery and self-discovery which is far from Kierkegaard's austere theology. Occultism was a great favorite among nineteenth-century poets: Victor Hugo, Baudelaire, Rimbaud, Mallarmé, Yeats were drawn to it in various ways, conceiving the Great Work of their poetry in terms which owed much to the ideas and vocabulary of magic, alchemy, and the kabbala. There has been a great deal of speculation concerning the influence of the occult sciences on these poets. To what extent were they actually initiated into the esoteric traditions? How accurate is their use of occult terminology in the poems? We know that Victor Hugo, during his exile in Jersey, spent long days turning tables and taking dictation from the spiritual voices he heard. We know that Villiers de l'Isle-Adam introduced Mallarmé into various occult circles; that Yeats experimented with occult symbols and belonged to Mme. Blavatsky's theosophy group.

It is clear, however, that their interest was of a special kind. Their Idumaean nights were not spent in alchemists' laboratories, or in reciting phrases learned from some traditional manual. They were spent in writing poems. The resemblance between Mallarmé's *Prose Pour des Esseintes* and the spells contained in the *"vieux grimoire"* of which the poem speaks is in no way obvious—if only because the poet knows how completely he must create anew what he inscribes on his page, saying for the first time something which he may call an "incantation" but which was found in no old spell book. What's more, the poets use interchangeably words and references which, for a practicing magician or alchemist, are vastly dissimilar. Baudelaire, Mallarmé, Rimbaud describe their use of language indiscriminately as a *sorcellerie évocatoire,* a magical operation, or an *alchimie du verbe.* For an adept, the practices of magic and those of alchemy are not at all equivalent. From another point of view, however, these technical differences—between the Magus, the alchemist, and the poet—lose their importance. According to Chaldean magic—the early Roman ancestor of Western occultism—all religions were one. In the nineteenth century, this old dogma of the perennial philosophy took on a more specialized meaning. As long as one "performed the work," one gave birth to one's own father. For the Great Work was the regeneration of the ego: alchemist, Magus, poet labored toward similar ends. And since, according to the old dogma, all the Works are one, the exchange of vocabulary on the part of poets betrays not ignorance but rather a kind of clairvoyance as to the true ends of their labor.

Victor Hugo wrote, "[The poet] is God's tripod. God did not make this marvelous alembic of the idea, the brain of man, in order not to use it." Through the alchemy of his poetic faculty, the poet brings messages from God. This resembles, dressed in new language, the old idea of the poet as *vates,* a vessel for divinely inspired messages. But Hugo's references are strangely crossed. The alchemist relies not on inspiration but on himself: his resourcefulness, his spiritual acuity, his recipes. If he succeeds, he does more than transmit messages from God: he changes his life, becoming himself a kind of God. In Hugo's phrase, God doesn't use the poet as he would a servant. The poet is the tripod on which God rests. Without the tripod, one can hardly imagine where God would be.

Mallarmé, in his poem "Les Fenêtres," makes it equally clear that the Work is none other than self-transformation, regenerattion of the ego. The window by means of which he turns his back on life is poetry. What he sees is what the poem's work has evoked for him:

> In their glass, washed with the eternal dews,
> And gilded by the chaste morning of infinity,
> I look and see myself an Angel.

Mallarmé's image renews the traditional trope of the mirror which reflects not the object itself but its ideal. Looking into the mirror, he discovers new reality and a new self. We remember the frequency of the mirror image in manuals of spiritual discipline. Like the mystic, Mallarmé has turned his back on life by choosing the view from his mirror. Unlike the mystic, however, he confirms a selfhood which he has renewed by this act of purification; he does not move out of the mirror's range— i.e., the range of poetry.

Mallarmé, in this poem, has simplified an insight which, for poets like Hugo and Baudelaire, opened up possibilities of a different kind. Hugo's poetic mirror also transformed the powers of the self, but it reflected a density of experience for which Mallarmé would have had no use: "Strange, it is within you that you must look at the outside world. The deep and somber mirror lies in the depths of man . . . When we look down into this well, our own mind, we see, an abyss away, the immense world, encircled by a tiny ring." Hugo, closer to the traditions of magic and alchemy, does not "turn his back on life." On the contrary, he asks his imagination to accord the rhythms of the inner world to those of the "immense world." By turning the mirror inward, Hugo turned to face life. Mallarmé's mirror was a window through which only the sky could be seen; it left behind the imperfect shapes of earth. Hugo's mirror is a well; it points downward, penetrating the earth. The goals are the same— regeneration of the ego; all the works are one. Yet Hugo follows the way down toward life, Mallarmé the way up away from life.

The Heraclitean paradox tells us that this difference is also not a difference: the way up and the way down are the same. But, as John Senior has pointed out in his interesting study, *The Way Down and Out,* the poets of the nineteenth century were, on the whole, unable or unwilling to turn their backs on the world. They were overwhelmed by life, half drowned in their own problematical selves. Even Kierkegaard, one of the few thoroughgoing Christians of the century, knew that the only solution lay inside of life itself; that one had to go down into the underworld in order to obtain the beloved.

Many men, during the nineteenth century, undertook this way down into poetry. Few succeeded in creating a life's work equal to their ambition. Of them Charles Baudelaire stands apart, a troubling combination of genius and failure. In his famous *Lettre du Voyant,* Rimbaud called him the King of Seers: Baudelaire's poems, he felt, opened a breach in the wall of familiar emotions, pointing to a place where, "an abyss away," other emotions took on shapes one preferred not to recognize. But it is Baudelaire's peculiar fate to have earned praise of another kind, from men as unlike Rimbaud as Paul Valéry and T. S. Eliot, who deplored the "perishable matter" of his poetry while praising the masterful discipline of his language, un- equaled in French poetry since Racine. Both of these extreme opinions betray their subject, for the rhetoric and the vision are uniquely mingled in Baudelaire's poetry. One is not intelligible without the other, as we mean to demonstrate in this chapter.

As with Kierkegaard, Baudelaire's descent into poetry began at that point in his character where the familiar emotions failed him, and something else—what Eliot called the "perishable matter"—filtered through the broken places. Kierkegaard named this failure his "thorn in the flesh" and explained how it had taught him, in his isolation, to leap higher and more gracefully. For Baudelaire, the solution was more elusive. Like Kierkegaard he knew that he had been condemned to a life of Unlikeness. He wrote to his mother, not without a touch of self-dramatization: "Understand one thing which you seem always to ignore: that truly, for my own unhappiness, I am not made like other men." Baudelaire, however, was not a Christian. Nothing as frankly heroic as the Category of Isolation could reverse his daily failures. Unlike Kierkegaard, he had always to begin again. He worked at poetry like Penelope at her weaving, unable to use yesterday's genius to help with today's failure. The letters to his mother are depressingly alike over a period of more than twenty years: the same complaints, the same nervous ailments, the same inability to organize his life "like everyone else." On the other hand, his poems and his critical writing have the same masterful beauty both early and late. In either case, no "progress."

The alchemist never finds the philosopher's stone, but each day's work shapes his life. He is forever beginning over again, so that failure seems to be part of his genius. Baudelaire, for whom poetry was a kind of alchemy, was no different. He explains this in a text which he liked well enough to publish twice: once as part of an essay entitled *La Morale du Joujou*, and again at the end of the life in the *Petits Poèmes en Prose*:

> On the road, behind the iron gate of a large garden, at the end of which you could see the whiteness of a lovely castle lit up by the sun, there was a child beautiful and fresh, dressed in those country clothes which are so fastidious.
> Luxury, freedom from care, and the habitual display of wealth make such children so charming that you could believe them

made of a different substance from children of an undistinguished or poorer class.

Beside him on the grass lay a magnificent toy, as beautiful as its master, varnished, gilded, clothed in a purple robe, and covered with plumes and beads. But the child paid no attention to his favorite toy; this is what he was looking at:

On the other side of the iron gate, on the road, in the midst of thistles and nettles, there was another child, dirty, frail, sooty, one of those child-waifs whose beauty an impartial eye might discover if, as the eye of a connoisseur guesses the ideal painting under a body varnish, it cleaned the child of the repulsive patina of poverty.

Through the symbolic bars which separated the two worlds, the main road and the castle, the poor child was showing his toy to the rich child who greedily examined it as if it were a rare and strange object. Now, this toy, which the small ragamuffin worried by shaking a wire box back and forth, was a live rat! His parents, for economy's sake doubtless, had gotten the toy from life itself.

As the two children laughed fraternally at another, they showed teeth of an equal whiteness.

The rich child and the pariah smile fraternally at each other with an irony characteristic of Baudelaire. The rich child has thrown aside his toy, for he sees outside the wall something he never knew existed: a toy drawn from life itself. By the end of the poem, the values have been strangely reversed; neither the child nor the pariah can be sure for which of them the wall was intended. This is undoubtedly what Eliot meant by the "perishable matter" in Baudelaire's poetry: we would be freer to enjoy the workmanship of the cage if it held something less dangerous, less willfully provoking than a living rat. This is tantamount to deploring Kierkegaard's "narcissism," calling his highly personal conclusions perishable and wishing that he had made better use of his genius. In the case of Kierkegaard we saw that the narcissism and the genius belong to each other; they are made out of the same material. If Baudelaire's parents had not given him a living rat, he would not have learned the difficult art of building cages.

Childhood played an important part in Baudelaire's *art poétique*. In the *Morale du Joujou*, he wrote, "The toy is the child's first initiation into art, or rather it is for him its first achievement, and, in his adult age, more perfect achievements will not give him the same warmth or enthusiasms, the same beliefs." The child has imaginative powers that fade as he grows older: out of a stick of wood and some cloth sewn together he makes a living creature. Later the poet tries to reawaken this forgotten energy. In a passage that psychoanalysts seem to have neglected, he declares, "Genius is only childhood rediscovered at will, a childhood gifted with virile organs to express itself." Too much has been written about Baudelaire's peculiar relationship to his mother for further elaboration to be necessary here. His mother fixation, his Oedipal troubles, his latent homosexuality, his difficulty with women are described amply throughout his work. Let us remark simply that the pain of Baudelaire's life, and the originality of his poetry, are made to spring from this unusual toy that once captured his imagination: no cheap doll, but something even cheaper, a living rat.

Baudelaire's *art poétique* makes even further claims. The poet who rediscovers childhood at will frees his imagination, but in doing so he risks his life. For the child, as he wrote elsewhere, "is closer to original sin," closer to those suppressed desires which can only trouble the decorum of the rich child's life, behind his wall. The genius must be a pariah, for he has rediscovered, enthroned in his imagination, the living rat that gave birth to it.

"If ever a man was ill, in ways that had nothing to do with medicine, that man is me." The letters he wrote to his mother over a period of twenty-five years are filled with similar descriptions of his "moral solitude," the "laziness that kills me, devours me, eats me alive"; "the frightful loneliness that surrounds (me)," the all-enveloping guilt, the doubts: "strange illnesses that somehow increase my hatred for everything and everyone."

And, worst of all, "in this terrible jarred existence, the fear of seeing the admirable gift of poetry disappear, used and exhausted, along with the clarity of ideas, and the power of hope which all together constitute my true capital." Baudelaire, like Kierkegaard, had a talent for self-exaggeration. And Sartre is undoubtedly right when he warns us not to read these letters too literally. They are written, after all, to his mother in order to pluck at her heartstrings and to punish her for not loving him enough, as well as to get some money from her. Yet the letters are convincing; the fears and obsessions he speaks of give an urgency to his language. If Baudelaire is acting out his pain here, if he is playing a part for the benefit of his mother, the part he invents is based on a reality: that of his erratic, self-destructive emotions. The impossible life he led, as well as the "perishable matter" of his poetry, are there to confirm and complete the inward landscape which his letters interminably describe and deplore.

This was the living rat his parents had given him: his own terrible character, of which he writes that it is "so strange I cannot recognize myself in it." The point of Sartre's brilliant essay on Baudelaire is that the poet "chose" his unusual fate, that, finally, he was overcome not by circumstances, ill will, or neurosis, but by his own decisions. According to Sartre, Baudelaire is truly the victim he describes in his letters, but he is his own victim: he could, after all, have refused the living rat; or—more to Sartre's point—he could have revolted against the world of the rich child, destroying the wall instead of living in the gutter to which the wall condemned him.

Baudelaire did choose, though in a way that Sartre does not recognize. He chose precisely to embrace his "bizarre infirmities," his obsession, the moral weakness that isolated him more and more completely from all human exchanges. He chose to build a cage for the living rat, transforming it from a low beast, a pariah among animals, into a work of art. Like Kierkegaard, he welcomed his fate; he made himself into what he already was, but with a difference. It is this difference that Sartre chooses to ignore.

In his poem "Le Mauvais Moine," Baudelaire asks, "When shall I learn to make the daily scene of my sad misery into my hands' labor and my eyes' love?" This is the aim of Baudelaire's genius: by this unusual work, and this more unusual love, to change the "sad misery" into something else: a spectacle, a finished language, ultimately a self regenerated through the skills of verbal alchemy.

Samuel Cramer, the hero of Baudelaire's only short story, sits for long hours in front of a mirror:

> He played wonderful tragedies for himself, behind closed doors, or rather tragicomedies. If he felt ever so slightly moved and tickled by gaiety, he needed to observe it, and then our man would practice bursting into laughter. If a tear swelled in the corner of his eye at some memory, he went to the mirror to watch himself cry. If some woman, in a fit of brutal, puerile jealousy, scratched him with a needle or a pocketknife, Samuel gave himself the private glory of a knife wound.

Samuel Cramer is a dandy. He is also a poet, but that is secondary: he is his own work of art. Baudelaire emphasizes the contradictory power of this art when he describes Samuel as a god of impotence, "a modern, hermaphroditic god" whose sterility is so colossal as to have become "epic." The self-enlacing hermaphrodite, traditional figure of plenitude and fertility, becomes the object of a new creed: the religion of "auto-idolatry," *le culte de soi-même*. "The Dandy must aspire to be sublime without interruption. He must live and sleep before a mirror." This continual vigil before the mirror is a kind of Great Work: it transforms the "natural" man, whose life is composed of a living rat, into a saint; like Mallarmé, the dandy looks into the mirror and discovers that he is an Angel. Baudelaire writes, in a phrase that recalls Kierkegaard's definition of the hero in *Repetition*, "To be a great man and a saint for *oneself*, that is the only important thing." Elsewhere he quotes, to the same effect, a phrase of Emerson's to which he was particularly attached: "The hero is he who is immovably centered."

Between Kierkegaard's knight of faith and the dandy, there is a curious resemblance. Both are entirely private, the dandy because of his "absolute simplicity," the knight of faith "by virtue of the absurd." They lead their lives unseen by any but themselves. There may be great numbers of them, yet they form no society. Each coincides so completely with his inward authority that he has succeeded in becoming his own "contemporary," tranquilly immured in his personality. Neither the dandy nor the knight of faith is a true hero. Their isolation is silent and self-contained: they need no witnesses. That is why the dandy must be sterile: his strength is precisely to make nothing happen. As for the knight of faith, he too, as we have seen, made nothing happen. One could not distinguish him from any other tax collector or shopkeeper. His adventure was so perfectly interiorized that he too, from a spiritual point of view, was sterile: the father of no faith, the gadfly of no sleeping masses.

Kierkegaard freely admitted that he was no knight of faith. After *Fear and Trembling*, the idea disappeared from his work and was replaced by the more properly heroic figure of the Isolated One. As for Baudelaire, his true dandyism was his poetry. The transformation which the dandy accomplished in the Great Work of the mirror Baudelaire undertook in his poems: to enclose the living rat—his thorn in the flesh—in a cage; not to mold the flesh itself, but to pass it through the alembic of his imagination, until the precipitate, the regenerated self, appeared before him. Sartre in his essay writes:

> The constraint of rhythm and verse forced him to pursue on this ground the spiritual discipline he practiced in his dress and his dandyism. He gave shape to his feelings, as he had given shape to his body and his behavior. There is a dandyism in Baudelaire's poems. In the end, the object he makes is only an image

of himself, a restoration of his memory in the present, which appears to be a synthesis between being and existence.

I would add only that Baudelaire's dandyism was not *also* in his poems, it was *only* in his poems. This, however, is an important difference, for the poems require witnesses; they make a claim for "glory," turning Baudelaire's Great Work of self-regeneration into an exemplary act, to be seen, and perhaps feared, by the men of moderation, by society. The rich child and the pariah smile fraternally at each other: one is holding up a living rat for the other to see.

There is another equally important difference. The dandy turns his back on life; he resembles Mallarmé's poet in "Les Fenêtres," even to the detail of his angelic sterility. *Les Fleurs du Mal*, on the contrary, is pointed downward toward the "abyss," where no repugnant detail is neglected: the poems describe, amplify, embody the living rat to its full measure of disgust. This is the price Baudelaire must pay. The road he has taken is certain, but it is a road down, and the god of his operation is a hybrid of evil and occult virtue: Satan Trismegistus.

Magicians, sorcerers, alchemists have long acted on a similar insight. The ingredients they mingle in their formulas belong invariably to the somber region of our sensibilities: menstrual blood, bits of hair, feces, ill-smelling chemicals like sulphur, rotted flesh. Among mythical heroes, Orpheus the poet was torn to pieces by the women of Thrace; while his more primitive counterpart, Dionysius or Thamuz, restored the earth's fertility by rotting first in its soil. This is an insight common to much great nineteenth-century literature. We remember Dostoevski's epigraph to *The Brothers Karamazov*: "Verily, verily, I say unto you, except a corn of wheat fall into the ground and die, it abideth alone: but if it die, it bringeth forth much fruit."

The same reversal is embodied in Baudelaire's poems. Their descent into vileness leads not to sainthood but to that vanishing point of spiritual ambition where opposites coincide. St. John of the Cross described the difficult journey *away* from illumination which he called the Dark Night of the Soul. It was only at the antipodes, at the far end of the valley of death, that the mystic encountered Life. Baudelaire's poetic journey is of the same kind. In "L'Alchimie de la Douleur," he writes:

> Unknown Hermes who are my helper, but of whom I ever went in fear, you make me the peer of Midas, the unhappiest of alchemists. Through you I transmute gold into iron and Paradise into Hell; in the winding-sheet of clouds I find the corpse of one I loved, and on the shores of heaven I build colossal tombs.

There is a muted irony in the neatness of the poem's reversals: Heaven for Hell, gold for iron, immortality for a tomb. With his strict, hieratic language Baudelaire is describing the price he pays: the terrible pattern of his character which makes everything he undertakes go wrong. In a letter he complained, "Can I ever know what wind will blow inside my mind?" The occult elegance of the poem transforms this thought about his failed life. The poet's alchemy works on human material—his own "bizarre infirmities"—converting them into the gold of artistic achievement. Only by this operation, this poetic descent into vileness, can his private failures be made to give birth to their opposite: the regenerated self, the Angel, the hero who is "immovably centered."

In his famous introductory poem "Au Lecteur" Baudelaire says this even more clearly:

> Satan Trismegistus soothes our bewitched minds for a long time on the pillow of evil, this expert alchemist dissolves our will's precious metal into vapor.

This passage brings us to the heart of Baudelaire's private hell: his constantly evaporating will; the perverse wind in his mind that, despite all his efforts, blew him where it would. *Mon Coeur mis à nu* begins with an idea distilled out of his life: "The distillation and the centralization of the self: that is everything." Baudelaire was haunted by a sense of his moral disintegration. For twenty-five years his letters spoke of little else: "perpetual laziness" and a hatred for that laziness; a disorganized wealth of images, ideas, projects, yet an inability to focus his energies on a single willful point. "This gap between the will and the ability is something I cannot understand—why, having so clear an idea of duty and of usefulness, do I always do the opposite?" He is forever making resolutions, swearing to reverse the pattern of his life by a single effort of the will: "If there is one thing that is certain, it is that I no longer wish to give anything in my life to chance; I mean for the will to occupy it wholly." Baudelaire's portrait of the dandy represents the perfect self-concentration of which he dreamed. In his dress, in his aristocratic manner, he tried to simulate his ideal, to make at least the gesture, as if that would be a first step toward the moral perfection—the willful self-sufficiency—of the dandy. But even here the perverse wind betrayed him. He overdid the elegance, became coolly provoking, and finally made himself into what a dandy could never want to be: an object of scandal. No, the genius of Baudelaire's imagination did not lead him toward the self-sufficiency of the dandy; it led him instead toward poetry: the perverse art of Satan Trismegistus. This "expert alchemist" performs *l'alchimie du verbe,* transmuting life into language. But Baudelaire, in "Au Lecteur," adds a new complexity. Satan Trismegistus "dissolves our will's precious metal into vapor." As in "L'Alchimie de la Douleur," the direction is from gold to iron, from the ideal of the life ("I mean for the will to occupy it wholly"), to the daily Hell that tormented him ("the distillation of the self"). It was only by losing the self that Baudelaire could find it again fashioned into an image of permanence and clarity.

Almost all of the poems in *Les Fleurs du Mal* describe this paradoxical descent. Think of the well-known sonnet "L'Homme et la Mer":

> O Man, so long as you are free you will cherish the sea! The sea is your looking glass . . . You love to plunge into the depths of your own image . . . And yet you two have warred against each other for untold centuries, with neither pity nor remorse.

The free man discovers his image, not—like Mallarmé—in a mirror, but in the "infinite movement" of the sea, in that chaos of unachieved forms which, for the mythical imagination, embodied death and rebirth. The image he seeks is not to be found on the surface of the water, as it was for Ovid's Narcissus. It lies inside the water and is the water; to find it, the free man plunges "into the depths of [his] own image." The ocean does not mirror him, it dissolves and destroys him. Yet the destroyed image is precisely what has been changed by the poem, shaped and made permanent by the poem's rhetorical grace.

Baudelaire's alchemical metaphor is perhaps a way of describing what all successful poems must do: out of the dissolving shapes to make something permanent, in which the formal mastery has coincided with the subject matter, or to use Freud's language, in which the conscious and preconscious elaboration has achieved a delicate but faultless harmony with the unconscious material. Baudelaire's own language, however, contains a nuance which we ought not to neglect. The transmutation he speaks of is, in his own eyes, not only aesthetic; it is spiritual. The "perishable matter" encounters the grace of language, just as the vile mixture of the alchemist encountered his chemical skill: the result is a new substance, disengaged from vileness; a substance which the vileness had always contained, like an embryo. If the earth is the mother of metals, alchemy is a kind of obstetrics, bringing to light the spirit of the metal.

The distinction Kierkegaard drew between the aesthetical, ethical, and religious stages on life's way would have meant nothing to Baudelaire. In "Les Petites Vieilles" he describes the following episode:

> Have you ever noticed that many old women's coffins are almost as small as those of little children? Cunning old death gives these similar coffins a strange and entrancing symbolism: when I catch sight of a flimsy ghost passing through the swarming Parisian landscape, I always have the feeling that this frail creature is gently advancing toward her second cradle.

In Baudelaire's imagination, opposites learn to coincide. In this poem, the withering human body recalls, at first ironically and then with a kind of tenderness, the first innocence of the body; the old women have shriveled until their coffins are like those of children. *Les Fleurs du Mal* is peopled with "crippled phantoms" like these: old prostitutes, wrecks of humanity, neurasthenic poets, criminals. Yet Baudelaire's art brings life out of their decay: their decrepitude becomes a metal on which he can work the changes of his imagination, until they appear in the poem, "gently advancing toward (a) second cradle." In their eyes, as in a mixing bowl, the alchemist sees the evidence of his skill: a sprinkling of the sought-for gold: "Those eyes are the wells of a million tears, crucibles spangled with cool metal."

The alchemical metaphor helps us understand the violence in Baudelaire's poetry; the pleasure he took in scenes of physical decay, as in "Une Charogne"—certainly the most "perishable" of the poems from Eliot's point of view. But even more striking than the poems of decay are those in which the violence is unmistakably sadistic or masochistic. Here the "distillation of the self" is translated into a strangely literal, erotic imagery. Orpheus was torn to pieces by the women of Thrace, Baudelaire's *alchimie de la douleur* required that the poet tear himself to pieces.

Baudelaire's violence breaks down the old forms and the old self, dissolving them into a kind of primitive fluidity, an ocean of pain. Pain, received and inflicted, becomes a spiritual solvent. It is an ingredient in the verbal alchemy: the fire which melts the elements together into their final harmony, just as, for the chiliasts, the resurrection of the earth could issue only from the catastrophe of the messianic pains. Another passage from *La Morale du Joujou* illustrates the link Baudelaire saw between violence and spirituality:

> Most kids want more than anything *to see the soul* (of their toy), some after a while, others right away. It is the more or less rapid invasion of this desire which determines how long the toy will last. I don't have the courage to find fault with this childish obsession: it is a first turn toward the metaphysical. When this desire has gotten itself stuck in a child's brain tissue, it fills his fingers and his nails with a strange force and agility. The child turns his toy over and over again, he scratches it, knocks it against walls, throws it on the floor. From time to time he starts its mechanical movements over again, sometimes backwards. The marvelous life of the toy stops. Like the people assaulting the Tuileries, the child makes a last effort; at last he opens it, he is stronger than the toy. But *where is the soul?* This is the beginning of sadness and encroaching stupidity.

Like the turbulent masses during the French Revolution, the child expresses a primitive metaphysical need in this first impulse to violence: he breaks apart his toy, not for the sheer pleasure of destroying, but because he is looking for the soul of the toy.

We must remember, however, that the child, for Baudelaire, was not simply an analogue of the artist. Creative genius endows the adult with "virile organs" which express, but also transform, what, as a child, he only vaguely apprehended. In order to discover the soul of the toy—i.e., his own soul, the living rat—the child destroyed it. Baudelaire, the adult, felt his life continually dissolving: his character was forever torn apart by some perverse wind that blew from inside him. Yet his genius enabled him to preserve the living rat; not to destroy it as the child would have, but to transform it, by allowing it to be destroyed symbolically, in the alchemical work of the poem. Another way of conveying this would be to regard Baudelaire's poetic labor as a kind of therapy. To look for the soul meant to to preserve oneself, to compose a vision of regeneration in which soul and self coincide, becoming what Kierkegaard or the mystics would have called the "true self."

In the poem "A Une Madone," the poet performs this work; through the alchemy of his self-inflicted violence he is looking for the soul. The poet's mistress, *la madone*, is enthroned in the "darkest corner of his heart." Piece by piece, he dresses the image in the baroque costume of his emotions: a coat of jealousy, a robe of desire, beautiful shoes made of respect, until the madonna has become an image of his own emotional life, "a monster swelled with hate and saliva," the Queen of Virgins. Then, out of the Seven Capital Sins the poet makes seven sharp knives: "And, like a circus knife thrower, I'll aim at the pure center of your gentle frame, and plunge those blades into your bleeding heart, your bleeding, suffering, palpitating heart." As often with Baudelaire, the poem generates a mood of suppressed irony which mitigates the violence. The governing figure of the poem, a mistress whose image is transformed into a madonna by the poet's devotion, recalls the courtly love poems of Provence; and this echo sharpens the transition in the poem from love to hate, while the image of the *jongleur insensible* subtracts just enough from the murderous act that follows for it to remain dramatic, and not simply self-indulgent—i.e., neurotic. A *jongleur*, in the courtly language of the Middle Ages, was a wandering poet, and this meaning lingers in the modern French word. Thus Baudelaire reminds us that the violence of the knives is symbolic; it is a poetic violence whose aim is not only to destroy but also to regenerate.

Poetry, for Baudelaire, was a matter of survival. His guilt, his self-destructive violence, the burden of his Unlikeness cried out again and again for some miraculous change, without which they would "eat [him] alive," turning him into one more "crippled phantom":

> Dissatisfied with everyone, including myself, I would gladly redeem myself and retrieve my pride in the silence and loneliness of the night . . . and you, O my Lord and my God, grant me the grace to produce a few lines of poetry which will prove to me that I am not the lowest of men, that I am not below those whom I despise!

We have seen how the very conception of the poems was meant to answer his prayer. There remains, however, a last point to be cleared up. In this passage from *Les Petits Poèmes en Prose*, Baudelaire prays to God; he pleads for grace, the pure gift which will enable him to save his life through poetry. But neither the Magus nor the alchemist needed to ask for grace; their art was their grace; the gods could not refuse them. The regeneration of the ego, according to Eliphas Levi, was not a product of grace; the Magus did the work and was reborn out of his own labor. Yet Baudelaire invokes God and speaks of prayer.

In *Mon Coeur mis à nu* he writes out a breviary of necessary virtues, beginning each time with the formula: "Hygiene, Conduct, Morality." The sentences have an almost military brevity:

> Nothing is irreparable. There is still time. Who knows, even, whether new pleasures . . . Fame, payment of my debts . . . Work necessarily begets wholesome habits, sobriety and chastity—and consequently health, wealth, a successive and progressive creative genius, and lastly charity.

Baudelaire never ceased to dream of a sudden reversal that would transform his life. Each time he fastened his hope on some new project: an apartment, a financial windfall, a single kind word from his mother, a literary success. These lines in *Mon Coeur mis à nu* reflect the same desperate hope: the "work" he invokes here becomes a kind of magical act to focus his energies and reverse the pattern of disintegration that governed his life. Prayer also has its place in this breviary of necessary virtues, alongside of "work": "An abbreviated wisdom. Dress, prayer, work. Prayer: charity, wisdom and strength." Although Baudelaire uses the language of the conventional virtues, he has changed the meaning of the words. "Prayer" as we normally understand it is an act of humility; the supplicant kneels down, acknowledging the full measure of his dependence on God. By becoming nothing and less than nothing, in the act of prayer, he pleads for grace.

But for Baudelaire prayer had another meaning. In *Fusées* he notes, "There is in prayer a magical operation" which is performed on "the altar of the will." It is less an invocation of divine aid than a regrouping of the poet's forces, according to his old wish to eliminate chance from his life, by strengthening the power of the will. Prayer taps a source of private energy which would otherwise be unavailable: "The man who prays in the evening is a captain who sets out sentinels. He can sleep." This is scarcely an image of humility. A few pages earlier he notes that "De Maistre and Edgar Poe taught me how to think." The debt to Poe need not concern us here. De Maistre, however, was an unorthodox and somber theologian, who describes the act of prayer in terms to which Baudelaire was surely indebted. When in *Fusées*, he wrote, "Pray, pray, endlessly," he was perhaps thinking of the count in De Maistre's *Les Soirées de Saint Pétersbourg*, who remarks, "Any nation that prays receives what it has prayed for." Prayer for De Maistre was a kind of spiritual medicine; to be effective it had only to be properly applied:

> I well believe not only that prayer is useful in general for curing physical ills but that it is its true antidote and natural remedy, and that it tends essentially to destroy physical ills, just like that invisible essence which comes to us from Peru hidden in the light bark of a tree: the bark, by virtue of its own essence, seeks out the source of the fever, finds it and attacks it.

The circuit of force which prayer has opened here leaves no room for the authoritarian God whose gesture toward man is thought of as a pure gift, a grace.

Baudelaire writes in a letter, "I have prayed at all hours (to whom? What definite being? I haven't the slightest idea)." Prayer organized his mind, concentrated his will, but the place toward which the prayer was directed was to be found nowhere outside himself; certainly not in any orthodox conception of divinity. Elsewhere Baudelaire is more specific:" Even if God didn't exist, religion would be Holy and *divine*. God is the only being who, in order to reign, need not even exist." Baudelaire varies this theme and even contradicts it, for his thoughts on the matter were far from clear. At one point he is willing to think of God as a "vast reservoir of energy" to which prayer would give him access. At another, he describes Him as "the eternal confidant in that tragedy of which each of us is the hero." Throughout these apparently contradictory formulas a single thought prevails: the true power of religion, of art, of spirituality lies not with God—whether He exists or not—but with man. Prayer, for Baudelaire, becomes a self-invocation, closer to Eliphas Levi's Great Work than to Catholicism: a ceremony in the new religion of "Auto-Idolatry."

In "Le Poème du Haschich," Baudelaire condemns the "black magic" of the drug because it depends upon a drunkenness whose effect is to dissolve the will, leaving a man helpless before the whirling passions that carry him off, "like a horse racing toward the abyss." The final pages of the essay, however, make it clear that what he is condemning is the method, not the goal; for the powers released by the drug can be obtained in other ways. He suggests that the "black magic" of hashish be replaced by the "white magic" of poetry and philosophy, "by continuous work and contemplation; by the assiduous labor of the will and the permanent nobility of intention." The *sorcellerie évocatoire* of poetry obtains legally, so to speak, what hashish smuggles illicitly into the mind.

Like poetry, hashish is a "pure mirror" in which a man discovers his superiority over all other men. He is "immovably
centered," divorced from all social intercourse. In this "terrible
marriage of a man with his own self," the mind, like a deforming mirror, learns to reflect all surrounding objects. Music,
language, color speak to him of himself. "All contradictions
dissolve . . . everything is material for joy . . . You are a king
unknown by those who pass, living in the solitude of his conviction."

This hidden superiority reshapes his memory of the past:
now even his faults have become sources of virtue, because of
the saintly honesty with which he confesses them. Caught up in
this moral exaltation, he thinks of Jean Jacques, the triumph of
his *Confessions,* and cries out, "I am the most virtuous of all
men." But the work of transformation cannot stop here. History,
knowledge, art, beauty, the universe itself take on new meaning:

> All these things have been created *for me, for me, for me!* For
> me humanity has worked, been martyrized and immolated—to
> become fodder, *pabulum,* for my implacable appetite for emo-
> tion, knowledge, and beauty . . . I have become God.

The delirium of the drug leads to this climax in which the poet's
"diabolical thirst for pleasure, glory, and power" finds an illusory
satisfaction. Hashish, he concludes, severs a man from his usual
obligations. It takes him on a solitary journey from which
he has no desire to return. The transformation has undone his
humanity; it has left him at the antipodes of all human intercourse, hovering like a spiritual hermaphrodite over the abyss:
"Hashish, like all solitary joys, makes the individual useless to
men, and society superfluous for the individual. It leads him to
admire himself unceasingly, hurrying him day after day toward
the luminous abyss where he admires his face of Narcissus."

By choosing to be a poet, Baudelaire rejected this sterile
beatitude, as he had already rejected the so-called heroism of the
dandy. Such were the poles between which his life and his

poetry were formed: on one hand the terrible flaw of the will, the "distillation of the self," exemplified by hashish; on the other the willful sterility of the dandy. Refusing both of these, Baudelaire struggled to find a middle ground: the ground of poetry, "the assiduous labor of the will and the permanent nobility of intention." He chose the paradoxical skill of the imagination, thereby refusing to remain sealed in his Unlikeness. From the antipodes, where his life had been stranded, he sent back messages. The hero, excluded from the common life, found this way to include himself again, at the greatest possible expense.

Part Five

13 THE SOCIOLOGY OF NARCISSUS

The emotional attitudes we have been describing are, each in its own way, highly dramatic. Baudelaire and Kierkegaard, Descartes and Montaigne, Tristan and the Gnostics lived far from the formless self-indulgence which our moral traditions have described as the sin of Narcissus. On the contrary, they were fighting for their lives. And the personal struggle which shaped and gave permanence to their "work" must, in turn, be grasped by us in its full context of contradiction and experience. This painful drama of the egotist has most often been neglected. The Narcissus we know best is an abstracted, sensuous creature, so perfectly turned toward himself that he has become all but timeless: a pure lyrical point about which no story can be told, for he is the beginning and the end of his own story. Gide seized on this nuance of self-love in an early lyrical composition, when he specified that "there is no longer any shore or running pool; no metamorphosis and no reflected flowers—there is only the one figure of Narcissus."

This theme of the "symbolist" imagination, taken up elsewhere by Mallarmé, Valéry, and others, describes the far limit of a tradition which has survived and renewed itself in the most varied circumstances, over the entire history of our culture. It is a tradition of heroic self-scrutiny and self-affirmation in the face of great odds, indeed because of the great odds. The subversive "egotist" responds to authority by disqualifying it, drawing out of his own idiosyncrasy another, better authority before which all else must give way. In its most extreme form, this attitude is not only anti-authoritarian, it is antisocial. The hero, like Kierkegaard or Baudelaire, is willfully solitary: he is one of the "great bachelors." Yet even at this far limit of unsociability there remains a need to send back signals, messages in a bottle directed back to the disdained continent. This is curiously apparent in the many "lives" of the saints: after a lifetime of the most extreme asceticism and desolation, spent among beasts in the desert, the saint, become half animal and half angel, happens on a wanderer to whom he tells his story. Just before his solitude is extinguished in bodily death, he sends back a signal across the ocean of history. Even this most unsocial of adventures, lived—or imagined—as far from men and companionship as the Egyptian desert could allow, had, by some trick of fate, to become public if it were to have any meaning at all. St. Antony is not only with his phantoms; he appeals out of a thousand paintings for us to know him. His extreme ordeal, and the victory he eventually wins, has, in the end, to become part of the way in which we consider our own experience; part of our location in the world.

Though a moment ago we spoke of a tradition, clearly the word applies only in part. We are dealing, rather, with a group of traditions, literary, philosophical, religious, whose debt from one to another is at times obvious, at times nonexistent. What is common to them, and what leads us to try to understand them together, is first of all the fact—characteristic, it would seem, of our civilization—that they all give the highest public significance to a most private range of emotions and situations. Second, and even more important, is the way in which these energies of self-preoccupation are turned consistently against authority and orthodoxy. To the extent that we learn to value what the men who adhere to these traditions value, we learn to resist the injunctions of society. Tristan and Isolde subvert the law of the land in defense of their self-exalting, self-generated passions. Against the hostility of King Mark and his allies, the lovers exert the genius of their "double narcissism" and, though it costs them their lives, their example is meant, by the authors of the legend, to inspire us.

There is a paradox in this notion of a "cultural" voice whose energies are directed against the institutions of "public" life. Though since the nineteenth century such attitudes have become so commonplace as to be now part of a new orthodoxy. Yet it was in full awareness of his "absurdity" that Kierkegaard promenaded his half-crippled figure of the Isolated One through the public streets and among the booksellers of Copenhagen. At the other end of Christian history, another lover of the absurd, Tertullian, must surely have known the extremity of his statement when he said of Christian morality, "No matter is more alien to us than what matters publicly." This refusal, on spiritual grounds, of the *res publica* was meant, of course, to have the greatest possible effect on public affairs, leading to developments far beyond anything even Tertullian envisaged. Institutions had to be created to socialize the "privacy" of the Christian; authorities had to exert themselves vigorously in order to keep the inventiveness of such self-preoccupation within "reasonable," durable limits. The new "privacy," by the very pressure of its unsociability perhaps, forced an increasingly authoritarian stance on the part of spiritual leaders. This first took a doctrinal form, in the early Councils, and then resulted in the most extreme contradiction of all when the Christian Church, under Constantine, took over the despotic apparatus of the Empire.

By choosing Gnosticism as a point of departure, rather than similar attitudes in early Christianity, we were able to describe, in all their unconstrained fantasy, the kinds of behavior and thought generated by this extreme self-rooted spirituality. To the extent that the Gnostic sects were "uncompromising" in their response to earthly and social exigencies, they were doomed to extinction once Christianity came to power. Yet the attitudes they expressed were later caught up into the needs and doctrines of the Church, passing, as we have seen, into an ensemble of traditions whose common insight exalts the authenticity of "inwardness" over all outward authority.

The method of this study, if there has been some degree of method in my approach to the problems it entertains, has been to seize on these traditions at the point where they have become entangled in the experience of certain exemplary individuals and have then been renewed or deepened by the "work" these individuals have done on and for themselves, whether in literature, philosophy, or religion. This, I think, is the only way to grasp an experience whose very life comes from the depth of its privacy: its single, unsymmetrical struggle for clarity; above all, for self-clarity. Because of this, however, certain questions have been left unasked or have been treated only peripherally. By reformulating the argument of the book, as these last pages have done, I find that such questions almost ask themselves. If the language of public privacy is permanent and important to us; if its intensity continues to move us and, in part, to shape our lives, we must finally ask why this is so. To what in our experience do these life-attitudes correspond? Why, and how, have they become one of those "cultural" facts which many people, including ourselves, have used to give shape and judgment to their experience?

Much social criticism written since the beginning of the nineteenth century has been concerned with this very problem, though in terms which at first appear quite distant from those I have been using. The focus of this criticism varies, but it is rooted in a common assumption which can be most simply stated as follows: there is a degree of harmony and wholeness to which men are entitled; yet modern society has consistently undermined every institution and social experience which could encourage such a flourishing of the individual. It has forced new conditions of life on its citizens—factory work, big cities, the cash nexus—which mutilate them in their innermost being. This modern industrial world has become, in fact, profoundly antisocial—satanical, according to Blake and Baudelaire—plunging its victims into an abyss of unsocial experience which cripples the humanity of those who succumb to it.

The argument, as it is developed and strengthened throughout the nineteenth century, owes much to Rousseau's original formulation in the *Discourses* and in the *Social Contract,* where it is declared that "man is born free, yet everywhere he is in chains." During the nineteenth century, however, the argument moves in new directions. Schiller, whose debt to Rousseau is well known, speaks of the "wound" which civilization has inflicted on modern humanity. But his indictment is more specific. According to Schiller, it is the modern division of labor which has mutilated man's natural possibilities: "Gratification is separated from labor, means from ends, effort from reward. Eternally *fettered* only to a single little fragment of the whole, man fashions himself only as a fragment." Detached from the context in which Schiller used it as a contrast to Greek civilization "where each individual enjoyed an independent existence and, if necessary, could become a whole," this argument was taken up in America by Emerson and in England by the romantic generation of poets and social critics. In their hands it is turned not only against the division of labor but, more specifically, against that most extreme enslaving of man's work capacities, the machine. The organic harmony of the faculties which, for the romantics, embodied the highest imaginative value, was everywhere corrupted by mechanization. Man was indeed fettered to a part, a single repeated gesture calculated to reduce him to the mindlessness of the machine he tended. As Carlyle wrote:

> Not the external and physical alone is now managed by machinery, but the internal and spiritual also . . . Men are grown mechanical in head and in heart, as well as in hand. Not for internal perfection, but for external combinations and arrangements, for institutions, constitutions—for Mechanism of one sort or another, do they hope and struggle. Their whole efforts,

attachments, opinions, turn on mechanism, and are of a mechanical character.

We can understand why Karl Marx so appreciated this aspect of
Carlyle's work. And in fact it is Marx who introduces into the
critical vocabulary the familiar concept of "alienation," in order
to describe the kind of "wound" Schiller and Carlyle are speaking of.*

Although Marx himself used the word in a limited sense, to
describe what happens to labor and its products in a capitalistic
economy, "alienation" has since been invoked in so many different contexts, and borne the weight of so many different insights,
as to have been all but submerged by its own ambiguities. It has
been used variously to describe the impoverishing effect of political institutions, of the money economy, the dehumanizing pressure of misery and insecurity, the psychological wounds inflicted
by authority, the difficulty in modern society of forming emotional relationships, etc. By meaning all these things, "alienation"
in the work of Fromm, Neumann, and others has lost its precision
as a critical tool. It has become part of an agreed-upon vocabulary, invoked rather than used, in order to identify the writer's
underlying moral assumption—namely, that society cripples man
instead of creating him; that it forces its members into a network
of antisocial circumstances which must, in the end, dehumanize
them and perhaps even "alienate" them in the purely clinical
sense.

By settling into a traditional pattern the argument has often
lost the urgency it had for those who first struggled to articulate
it. It is particularly useful, in the context of our own study, to
avoid the more general indictment contained in the word "aliena-

---

*The actual father of "alienation" is, of course, Hegel; but his use of
the term is of only partial interest in this immediate context since, in
his eyes, it described not a process of impoverishment but part of man's
inevitable experience in the world: that painful but unavoidable process
by which man's inward energies become part of the world around him,
taking form, making objects, creating.

tion" and to return instead to some of the divergent formulations which, during the nineteenth century, described and condemned the dangers of the then new society. Among these dangers is one described by Tocqueville in *La Démocratie en Amérique.* Tocqueville, in this book, sets out to explore the effects of "democracy" on those forms of public life which, he felt, encouraged men to desire true excellence in themselves and to admire it in others. By "democracy" Tocqueville referred not only to the new institutions but to the spirit of change which had begun everywhere to dissolve the old forms of community, replacing them by a generalized equality between citizens. Of this new society Tocqueville wrote:

> Among democratic peoples, new families are always rising out of obscurity, others are always falling back, and those that remain are changing; time's pattern is broken at every moment, and the remains of past generations are obliterated. We forget easily those who have preceded us, and have no idea of those who will follow. Only those who are closest appear interesting. Each class moves closer to the others and mixes with them, its members become indifferent and like strangers to each other. Aristocracy had made of all its citizens a long chain climbing from the peasantry to the king; democracy breaks the chain, setting each link apart from the others . . .
>
> Thus not only does democracy make each man forget his ancestors, it hides his descendants from him, and divides him from his contemporaries; it continually turns him back into himself, and threatens, at last, to enclose him entirely in the solitude of his own heart.

Beneath the exuberance of the new institutions, Tocqueville saw an unprecedented danger. This democratic society, whose goal was to create a noble balance between the private and the public, between the individual's freedom and his social responsibility, enclosed its citizens in an isolation whose psychological consequences could be devastating.

Tocqueville's account is all the more enlightening, since America in the 1830's displayed, as yet, few of the iniquities of early industrial society. Thus he could observe how the energy released by economic self-interest was indeed able to enhance material prosperity, as if the entire society were guided by Adam Smith's "invisible hand." But it was nonetheless clear to him that this "invisible hand" was not a serviceable bond between the individual and his community. Unlike many nineteenth-century social critics, Tocqueville is willing to acknowledge the advantage to be gained from the kinds of relationships described by Smith's famous formula: "It is not from the benevolence of the butcher, the brewer, or the baker that we expect our dinner, but from their regard for their own interest. We address ourselves, not to their humanity but to their self-love." At the same time he knew all too well that the broken links of the chain could not be reunited in this way, and that the individual had therefore to suffer from the fact that a whole portion of his emotional life, his values, his aspirations was excluded from the arena of social exchange.

Wherever the social critics of the nineteenth century looked, they discovered isolation: men broken apart from each other, subjected to harsh economic pressures, then left to themselves. It is in these words that Engels describes the prosperous, expanding city of London in the 1870's:

> The more that Londoners are packed into a tiny space, the more repulsive and disgraceful becomes the brutal indifference with which they ignore their neighbors and selfishly concentrate upon their private affairs. We know well enough that this isolation of the individual—this narrow-minded egotism—is everywhere the fundamental principle of modern society. But nowhere is this selfish egotism so blatantly evident as in the frantic bustle of the great city. The disintegration of society into individuals, each guided by his private principles and each pursuing his own aims, has been pushed to its furthest limits in London. Here indeed human society has been split into its component atoms.

Engels, like Tocqueville and many others, was convinced that society had failed to provide what the very word "society" seemed to imply: a meaningful exchange of emotions, talents, ambitions —a community. Instead of this the new industrial world produced an anti-society, whose members met only at points where their humanity was irrelevant: exchanging money instead of emotions; working not together but in parallel lines of production; cultivating their self-interest while leaving the work of "community" to some hypothetical, and very distant, "invisible hand."

This returns us to a problem raised earlier in the chapter. If we now ask what kind of social experience could have given urgency and currency to the antisocial stance assumed by so many exemplary minds, especially from the late eighteenth century on, we are able to give a tentative answer. The "modern" world had, in the eyes of many, become a veritable anti-society; instead of forming the individual, it oppressed him. The problem then became either to change the society—that was the goal of Rousseau, the social critics, the revolutionaries—or to teach the individual how he might resist a society whose inhumanity threatened to overwhelm him. Raymond Williams has described how the word "culture" in nineteenth-century England came to refer to an ideal of perfection and spiritual strength which could act as a bulwark for the individual against the pressures of his social milieu. By "cultivating" himself, the individual resisted those influences which otherwise would have diminished his humanity, i.e., "alienated" him.

This "aesthetic" response, which is also that of men like Schiller, Burckhardt, and Nietzsche, springs from the same moral ground as Marx's revolutionary politics. Since Rousseau, the most incisive and morally responsible minds in Europe and America had begun to judge their society according to what was apparently a new scale of values. Their judgment was explosive. The private individual—the "natural" man—self-cultivated and aggressively articulate, was placed at the center of the public stage. His very presence on the scene became a political act: an act of resistance, a condemnation, setting the highest common value on a range of experience which he located beyond society, beyond the reach of the alienating, mechanizing, isolating enemy.

This kind of explosive reaction, however, did not originate with Rousseau, nor with the romantic generation that followed him. Its roots, as we have seen, reach far back into the history of Christianity. The hero, the saint, the lover stand out among the images of our culture, reflecting an absolute requirement of self-perfection, a refusal to acknowledge the crippling barriers of "this world."

In the preceding chapters we described the richness and the constancy of such responses to the dilemma of our social experience. But this, in turn, complicates our initial question. We began by asking what kind of social experience could have given power and resonance to the language of self-affirmation. The answer we must now consider is that the power may well come not from the social conditions—as "alienating" as they may objectively be—but from a traditional refusal to accept, not only these conditions, but any conditions whatsoever. Jacob Burckhardt was among the first to recognize how much this flourishing of extreme individuality in the West depended at different times on such different social arrangements as to prove bewildering to the sociological historian. He acknowledges, what Schiller and Winckelmann had seen before him, that "it was . . . in a *Greek* cosmos that all the powers of the individual, released from his bonds, reached that pitch of sensitiveness and strength which made it possible to achieve the highest in every sphere of life." But he goes on to recognize that the cultural freedom of the individual has since flourished "more under durable tyrannies than in freedom"; that, under Roman despotism, the very indifference of the bureaucracy to affairs of the individual was a bulwark for culture; that during the Middle Ages, on the contrary, culture and individuality—for Burckhardt these were closely related—

were protected by the fact that the state "commanded a very restricted sphere of activity, being surrounded by the Church, universities, knightly orders, cities and corporations, all of which were republics protected by privileges and statutes." And, in general, that culture was blessed by the good luck that "in the West, at any rate, state and Church did not fuse into one oppressive whole."

The languages of public privacy attain a richness and a variety in the diverse Western traditions which are unequaled elsewhere. From this richness, Burckhardt derives the genius of Greek and European theater, as compared, for example, to Indian drama, whose "chief limitation—and in this it is instructive —consists in the slight value it placed on earthly life and its conflicts, and in an inadequate awareness of strong personality wrestling with fate."

It is possible to argue that this "awareness of strong personality," the great discovery of the Greeks, grew out of an ensemble of sociological circumstances whose main expression was the famous cultural-political arena of the Greek *polis.* Yet, imbedded in the Greek language itself, we find a strangely individualistic predisposition, illustrated, for example, by the fact that the Greek word for "everyone," *hekastos,* is derived from *hekas,* meaning "far-off." His language itself prepared the Greek for a far less homogeneous social experience than any known before him.

Our argument to this point has concluded in two directions which appear contradictory. The attitudes of "public privacy" oppose their language and emotions to those elements of worldly —i.e., social—experience which, during the nineteenth century, threatened to become overwhelming. Yet these same attitudes, as we have seen, belong to a tradition of subversive individualism which extends, in one form or another, throughout our civilization.

There is an aggressiveness and a revolutionary potential in Christian asceticism, for example, which is entirely foreign to

Buddhist ascetics, except to the extent that their religious attitudes have been Westernized, as has been the case in Vietnam, for example. It must surely have been disturbing for the newly legalized Church, during the fourth century, to have ascetic "heroes," like Shnoudi and others, arrive from the saintly isolation of their deserts, armed with stones and clubs, to beat pagans into the next world or, on occasion, to spread havoc and violence in the synods of the Church itself.

The point will be clearer, perhaps, if we again consider the experience of isolation which has so preoccupied modern social philosophy. It is probable that any society which has needed to organize large numbers of people over a wide area has faced problems similar to those encountered in modern Europe: notably, the problems caused by the breaking down of local community life and the imposition from afar of a more abstract form of social discipline, usually based on coercion. The political conservatism of men like Tocqueville and Burckhardt is based, for this reason, on a distrust of the great nation-state, which by its very nature breeds power, the weakening of community life, isolation, and finally, in one form or another, tyranny.

It is precisely this kind of non-European nation-state that Karl Wittfogel describes in his study *Oriental Despotism*. The political animus of Wittfogel's study, apart from his brilliant analysis of the "agro-managerial" economy and bureaucracy, comes from a tradition whose greatest debt is to Montesquieu and, especially, to an insight in *L'Esprit des Lois* which Hannah Arendt has summarized as follows:

> Montesquieu realized that the outstanding characteristic of tyranny was that it rested on isolation—on the isolation of the tyrant from his subjects and the isolation of the subjects from each other through mutual fear and suspicion—and hence that tyranny was not one form of government among others but contradicted the essential human condition of plurality, the acting and speaking together, which is the condition of all forms of political organization.

Wittfogel documents this judgment with material from most of the large non-European societies we know of: Chinese, Persian, Egyptian, Aztec, Inca. The solution found by all these civilizations to the problem of large-scale political-economic organization was, he demonstrates, bureaucracy and, finally, despotism, or "total power." Because his analysis is also an accusation, Wittfogel develops the contrast between the European "open" society and "oriental despotism," showing, among other things, the extent and varieties of isolation, terror, and illegality which characterized the political fates of all citizens under an agro-managerial tyranny. An Egyptian papyrus preserves what is thought to be the advice of a Pharaoh to his son; but it might be advice for all those who were touched in any way by the apparatus of total power. The message reads:

> Hold thyself apart from those subordinate to [thee], lest that should happen to whose terrors no attention has been given. Approach them not in thy loneliness. Fill not thy heart with a brother, nor know a friend . . . [EVEN] WHEN THOU SLEEPEST GUARD THY HEART THYSELF, because no man has adherents on the day of distress.

Authority edged with coercion—a power of life and death over those it mastered—held the members of society in a state of submission and mutual distrust. This power of coercion was doubled by a network of secondary authorities who drummed their message into the very personality of the citizen:

> In ancient Mesopotamia "the individual stood at the center of ever wider circles of authority which delimited his freedom of action. The nearest and smallest of these circles was constituted by authorities in his own family . . . And obedience to the older members of one's family is only a beginning. Beyond the family lie other circles, other authorities: the state and society." Each and every one of them "can and must claim absolute obedience."

According to our scale of critical values, these oriental despotisms are profoundly antisocial; they negate the necessary conditions of "community" even more thoroughly, perhaps, than the industrial society of the nineteenth century. Surely the experience of isolation has never been imposed on large numbers of people. Yet nowhere in these societies did the private desolation find a public voice, as it did in the West. The individual's "privacy" belonged only to himself; it was worn on the inside of his personality, but nowhere, or as little as possible, on that part of him which he turned outward in order to perform his social duties. Wittfogel compares, in passing, what he calls the "introverted" architecture of private Chinese houses with the "extroverted" style characteristic of European architecture. The tendency, in "agro-bureaucratic society," was to "hide luxurious courtyards and dwellings behind a noncommittal façade," and this not only among wealthy commoners but among officials as well. What a man amassed and enjoyed privately concerned only himself; its consequence on the course of public affairs, and on the power he wielded publicly, was nonexistent. Compare this with the careful outward elegance of European architecture: the Renaissance chateaux, the aristocratic town house, etc. In purely economic and political terms, a man's private strength—his property—has, in the West, been immediately translatable into the language and duties of the public realm. More crudely, money —or aristocratic property—meant, and means, power. We might point out, in addition, that the growth of the state and the increasing centralization of power since the eighteenth century have been accompanied by a marked decline in the standards of private architecture, as if the wealthy had begun to sense the public irrelevance of their fortunes when faced with the hugeness of national politics.

It is possible now to define more precisely the aim of this study. Our subject has not been culture or individuality in general, but those moments in our cultural history when the values of "public privacy" have been most powerfully and most paradoxically asserted. We have chosen to describe men whose character and genius led them close to the danger point of silence, yet not beyond it. For the hero's ordeal is worth nothing if he cannot find his way back among men to tell what he has done. Between the hero and the madman there is this difference: the hero carries not only his own solitude but the solitude of his countrymen as well. Even at the farthest point of his journey, he is sustained by the community to which he will return. The madman, one might say, is a hero who has lost his way; the hero, a madman who can and will still speak to us.

Nor is the distinction always a clear one. Men like Luther, Montaigne, Pascal, Hölderlin, Kierkegaard lived close to danger, and were themselves in danger. The tone of urgency in their work makes it clear that they were, in some sense, fighting for their lives or, at the very least, for their sanity. At the heart of their struggle was the isolation—both psychological and social—which threatened to overcome their humanity. They responded by turning their isolation into an ordeal, a journey into the underworld from which they sent back news.

It is not only the extremity of their response that characterized these men. Their work reveals a choice: a decision to cultivate their danger in order to defeat it. For like Baudelaire they knew that the way down could also be a way out. By cultivating their death, they could defeat dying. To overcome their isolation, they turned it into a principle: they made it work, and made work out of it, creating thereby a new "cultural" link with a world clarified by their ordeal. This is precisely the distance between Kierkegaard's neurotic loneliness and the figure of the Isolated One into which he made his life.

This choice of the way down characterizes the cultural response of men like Baudelaire and Kierkegaard, Nietzsche and Dostoevski. In their refusal to be conditioned by the "failure" of their lives, they turned the failure into a transforming mirror; they made the danger worse, in order to make it better.

The alternative to their choice is one proposed by Wordsworth, for whom the artist was meant to be "an upholder and

preserver, carrying everywhere with him relationship and love."
In a world where society and institutions had failed, where "getting and spending" had become the only communication between
men, it was the poet, according to Wordsworth, who carried the
gift of community. Faced with isolation and distrust, he used his
imaginative gifts to create, through poetry, that *transparence des
coeurs* imagined by Rousseau in the *Social Contract*. When Shelley declared poets to be the unacknowledged legislators of the
world, he expressed a similar insight. The failure of society,
devoted to the pursuit of self-interest, was to be rectified by the
pure generosity of the imagination: "Poetry and the principle of
self, of which money is the visible incarnation, are the God and
Mammon of this world." Shelley and Wordsworth wrote out of
a utopian tradition. They refused to follow the paradoxical way
down into the self which we have described. Instead, they devoted their poetic gift to a vision of "relationship and love," a
vision in which poetry was the promoter of an ideal community
between purified selves. Their true companions in imagination
are men like More, Campanella, Rousseau, and Fourier, with
this difference: Wordsworth and Shelley were less interested in
the political requirements of community than in the quality of
utopian emotions, as they expressed them in their poetry.

It has often been remarked that the utopian imagination has
only rarely given rise to masterpieces. The dream of "relationship
and love"—the dream of community—has proved remarkably
elusive, except in those rare cases when it has unlocked in a man
imaginative energies which have renewed the dream. More
often the utopian imagination drifts over the surface of experience, contents itself with formulas or, in the case of Shelley, with
vague invocations. It is at the point where "relationship and
love" fail, where utopia, by some hidden fatality, destroys itself,
that our most powerful response seems to be awakened. In Dostoevski's little known short story, "The Dream of a Ridiculous
Man," the hero reacts to his utopian dream in a way which we
understand. At first he is overwhelmed by the vision:

Everything seemed to be bright with holiday, with a great and
sacred triumph, finally achieved . . . tall splendid trees stood in
all the glory of their bloom, and I am convinced that their innumerable leaves greeted me with a sweet caressing sound, as
though they uttered words of love . . . At last I saw and recognized the people of that happy land . . . Never on earth have
I seen such beauty in man. . . .

Yet the only adequate response he finds in the world of his own
emotions is to destroy the dream. A perverse energy takes hold of
him. "Like a filthy germ, like an atom of pestilence, infecting
whole peoples, so did I infect with my soul that happy land, that
knew not sin before me." Into this world of natural felicity,
which strangely resembles Rousseau's utopian fantasy in the
Dialogues, and beyond that the vivid evocations of Parousie in
Christian eschatological literature, the Ridiculous Man injects
the "sin" of isolation. It is only through the "sin"—i.e., through
the ordeal of guilt and loneliness—that he reaches the "turning
point" in his character whereby the harmony becomes human
and relevant.

In earlier chapters we were led to draw a problematical line
between the "cultural" attitudes we have been describing and
psychotic madness. The distinction is blurred and undependable,
yet common sense and our own feeling of implication in the
experiences we have described tell us it must exist. That the
problem should need to be raised at all points to a similar blurred
line in our own lives, as if we too, faced with failures of "relationship and love," lived closer to a danger that we try, with all
our resources of character and conformity, to forget.

Karl Jaspers, in his study *Strindberg and Van Gogh,* won-
ders whether schizophrenia is not the exemplary mental failure
of the modern world just as mass hysteria was, he felt, for the
Middle Ages. Yet Jaspers' query can be taken in a more troubling
sense. We know that schizophrenia is a diagnosis made fre-
quently by psychiatrists. But what if those of us who remain

"healthy" do so nontheless in the face of dangers which inject into our familiar experience a shadow of instability, a glimpse of the "underworld" into which we haven't fallen. We are not mad, yet we live in the shadow of madness, it reminds us of ourselves: of those failures of "relationship and love" which we spend our lives mending precariously, insistently.

Schizophrenia is the malady of isolation. The schizophrenic is a man for whom the world has become so comfortless, so empty of "relationship and love," that, in order to preserve himself, he retires to some inaccessible place in his mind, conversing no longer with others now, but with his own fantasy. Yet even here, in his retreat, the world finally breaks through, forcing further retreats, until the inner world is no longer viable, having itself become now a world of death. Dostoevski's Ridiculous Man retreats from his isolation into a marvelous vision of love. But then his fantasy betrays him; the germ of isolation finds him again, making his guilt and loneliness even greater than before. It is at this point, however, that the character in Dostoevski's story becomes truly "ridiculous" and merits his name. He awakens from the dream and sets out on a course which, though it may be foolish—i.e., ridiculous—obeys another, equally imperious logic. He sets out to preach the "relationship and love" he dreamed of and destroyed. He finds a way to do a new thing in his life: to speak to people instead of to his fantasies. By becoming "ridiculous," he tries to become sane.

The schizophrenic is a man who cannot risk becoming ridiculous, for he is so unsure of his location in the world that the slightest shock could make him lose all sense of direction. The world as such has become inhospitable for him, like "a prison without bars (or) a concentration camp without barbed wire." He reacts to his worldly insecurity by withdrawing from the world: by devaluating those parts of himself which deal with the world—i.e., his body—and by establishing residence in the part of himself which he feels to be impregnable—i.e., his mind or, alternatively, his spirit. This is how R. D. Laing, in *The Divided Self,* characterizes the "split" between body and mind which becomes progressively deeper as a man fails to anchor his personality, until it finally overcomes him and he becomes properly "mad." Laing suggests that we have all experienced this worldly insecurity—he calls it, using the language of existentialism, an "ontological insecurity"—to varying degrees and, without necessarily going mad, form our psychological responses (our characters) in order to deal with it. Most of us fail some of the time in our life-strategy, experiencing anxiety, depression, etc. The schizophrenic is a man whose failure has become permanent, until it has completely disorganized his personality.

It is not difficult to recognize this worldly insecurity in the experiences we have been describing. It is formulated with aggressive clarity by the Gnostics, for whom the world and its human counterpart, the body, were prisons from which they needed to escape. Later this became a part of traditional Christian morality, reinforced by Luther and even more so by Calvin. Descartes's dualism is equally explicit. While the emotional urgency in the work of men like Pascal, Kierkegaard, Rousseau, Baudelaire, and Nietzsche is compelled by a sense of the danger which lay close to the surface of their lives. The traditions of modern social criticism are also rooted in a feeling of worldly insecurity which the social critics ascribe to failure on the part of society and hope to solve by changing society or, alternatively, by arming the individual against its dangers. What we must emphasize, here as before, is not only the worldly insecurity—which was surely not invented by Western society—but the attention we pay to it; and the need, expressed in our most stable cultural values, to overcome it. What characterizes schizophrenia is this: that it lies beyond the far limit of viable answers to the isolation and the worldly insecurity which we agree to recognize as our daily problem. To that extent it is exemplary. But then, we must not be surprised to discover a number of similarities between the madness and those responses which have remained sufficiently

social as to become public property; we should not be surprised
to discover something of ourselves in the world of schizophrenia.

Laing's account of the schizophrenic process helps us to grasp
even more clearly some decisive similarities and differences between the hero, as we have described him, and the madman.
The person whose sense of worldly insecurity has become overwhelming "*feels* . . . persecuted by reality itself. The world as
it is and other people as they are, are the danger." The danger,
more exactly, is that surrounded by these hostile influences he
will disintegrate, become nothing; that his self, unable to resist,
will die. The schizophrenic responds to this overwhelming threat
in a particular way: he defeats the danger by depersonalizing
himself; in order not to "die," he finds a way of becoming anonymous, of "playing possum." Laing quotes from the description
given by a young girl, who acted in just this way in order to
overcome her fear:

> I was about twelve, and had to walk to my father's shop
> through a large park, which was a long dreary walk. I suppose
> too that I was rather scared. I didn't like it, especially when it
> was getting dark. I started to play a game to help pass the
> time. You know how as a child you count the stones or stand
> on the crosses on the pavement. Well, I hit on this way of
> passing the time. It struck me that if I stared long enough at
> the environment I would blend with it and disappear just as if
> the place was empty and I had disappeared. It is as if you get
> yourself to feel you don't know who you are or where you
> are. To blend into the scenery so to speak. Then, you are
> scared of it because it begins to come on without encourage-
> ment. I would just be walking along and felt that I had blended
> with the landscape. Then I would get frightened and repeat my
> name over and over again to bring me back to life, so to speak.

The young girl, at the time of her experience, had not crossed the
line into psychosis. She was able to solve her anxiety by playing
a game—the game of depersonalization—and when the game
itself became a danger, she could apply a remedy: repeating her

name, she reassembled herself, and returned to the world. But, as Laing points out, there may come a time when the game goes out of control and the name disintegrates. The refuge of anonymity becomes a prison, and the game a fate of solitary confinement.

This girl's story throws an interesting light on the experience of isolation, and on the "heroic" response to it which we have described. Laing comments on this intriguing document in the following way:

> A securely established sense of identity is not easily lost, not as readily as this girl of twelve was able to lose hers in her game. It is, therefore, probable that this very ontological insecurity at least partly occasioned her anxiety in the first place, and that she then used this source of her weakness as her avenue of escape.

The girl faces her danger, not by removing herself from it, or by trying to think of something else—this would be analogous to the "utopian" response we have described; instead, she uses the danger itself as an escape: she plays the game of disintegration, in order not to disintegrate. But the game is not without its own dangers, and therefore the girl descends into the "abyss" armed with her name, which she can invoke at the proper moment. Her name, like Ariadne's string, can lead her out of the labyrinth and back into the world where names mean something: the world of society.

Walt Whitman wrote that he was like a child, endlessly repeating its own name. As long as he could do this, he remained in control of the game: he let himself down into the "underworld"—into the isolated world of his fantasy—confident of finding his way back. Laing's description of the imprisoned fantasy self bears a strong resemblance to the self in *Leaves of Grass:* "The [schizophrenic] self being transcendent, empty, omnipotent, free in its own way, comes to be anybody in fantasy and nobody in reality." The point is that Whitman, although he became anybody in fantasy, remained somebody in reality. By repeating his name, which is to say by writing poetry, he could deliver himself up more and more completely to the danger, while becoming increasingly someone in reality—i.e., the poet Walt Whitman, who had traveled deliberately into the storm of isolation, and returned to bring us news.

In Baudelaire's *Journaux Intimes* we read the following passage: "Commerce is, in its essence, *satanic* . . . because it is the lowest and most vile form of egotism." Baudelaire no less than Wordsworth execrated a society based on "getting and spending," and condemned the deepest failure of such a society: the failure of community. Like Wordsworth, Baudelaire turned to poetry to create a livable center for his life. But Baudelaire's poet did not bear "relationship and love"; he was instead an "alchemist," cultivating in himself the satanism and the egotism, in order to overcome them. Elsewhere he notes: "I have cultivated my hysteria with joy and terror." Like the schizophrenic, he cultivates his death, in order to master the death that threatens him on all sides. By transposing the satanism and the egotism into poetry, he does what the little girl does: repeating his own name, he becomes somebody in the real world; above all, he becomes somebody for us, something of which the schizophrenic is no longer capable.

14 CONCLUSION

"Out of the argument with ourselves we make poetry, out of the argument with others, rhetoric." If we accept Yeats' definition then the subject of this book has been a poetry of sentiment and inner violence which has never ceased to nourish the cultures of Europe and America. The hero and the poet have become inseparable. Divided from the world by the violence he dreams of committing upon it, the hero needs a new language, a style appropriate to what he has shaken loose in his own life. It is surely no accident that our civilization, obsessed with material progress, engaged in perpetual warfare with "nature" and thereby isolated from it as few civilizations have been, should also have produced a repertory of languages for self-discovery, a "poetry" on which its very politics have been founded.

The nature of my subject has led me to consider works of religion, philosophy, literature, and social criticism as if they were elements of a single discourse. It seemed proper, and indeed inevitable, that I should move freely in my study from one strain of this discourse to another. The travail of self-discovery; the need to shape a human response to a world which we have neither wholly made nor wholly received; the comfort of locating one's own self on the difficult map of the emotions: these common impulses have shaped our cultural traditions. I have attempted therefore to grasp these traditions as if they were a kind of living speech, still rooted in their own, and our, humanity.

Since the nineteenth century the colloquy with self has widened and become more desperate. It shaped the revolutionary self-scrutiny of Freud and the psychoanalysts who advanced further into the obscurities of the *coeur humain* than Stendhal or Rousseau ever dreamed possible. It has given impetus to the formal modernism of the novel.

Indeed, if the twentieth century has invented a form of discourse—as, in the twelfth century, Provence invented the new poetry—it is surely the modern novel. Stendhal still believed that the "human heart" revealed itself in action, in a continual exchange with a world of social obligations. Such a world was questionable, perhaps, and unsatisfying, yet it was terribly present and ultimately the only field a man possessed to display his virtues and discover his own individuality. The colloquy with self, for Stendhal, as for most novelists of his century, *was* a colloquy with others. A man was none other than the story, or stories of his life; he had a plot, a subplot, a beginning, middle, and end; and the traditional novel was a "mirror" trundling down a road, reporting the reality.

The formal changes in the novel—by Joyce, Proust, Kafka, Hesse, Faulkner—correspond to moods of understanding which have little in common among themselves. Yet they all reflect a growing suspicion that men, in their commerce with others, trade on used words and flimsy gestures. Their "story" is precisely what doesn't count, because it is in the language of what cannot be trusted. The "epiphany," the moment of truth, the leap into or out of grace, engages an obscure grammar of images; it happens where the words of the "story" are endlessly disordered and recomposed by warring pieces of the self. A novel governed by this suspicion cannot, therefore, "narrate" anything. What goes on "in the world," between people, moves to the periphery. Proust's descriptions of the Faubourg St. Germain are brilliant. Yet they cannot shape his novel. He equals Balzac, in places, only because the intensely composed self-scrutiny, the shifting planes of memory and experience, catch up into themselves solid pieces of world, so to speak. But this net in which the world is caught is radically new. It is a language whose genius is to recompose the fleeting moments of the self. It is ceremonious and protean because the region where Marcel's truth is revealed obeys energies to which the causal grammar of our sentences is only barely appropriate.

In order to meet the demands of this insight into the "inauthenticity" of social—worldly—obligation, the novelist contrives new conventions of style. Joyce's stream of consciousness is a convention of this kind. It describes the contours of the inner landscape, telling us what the characters cannot tell each other because there is no way of saying, perhaps even of knowing, such things socially. If the modern novel has become "symbolic," "poetic," in Yeats' sense, it is because it has had to find ways of rendering this colloquy of self with self.

The danger of such novels may be that they slip all too easily from the Self into the self; from the clear transparency of which Kierkegaard writes, into the rehashed memories and obsessions which lie like a tangle of roots along the under-surface of experience. How easily the surrealists shifted unaware from one to the other! How much of the experimental prose of the 1960s lapsed into anecdote and pastiche, as if taking the ripples on the water—Stendahl's *cent folies*—for the unifying vision that underlies them! Heroic retreat from the world and from society has come at last to seem impoverishing and self-defeating. The great age of the "subjective novel" lies behind us now. What is left is disarray, a feeling of discontent with the Romantic language of the hero.

Norman Brown (*Life Against Death*) and Herbert Marcuse (*Eros and Civilization*) attempted to refocus this feeling of discontent by rereading Freud and Western philosophy. Criticizing the drama of estrangement, and self-estrangement—"repression"—which Freud placed at the heart of the civilizing process, they proposed a profoundly reconciling vision of the psychic life: a form of secular salvation, rooted on the one hand in biology, and on the other, in political reform.

The recent fascination with oriental religions comes, I think, from a similar desire. Zen, Tibetan Buddhism, the high traditions of Hinduism, offer a philosophy of self-liberation which is founded on the ancient mystical precept: in order to gain the self, you must lose it. Instead of cultivating the life-long isolation of the romantic philosopher, the heroic pain of the individual perched in a dark world, as Kurtz was perched in the heart of

Congo darkness, the Eastern religions propose an emptiness of self into which the world flows unimpeded, spontaneous. The self must give up its "egotistical" need to be subtracted from the implacable rhythms of nature by its ever-renewed struggle for self-awareness. Instead, through hard spiritual discipline, it must learn to "let go," it must become "lost," because the nature it thus liberates in itself is none other than the God-infused order of all things. Whitman approaches this attitude when he declares himself "the greatest lover of the universe," lover of the "bad" as well as the "good." Nietzsche's *amor fati* also resembles the Oriental confidence in "fate," i.e. Nature, or God.

We find ourselves today caught in a moral dilemma: ill at ease with the conformities of patriotism, national honor, authoritarian religion, yet wary of the old poetry of alienation, with its overtones of self-punishment and isolation. This uneasiness has fueled the recent concern with "narcissism" as an affliction not only of individuals but of society. Stranded midway between unpromising forms of the social bond and the icy strictures of an aloneness which has been drained of cultural drama, the "self," in today's parlance, has come to resemble an oddly palpable, almost autonomous homunculus. An enormous psychiatric establishment works overtime to keep it intact. Social moralists deplore its bad influence on virtually every form of sociability. Autobiography has become the most prolific contemporary form of narrative, influencing fiction as well as non-fiction reportage.

Are these signs that our society is collapsing into a ruin of splintered relationships and aggressive egotism, as some critics contend, echoing two millennia of ecclesiastical and social moralists? Or are we repeating yet again the essential drama of our history: an ambivalent warfare—call it a dialectic—between subversive individuals and the large, moralized embrace of society?

Yet again it seems individuality is redefining itself in our day, therefore redefining the ways in which we can be together, as well as alone. Yet again Narcissus, with his complex challenge and his pain, is at work in our midst.

Suggested Reading

Brown, Norman. *Life Against Death*. Middletown, Connecticut: Wesleyan University Press, 1959.

Burkhardt, Jacob. *Reflections on History*. Indianapolis, Indiana: Liberty Fund, 1979. (Original title: *Force and Freedom: An Interpretation of History*, 1955.)

Caillois, Roger. *Le Mythe et L'Homme*. Paris: Gallimard Idées, 1972.

Carlyle, Thomas. *On Heroes, Hero-Worship and the Heroic in History*. London: Oxford University Press, 1965.

Cassirer, Ernst. *The Myth of the State*. New Haven, Connecticut: Yale University Press, 1961.

——. *The Philosophy of the Enlightenment*. Princeton, New Jersey: Princeton University Press, 1951.

Cohn, Norman. *Pursuit of the Millennium*. New York. Oxford University Press, 1970.

D'Arcy, M. C. *The Mind and the Heart of Love*. Revised edition. New York: Henry Holt, 1956.

Dasgupta, S. N. *Hindu Mysticism*. New York: Frederick Ungar, 1959.

De Rougemont, Denis. *Love in the Western World*. New York: Harper and Row, 1974.

Eliade, Mircea. *Myth of the Eternal Return*. Princeton, New Jersey: Princeton University Press, 1954.

Erikson, Erik. *Young Man Luther: A Study in Psychoanalysis and History*. New York: Norton, 1962.

Foucault, Michel. *Madness and Civilization: A History of Insanity in the Age of Reason*. New York: Random House, 1973.

Grant, R. M. *Gnosticism and Early Christianity*. Columbia University Press, 1959.

Hill, Christopher. *The Century of Revolution*. New York: Norton, 1966.

Huizinga, Johan. *Homo Ludens*. Boston: The Beacon Press, 1955.

Inge, W. R. *Christian Mysticism*. New York: Meridian Books, 1956.

Jonas, Hans. *The Gnostic Religion*. Enlarged second edition. Boston: The Beacon Press, 1963.

Laing, R. D. *The Divided Self*. New York: Penguin, 1965.

Lewis, C. S. *Allegory of Love*. New York: Oxford University Press, 1936.

Lovejoy, Arthur O. *Essays in the History of Ideas*. Baltimore: The Johns Hopkins University Press, 1948.

Marcuse, Herbert. *Eros and Civilization*. Boston: The Beacon Press, 1955.

Martz, Louis. *The Poetry of Meditation*. Yale University Press, 1954.

Michelet, Jules. *La Socière*. Paris: M. Didier, 1952-56.

Otto, Rudolph. *The Idea of the Holy*. New York: Oxford University Press, 1958.

Pagels, Elaine. *The Gnostic Gospels*. New York: Random House, 1979.

Praz, Mario. *The Romantic Agony*. London: The Fontana Library, Collins, 1960.

Robinson, James, ed. *The Nag Hammadi Library*. New York: Harper and Row, 1978.

Senior, John. *The Way Down and Out*. Ithaca, New York: Cornell University Press, 1959.

Starobinski, Jean. *Jean-Jacques Rousseau, La Transparence et L'Obstacle*. Paris: Plon, 1957.

Valency, Maurice. *In Praise of Love*. New York: Macmillan, 1958.

Whitehead, Alfred North. *Science and the Modern World*. Boston: Free Press, 1967.

Willey, Basil. *The Seventeenth Century Background*. New York: Columbia University Press, 1942.

Wittfogel, Karl. *Oriental Despotism*. New Haven, Connecticut: Yale University Press, 1957.

Index